The Films of Peter Weir

Also available from Continuum:

Bondanella: *Italian Cinema, 3rd Edition*
Jones: *The Guerilla Film Makers Movie Blueprint*
Jones and Jolliffe: *The Guerilla Film Makers Handbook*
Kagan: *The Cinema of Stanley Kubrick*
Lanzoni: *French Cinema*
McMahan: *Alice Guy Blaché: Lost Visionary of the Cinema*
Schroeder: *Cinema's Illusions, Opera's Allure*
Vincendeau: *Stars and Stardom in French Cinema*

Forthcoming:
Kickasola: *The Films of Kryzstof Kieslowski*
McMahan: *The Films of Tim Burton*

The Films of Peter Weir

2nd Edition

JONATHAN RAYNER

NEW YORK • LONDON
www.continuumbooks.com

The Continuum International Publishing Group Inc.
15 East 26 Street
New York, NY 10010

The Continuum International Publishing Group Ltd.
The Tower Building
11 York Road
London SE1 7NX

www.continuumbooks.com

Printed in the United States of America.

Library of Congress Cataloging-in-Publication Data
Rayner, Jonathan.
    The films of Peter Weir / Jonathan Rayner.—2nd ed.
        p. cm.
Filmography: p.
Includes bibliographical references and index.
    ISBN 0-8264-1534-2 (hardcover : alk. paper) — ISBN 0-8264-1535-0
(pbk. : alk. paper)
    1. Weir, Peter, 1944—Criticism and interpretation. I. Title.
    PN1998.3.W44R39 2003
    791.43'0233'092—dc21
                                                              2003008895

Contents

List of Illustrations

Dedication

For Sarah this time

Acknowledgments

I would like to thank the following people for their assistance in the development and completion of this book: Dr. Bryan Burns; Prof. Steve Neale; Prof. Tom Ryall (for making me rethink Hitchcock again); David Barker at Continuum Books; and my students and colleagues at the Sheffield universities.

Preface

Five years ago, the first edition of this study of Peter Weir's films did not seem to need a preface to vindicate its subject or justify its approach, any more than the original research, begun several years earlier, did at its inception. The study of film texts grouped on the basis of their authorship remains as critically controversial now as then, and yet if anything the currency and recognition of filmmakers in relation to their work continue to increase in popular commentary as well as academic enquiry. Despite a controversial half-century of usage, the auteurist approach maintains its importance for filmgoers, academics, and students as one of the few reliable and enlightening organizing principles for textual appreciation. Along with the identification of generic consistencies, it is one of the most obvious and pervasive ways in which film study is undertaken and considered.

As a subject for such an examination, Peter Weir may have become more rather than less relevant since the first edition, which appeared at the time of the director's most recent critical and commercial success, *The Truman Show* (1998). Similarly, and unfortunately, this edition is set to appear before the release of Weir's next feature, which may represent a new direction in his work. However, the development of this book has also run parallel with an expansion of interest in Australia and its cinema. My own experience of discussing Australian films with undergraduate and postgraduate students and with colleagues has underlined their importance and fertility.

Inevitably, Weir's films form a significant part of the story of the Australian film revival, but while their inclusion in the university curriculum may be predictable, the response they prompt is not. Weir's films such as *Picnic at Hanging Rock* (1975) and *Gallipoli* (1981) enjoy a critical reputation that *Homesdale* (1971), *The Cars That Ate Paris* (1974), and *The Last Wave* (1977) cement, but the appearance in the 1990s of *Fearless* (1993) and *The Truman Show* does, after T. S. Eliot, literally change as well as change our grasp of the earlier feature films. The interdependent studies of national cinema, genre filmmaking, and the auteur's output are, I hope, connected here with good reason and relevant result.

Introduction

> No trait we could assign to an implied author of a film could not more simply be ascribed to the narration itself: it sometimes suppresses information, it often restricts our knowledge, it generates curiosity, it creates a tone, and so on. To give every film a narrator or implied author is to indulge in an anthropomorphic fiction.[1]

The seeking of an author for filmic discourse has a long and varied history, and a critical distinction has been drawn between commercial (American) and art (European) cinema in the role and responsibility of the director in creating the meaning with which a text is imbued. The authentication of film authorship is closely linked with arguments for granting certain films the status of art-works, on a par with individual oeuvres of literature, painting, music, or drama. The supposed artistic autonomy of a European writer-director, whose works express a personal vision and appeal to an informed minority audience, is contrasted with the apparent slavery of contracted journeyman directors working in Hollywood:

> With rare exceptions . . . the Hollywood cinema does not give directors, or even producers, authorial status. Consider by contrast the European art cinema, which has created a complicated set of processes (criticism, film festivals, retrospectives) to fix "Bergman" or "Fellini" as trademarks no less vivid than "Picasso."[2]

3

The categorization of films (in the minds of makers and view-ers) becomes dependent on their point of origin and their intended receivers. The films of "trademark" directors can be advertised and criticized on the basis of their reputation and comparison to past work, whereas Hollywood features may be compared with estab-lished genres (the western, horror, science fiction) or with similar films featuring the starring actors. Hollywood's films can be di-vided into several conventionalized genres within a standard mode of linear narrative filmmaking, whereas art cinema (and all non-American, and particularly non-English–language, films, irrespec-tive of their "artistic" or "industrial" circumstances of production, are circulated or received "like art films"[3] outside their countries of origin) can have as many genres as author-directors and an equal number of modes that may or may not conform to Hollywood nar-rative. As Bordwell's equation of narration and authorship suggests, the audience or "readership" of the text is of equal importance to authorial intention in determining a film's European (author) or American (genre) classification. Readings of authorship also are in-separable from critical debates on the characteristics of national cinematic movements, particularly in relation to film authors whose work weds popular genre appeals, cultural specificities, and individual emphases and who come to define both the national and the authorial:

> We must come back to Kurosawa's authorship as a question or a site of negotiations. The author "Kurosawa" is a discursive product, the critical meaning and social function of which are constantly negotiated by Kurosawa, critics, and audiences. The reception and interpretation of his films cannot but be influenced by a particular construction of Kurosawa as an au-thor. At the same time, a close analysis of his films may give rise to a more complex, contradictory model of authorship.[4]

In the study of auteurs and national cinemas, genre criticism ex-ists as a coterminous rather than tangential activity. The concept of genre facilitates film classification for producing studios, the foun-dation of narrative structure for filmmakers, and interpretation for viewers, with the recognizable formulas creating a framework for ongoing communication. The genre notions within a film's narra-tive are recognized and read by an audience, whose subsequent creation of meaning represents the authorship as well as the interpretation of an "authorless" genre film. Like an art film's association with an authorial canon, a film's genre labeling before and during viewing prompts patterns of expectation and interpretation within the viewer. Knowledge and recognition of a film type's conventions and the formation of audience expectations from previous viewing experience allow for the genre definition of all film texts and validate an audience's role, comparable to that of the filmmaker's, in social and cinematic discourse:

> the genre concept is indispensable in more strictly social and psychological terms as a way of formulating the interplay between culture, audience, films, and filmmakers . . . genre is a conception existing in the culture of any particular group or society; it is not a way in which a critic classifies films for methodological purposes, but the much looser way in which an audience classifies its films. On this meaning of the terms "art movies" is a genre.[5]

If seamless film narration in a Hollywood narrative spells the death of the film author, then the non-narrative art film emerges as an authorial and non-conformist genre of its own. The viewer holds joint responsibility for genre definitions and full responsibility for an authorial act of interpretation when responding to genre-structured American cinema and individually created art film. Both the writerly Hollywood text, whose linear narrative and genre conventions appear to prevent alternative methods of decoding, and the readerly non-narrative and allusive art film are opened for individual interpretation by this application of genre notions to auteur films.

Distinguishing films by the principal contribution of a director to one film or that of a producer or a star to another underlines the fact that all film production is a communal exercise, irrespective of the attribution of the text's qualities to one or more persons. Consideration of the cinema's artistry must always encompass an awareness of its industry and the attendant difficulty of isolating the input of one artist or technician. The problem of identifying individual expression in a collectively created artefact has been exacerbated by the convergence of Hollywood and European film products since the 1960s.

It may appear self-evident that an individual director who chooses, writes, or even edits his own material has a greater degree of creative control over his credited works than a salaried craftsman working on films assigned to him within the American industrial edifice. Genre-based consideration of Hollywood films (classifying and comparing musicals of the 1930s, film noir of the 1940s, science-fiction films of the 1950s) implies formulaic filmmaking (and film reading) antithetical to the unique inspiration and individual interpretation of art film.

However, the *politique des auteurs* (proposed by French critics of the *Nouvelle Vague* [New Wave] in the late 1950s), which prompted the first studies of film authorship, was based on analysis of the studio output of certain salaried directors. Their status as individual authors within the studio establishment was justified by the detection of recurrent thematic and stylistic features, which individualized the staples of genre filmmaking. These first auteurs were credited with crafting repetitive genre narratives with individual style, whereas the works of later art-film auteurs, such as Bergman, Godard, and Antonioni, link dissimilar subject matter with idiosyncratic but repetitive style. Differentiation between the first Hollywood auteurs and the later European generation rests on the perceived freedom of the latter from commercial imperatives and external interference.

Directors have always been associated with their films, in a conception of personal vision impeded by or realized in spite of outside influence. With studio control over choice of personnel and subject matter and the final product refined by commercial concerns, the American auteur's creativity became channeled into the formation and transformation of genre formulas and individual visual styles, spurring on the evolution of both. Ironically, the recognition of the first auteurs bringing personal concerns and individual styles to genre cinema accompanies their association with (and definition of) specific American genres: John Ford with the western, Howard Hawks with the screwball comedy, Vincente Minnelli with the musical. Genre cinema conventions represent the critical, commercial, and artistic framework in which an auteur's films can be defined and appreciated. Hollywood narrative provides the model of editing, point of view, and diegetic reality from which art films diverge; genre staples first filmed by studio directors become modified in later works, revising the formulae while establishing an authorial signature; and recurrent narrative or allusive structures, based in the art-film director's personal genre of expression or in the evolving genre format of the Hollywood narrative filmmaker, provide keys to the experienced audience's decoding of the text.

Recurrent structures, images or allusions in an art-film director's canon are isolated for consideration in the same way that genre conventions are identified and interpreted (the landscape, iconography, and morality of the western, the urban twilight setting and moral conundrums of film noir, the levels of diegetic reality of "rehearsal" and "performance" in the backstage musical). Genre cinema represents a facilitating framework for individual expression rather than a convention-ridden practice. The close association of certain filmmakers with specific genres illustrates their gradual revision of genre staples during their careers. This can be seen in the treatment of the U.S. Cavalry in the films of John Ford. The army is seen first as a protector (*Stagecoach* [1939]), later as an organization riven by class rivalry and racial tension (*Fort Apache* [1948], *Sergeant Rutledge* [1960]), and lastly as a blunt instrument of government policy (*Cheyenne Autumn* [1964]). Characterization of Native Americans also alters significantly, from faceless aggressors in the early films to noble victims in the later. The western is Ford's most accomplished (but not only) genre, and his output represents a career-long development of personal style and theme within its narrative structure, defining and reviewing the traits of the former and the tropes of the latter until narration, authorship, and genre are inseparable.

A more recent example is the recurrence of the Nazi Party lapel badge in Steven Spielberg's films. Its automatic appearance on the coat of a stereotyped Gestapo agent in *Raiders of the Lost Ark* (1982) is succeeded by its embodiment of moral and spiritual ruination in *Indiana Jones and the Last Crusade* (1989), through association with an American traitor. The significance of the badge as symbol culminates in its talismanic and potentially subversive value in *Schindler's List* (1993).

Genre criticism and auteurism derive meaning from consistent elements of theme and style and extend their findings to other related works. In either case, the proof of intention or authorship behind the presence of the identified structures is difficult to establish. It is simpler to ascribe their recurrence to imperatives of studio-produced narrative or the filmmaker's unwitting inspiration. Both schools of thought require greater emphasis on the viewer's contribution to the creation of meaning, whether or not the text is addressed with the benefit of knowledge of the requisite genre or auteur. Such an emphasis should go beyond the concepts of "closed" texts (whose encoding permits only limited readings) and "open" ones that allow unlimited subjective interpretations and consider the connections between film texts, their makers, their readers, the makers' readings of other films, and the culture that they reflect and to which they contribute:

> [A] consideration of any film should recognize (a) that it is the creation of a person or group of persons reflecting the contribution of that person or persons (authorship); and (b) that the film does not exist in a cultural vacuum—that it must of necessity have roots in other works that surround it or have appeared before it (genre).[6]

The films of Peter Weir demand a close textual study and thorough structural analysis because of their amalgamation of the features of art and genre film. His films of the 1970s, like European films of the previous decade, allude to a wide variety of material from other art forms (some being adapted from novels, others deriving elements of scripting and mise-en-scène from visual art, and nearly all quoting classical music on their soundtracks), while the subsequent Hollywood features use generic tropes in more conventional and commercial narratives. All the films, whether Australian art films or American genre pictures, show an awareness of genre conventions, and consistently such staples are revised or subverted in ways reminiscent of the art-film genre. In the lack of narrative closure and features of mise-en-scène, editing, and music carried from film to film, Weir establishes his own visual and thematic hallmarks and, through their inclusion in his contracted Hollywood commercial material, unites European auteur style with the American auteur's genre revision.

The ascendency of narration over authorship in Bordwell's examination of narrative film illustrates the tension between Hollywood genre cinema (the origin of film authorship) and European auteurism (the genesis of film artistry). Weir's films and others of the Australian film revival bridge these cinematic opposites by modifying the style of the art film and revising the ideology of the genre film, appealing to mass and minority audiences simultaneously. The critics and filmmakers of the Australian revival were divided over the orientation (and politicization) of the renascent film industry, with a polarization between "film as industry and commerce vs. film as art,"[7] and with the desire for a cinema of national culture conflicting with the economic necessity of challenging the dominance of Hollywood. The maintenance of Weir's individual style throughout the Australian art and American genre phases of his career is evidence of the successful union of these aspirations, with the development of characteristic themes and treatments accompanying the adaptation of genre motifs to new films and present-day social concerns in an individualistic mode of filmmaking.

Conditions in the Australian film industry prior to the revival prefigure the contemporary ambiguous stance both for and against the influence of American cinema noted by Susan Dermody and Elizabeth Jacka. The most prolific period of Australian film production took place in the silent era, when the country's physical remoteness allowed the development of a truly national cinema. The Australian audience was served exclusively by the films of indigenous producers, without the influence of foreign conventions or practices.[8] Unfortunately, this infrastructure withered in the wake of World War I because of the rise of Hollywood to international economic dominance and because of altered circumstances of distribution and exhibition. Monopolized Australian film companies, owned by American or British chains, began to favor cheap British and American imports over indigenous films. Once Hollywood was established as the main film producer and exporter, Australia was reduced to consumer status. The few locally made films looked to America for style and subject: To recoup their costs in the home market, they had to appeal to an Australian audience that was most acquainted with and that preferred to watch American products. The decline continued unabated for the next thirty years. Australia was used as an inexpensive foreign location for American and British productions, employing cheaper Australian crews in the making of stereotyped Hollywood films.

Growing up in Sydney during the 1950s, Weir was an enthusiastic if not avid cinemagoer, enjoying imported westerns, serials, and the few contemporary Australian features of Charles Chauvel.[9] Without an established Australian film culture to impress its traditions or works upon them, Weir and his contemporaries appreciated the popular foreign films that were available:

> There is the thrill, particularly for my generation, a pretelevision generation, that the first movies you saw were American, the first ones you loved and touched you were American, from the matinee B-grade movies to horror films, and including British movies, too.[10]

The lack of a vital Australian cultural life led Weir to travel overseas to discover the European foundations of Australian society. These trips gave him an understanding of Australia's distance from its cultural heritage, personal experiences that formed the basis of three early films, and first contact with writing and filming through his participation in revue shows aboard his passenger ship.[11] Upon his return to Australia in the late 1960s, Weir decided on a career in television: Film did not occur to him since no Australian industry, training, or film school existed at that time.

Weir was ideally placed to benefit from government legislation enacted to recreate an Australian film industry. Having left television for the Commonwealth Film Unit (CFU), he was among the first to profit from those initiatives. After initial work in documentaries, he was one of three young directors enlisted for the CFU's first feature film (*Three to Go* [1971]), and he later received a grant from the Experimental Film Fund for the independent production *Homesdale* (1971). In this period, Weir continued to work with his collaborators from the ship revue shows, and his writing and direction at this time are distinct from mainstream Hollywood styles. The television revue show format is discernible in the vignettes and film clips on which *Homesdale* and *Michael* (1971), his segment of *Three to Go*, are based. Without a film-school background, Weir learned the required skills on set, and the resultant style reveals a mixture of expediency, experimentation, and imitation of contemporary foreign film. Acknowledgment of his early influences provides insight into the director's first Australian features and underpins his subsequent combination of popular and art film techniques in his American films. Weir's absorption of popular and art cinema influences in the late 1960s and 1970s parallels contemporary developments in America, with Arthur Penn and Robert Altman making "popular genre films transformed by modernist techniques."[12]

From early viewing of imported features, Weir progressed to a preference for those directors who "were working in the commercial cinema in an interesting way."[13] His list of these filmmakers reveals an eclectic taste and gives some indication of sources for his later films. Admiration for Alfred Hitchcock encourages the merging of thriller and horror materials in *The Last Wave* (1977) and *The Plumber* (1979), and appreciation of the films of Stanley Kubrick and Roman Polanski emerges in *Homesdale*'s black comedic tone, monochromatic photography, and mise-en-scène. Other directors cited—Joseph Losey, Ingmar Bergman, and Akira Kurosawa[14]—can hardly be classed as commercial filmmakers, and their art-film reputation fuels Weir's classification as an art-film director when his work evokes them. *Picnic at Hanging Rock* (1975) recalls *The Go-Between* (Joseph Losey, 1970), and the connection of the peasant community to the landscape seen in *Seven Samurai* (Akira Kurosawa, 1954) colors the western basis of *Witness* (1985). Imitation of the techniques of others is evident in some of Weir's most critically and commercially successful pictures, with *Picnic* portraying a mastery of the non-narrative mode of European art film and *Witness* maintaining traditions of genre revision by Hollywood auteurs.

Taking inspiration from a variety of foreign, popular, and art filmmakers, Weir's cinematic idiom eschewed the aspirations of some critics and directors of the revival for a uniquely Australian film language. Ironically, national cinema movements defying the cultural imperialism of Hollywood can become conformist and hegemonic projects in their own right.[15] The development of Weir's characteristic visual expression highlights his evaluation of the Australian film (and Australian culture in general) as "caught between influences—American cinema and European cinema."[16] The director's position between these creative and cultural influences lies behind the international and intertextual aspects of his films. Weir's working methods (gathering artwork, literature, and music for inspiration in pre-production, using music in rehearsal and on set that may be included in the film's soundtrack) underpin his intuitive style and give his Australian films a distinctive art film bias:

> Formally, the art cinema employs a looser, more tenuous linkage of events than we find in the classical [Hollywood] film. . . . What takes up the forward causal momentum is an exploration of the nature and sources of psychological states. The art cinema is concerned less with action than with reaction; it is a cinema of psychological effects in search of their causes.[17]

This patterning, with lack of narrative closure, allusive and pertinent design elements, characteristic lighting and framing, and a mystical and philosophical approach, is discernible in Weir's most famous Australian films. These films were accepted at home and abroad as art films and as representatives of the new national cinema. Yet the same approach and stylistic qualities persist in Weir's American films—(the imitation of visual arts, editing, and use of music in *Witness, Green Card* (1990), *Fearless* (1993), and *The Truman Show* (1998).

Weir's oeuvre exhibits a stylistic unity in which European and American concepts of auteurism converge. His career is marked by a European brand of art-film auteurism, based on personal writing and visual expression, in Australia, and by an American brand of auteurism, based on genre revision, in Hollywood. In both phases, an awareness of genre conventions (from the Hollywood industry and the art-film genre) elucidates personal themes and preoccupations articulated by the individual visual idiom. Equipped with an idiosyncratic style and versed in genre modification, Weir was well suited to enter the Hollywood establishment in the early 1980s, at a time when the industry was populated with contemporary American directors who also acknowledged the influence of the European art film and sought to direct in innovative and individual ways.

Hollywood studio history is punctuated by the outstanding films of non-American directors (Fritz Lang's contribution to film noir, along with the films of Michael Curtiz, Max Ophuls, and Jacques Tourneur) who established and transformed genre cinema with individual signatures. The popularity of Weir's films at home and abroad and his subsequent invitation to work in Hollywood require a consideration of the aptness of his work to the aspirations of the Australian revival and his compatibility with contemporary trends in American cinema.

Behind the revival's twin ambitions of art (national) and commercial (international) cinema was a desire for differentiation from Australia's previous cultural dependency. The country's colonial origins under British rule and the recent American cultural influence fostered a requirement for an identity underpinned by a national culture. A new film industry would give the clearest indication at home and abroad of burgeoning cultural independence. The aspiration for a national film industry, even for a national film language, was tempered by the economic imperatives of recovering costs and selling films overseas. The revival's first commercial successes, the "ocker" comedies, were adventurous and peculiarly Australian only in their choice of material (scatological humor) and subsequent X ratings. Later films attempted more refined expositions of Australian society (*Sunday Too Far Away* [Ken Hannam, 1974], *The Devil's Playground* [Fred Schepisi, 1976], *Don's Party* [Bruce Beresford, 1976]), but it was not until the advent of the "period" film and adaptations from literature that Australian cinema attained cultural respectability. The alleged ideological motivation behind this development would bias Australian film production for years to come.

Unwittingly, Weir's *Picnic* reflected and inspired this trend. The film's elevation as an artistic and original Australian film, based on an Australian novel, overlooked its debt to earlier European art film and its distinction (in its unclosed narrative, artistic allusiveness, and reflexive editing style) from the technically unadventurous and stereotyped period films that imitated it. The revival's need for cultural identity and cinematic worth transformed *Picnic*'s innovations into conventions, when in fact its images of landscape and individual freedom embodied a more sophisticated avowal of difference and escape from cultural dependency than the excesses of the "ocker" comedies. Weir's films became landmarks in the revival, but his mixture of modes and intertextuality were more closely attuned to contemporary American developments. His synthesis of art film and adaptation in *Picnic* and his revision of genre conventions in the preceding *The Cars That Ate Paris* (1974) and the succeeding *The Last Wave* are comparable to the works of the Young Lions in 1970s Hollywood (Brian DePalma, Martin Scorsese, Francis Coppola, Steven Spielberg, and George Lucas).

Bordwell identifies a shift in Hollywood productions in the 1970s to accommodate the auteur-based style of the art film:

> The force of the European art film lay in large measure in making not genre but the author's oeuvre the pertinent set of transtextual relations, but the Hollywood cinema absorbed those aspects of art cinema narration which fitted generic functions.[18]

Features such as the freeze-frame, slow motion, and elliptical narrative structuring (all found in *Picnic* and *Wave*) began to appear in American productions, under the influence of filmmakers well acquainted with past American genre and present art film from their background in film school. Combining their knowledge of classical Hollywood genres and narrative discipline with admiration for European art-film style and the work of individualistic commercial filmmakers such as Kubrick, the films of Hollywood's Young Lions of the 1970s exhibit an eclecticism and intertextuality comparable to Weir's.

Despite Weir's lack of film-school training, his work parallels and exceeds that of the Lions in many respects. *Wave* and *The Plumber* are more sophisticated Hitchcockian essays than De Palma's recapitulative thrillers, and *Green Card* and *The Year of Living Dangerously* (1982) enact a revision of genre material that is largely absent from Spielberg's pastiches of film serials (the *Indiana Jones* trilogy, 1981, 1984, 1989). Weir's male heroes, in both his American and Australian films, are prone to indecision, and their actions are of questionable morality and value. They are therefore in keeping with the Fordian/Hawksian materials and genre subversion of the films in which they appear (a modern-day mixture of western and cop film in *Witness*, a western frontier family transplanted to Central America in *The Mosquito Coast* [1986], a community of journalists in an exotic posting in *Year*). The rejuvenation of genre in Spielberg's films is an undertaking of wider scope and bigger budget rather than a questioning of the hero's role and motivation, as in Weir's. Ironically, Spielberg's acts of authorship follow genre patterns without alteration, the personal element of the project being limited to revamping a past pattern defamiliarized by age rather than modification. Guy Hamilton, the hero of *Year*, eventually abandons his attempt to intervene in the Indonesian civil war when no clear course of action is available to him; by contrast, the relentless and apparently unproblematic heroic action of Indiana Jones in Spielberg's films deserves scrutiny.

Although they make use of genre structures, Weir's American films eschew simplistic or anachronistic treatment of the contemporary issues held within them. *Witness* questions the western's and cop film's morality of violence, justice, and communal unity, *Dead Poets Society* (1989) combines bildungsroman with an allegorical tale of authoritarianism. *Green Card* addresses isolationism and racial intolerance within a comedic narrative. *Fearless* and *Truman* continue Weir's unsparing analysis of American family, society, and film institutions, revising genre in the light of current sociological concerns. In this respect, Weir's output mirrors that of Wim Wenders, another art-film director brought to Hollywood, whose films incorporate genre materials in ambivalent or critical ways.[19]

The intertextuality and postmodern criticism of artistic and social constructs that characterize Weir's filmmaking can be seen to outstrip the ideological confines of the Australian revival and the uncritical impetus of entertainment driving comparable American films, and Weir emerges again as an old-style Hollywood auteur, revising genre by injecting personal style and subject matter. Working with genre materials in unconventional ways, from outside as an Australian director and from inside as a Hollywood filmmaker, Weir evinces the potential rephrasing and redirection of American cinema that is open to audiences and artists within other national film cultures, producing

> a new cultural hybrid integrating, at the level of national specificity, two national cultures (one of global proportions, the other more local) through a process of mental bricolage. . . . they [cinemagoers] engage with these movies as American, and will tend to bring their understanding of the U.S. (admiring, exotic, sceptical, dismissive, hostile and so on) to bear, more or less directly, on their interpretation of what they are watching. At the same time . . . national audiences will apply the optic of their own history, identity, and values in a process involving a decoding and reframing of the film's content and "message."[20]

Peter Weir is a director with definite and discernible intentions, even if he does not necessarily have a specific "message" to transmit. In extracting meaning from the delineated set of Peter Weir texts, a balance must be struck between the freedom of individual interpretation and wider intertextual associations on the one hand and an acknowledgment of deliberate textual construction and intertextual reference enacted by the director and his collaborators on the other.

Because Weir's films combine an awareness of the conventions of popular cinema with the art film's subversion of the same expectations, and yet with a stated preference for simple, entertaining, cinematic "storytelling,"[21] any evaluation of Weir's American films depends ultimately upon one's view of auteur criticism. The distinction between the selectivity of the auteur—either in rejecting certain projects in favor of others more in tune with his artistic temperament or in writing his own source materials—and the choiceless position of the salaried director has special significance for Weir. He accepted work as a journeyman director on *Witness* in place of more personal work and found the project rewarding for the public and private advancement of his career.

Contradicting his reputation as an art-film director after the European fashion, Weir appears to favor the classical mode of Hollywood auteurism. This explains his wish to work in America and returns to the theories of the French critics who first recognized Howard Hawks and John Ford as authors with a unique vision:

> I felt really comfortable in a particular American context, which was that of the '30s and '40s, and I think I would have flourished there. I would have gone over, or been taken over, and worked for one or other of those big people.[22]

This may not be conclusive proof of auteur status, but it is evidence of authorial intention and career planning in emulation of the first filmmakers categorized as auteurs.

Along with the difficulties associated with gaining a working knowledge of the medium, Weir has indicated that he finds strict adherence to conventional storytelling to be "the hardest form of filmmaking."[23] In their analysis of the parallels and disparities between Australian cinema and the film products of Britain and America, Brian McFarlane and Geoff Mayer define Hollywood's melodramatic mode of film narrative:

> The commercial appeal of the classical cinema resides in its ability to emotionally involve a larger number of people. This is partly achieved through character-centred, goal-oriented

stories, but it is also a product of a specific narration process that encourages the successive formation of hypotheses concerning future developments, hypotheses that are essentially based on audience expectations that have been formed, or learned, through repetitive narrative conventions. Central to these expectations is the role of the climax, the emotional and/or physical pivotal moment within the narrative structure that occurs just prior to resolution. The Australian cinema of the 1970s and 1980s . . . is characterised in a great many cases by its inability, or refusal, to exploit these crucial aspects of the classical cinema.[24]

Examining Weir's films, the same authors draw a distinction between the director's Australian and American features based on the linearity and impact of melodramatic narrative:

His main Australian films end with an off-screen death recorded in a mock-authentic caption (*Picnic at Hanging Rock*), in an underfunded and ambiguous rendering of apocalyptic vision (*The Last Wave*), and a freeze-frame, perhaps to denote the futile waste of youth (*Gallipoli*). Compare these oddly low-key endings to the emotional frissons generated by some of his American films: by the shoot-out in which Harrison Ford emerges unequivocally as victor in *Witness*, as protector of innocence, and, more powerfully still, in the inspired last moments of *Dead Poets Society*, in which the students' tribute to their departing teacher hero ends the film on a note of affirmation of goodness. Coincidence no doubt: but the enigmatic Weir of his Australian films has responded with melodramatic flourish to the melodramatic challenges of two of his American films.[25]

Admittedly, the formation of hypotheses, based on acquaintance with film narrative in general and Weir's films in particular, is a problematic exercise in the Australian films. *Cars* and *Wave* offer few clues as to their endings (hardly resolutions in the accepted sense), and attainment of the goals of discovery and explanation in *Picnic* is forever frustrated. However, the examples of melodramatic resolution cited by McFarlane and Mayer are also highly qualified: The innocence protected by John Book (Harrison Ford) is a quality the inner-city detective no longer possesses, in comparison with the Amish community he can defend but not join, and the affirmation of goodness concluding *Dead Poets* is seen against a backdrop of authoritarian triumph for a regime founded on unthinking conformity. Weir's later films (especially *Fearless* and *Truman*) clearly continue to compromise or evade the melodramatic demands of clarity and closure.

The evidence that Weir continues to eschew convention is found in his other American films as well. *Mosquito Coast*'s subversion of Harrison Ford's usual heroic persona, within a pseudo-western narrative of failure and acrimony rather than success and unity, doomed that film to critical and commercial failure. Even the commercially inspired production *Green Card*, a romantic comedy in the traditions of the 1930s, ended with the lovers parted rather than united, and the editing and imagery of *Fearless* and resolution of *Truman* further this divergence from the narrative norm. Weir continues to revise the conventions of genre and the hypotheses of audiences and creates contrary conventions for a "Peter Weir film", in which the expectations of the art cinema and their mirror image in the mainstream genre film are equally likely to be satisfied:

> Movies may be commercially successful without being widely or greatly enjoyed. A film that fails does so in the terms set by the structures of the industry and not necessarily because it is incapable of offering pleasure. Thus "popular" may be thought to evade—where "commercial" would confront—the difficulties of characterizing the products of a mass medium as a cinema of the people.[26]

The marked absence of Weir's hallmarks from *Mosquito Coast* and *Gallipoli* (1981) underlines their ubiquity in the director's other work. Their omission is a matter of choice on Weir's part, showing a desire to master narrative craft and avoid becoming "trapped by style."[27]

However, the characteristic forms of visual expression return despite their repeated excision, aided not only by Weir's intuitive methods but also by the continued presence of trusted collaborators. Discussing the film work that Peter Weir has written, produced, and directed and ascribing its thematic and stylistic qualities to him alone prompt consideration of the group of collaborators he has worked with in Australia and America. Weir acknowledges their influence and assistance, describing the collective creative process as "completely open to suggestions and to chance."[28] Critics have noted specific contributions, such as that of editor Max Lemon, who suggested the step-printing and repetition of the picnic sequence at the ending of *Picnic*.[29]

In view of this, certain trademarks of Weir's work (visual style, use of editing and music) can be credited to key technical personnel with whom Weir has chosen to work on several occasions. Their talents complement the director's and facilitate a definitive artistic expression. Hal and Jim McElroy produced four Weir films (*Cars*, *Picnic*, *Wave*, and *Year*) over a nine-year period, Russell Boyd was director of photography on four features (*Picnic*, *Wave*, *Gallipoli*, and *Year*), with John Seale as his cameraman for three (*Picnic*, *Wave*, and *Year*). Seale subsequently became director of photography for Weir's first three American features (*Witness*, *Mosquito Coast*, and *Dead Poets*). Maurice Jarre composed the scores of *Year*, *Witness*, *Mosquito Coast*, *Dead Poets*, *and Fearless*; and Weir's wife Wendy (Weir/Stites) is credited with production design and art direction on numerous films, from *Picnic* to *Green Card* and *Truman*. It is logical that films emanating from this consistent group of collaborators should share common facets of theme, style and construction.

While admitting the director's responsibility for the "overall tone of a piece,"[30] Weir dislikes being labeled an auteur, even within the limited definition of the term as a writer-director, despite having written, either alone or with other screenwriters, the screenplays of six of his features. At the same time, Weir has asserted that national cinemas such as Australia's industry "depend for their reputation on a highly talented group of individuals—writer/directors, essentially."[31] Instead of crediting the director alone for the stylistic and thematic consistencies of this group of feature productions, we could discuss their recurrence as evidence of joint authorship in a qualification of auteurism.

In pursuing this line of argument, however, we must credit the director, as the only artist collaborating on all these films, with the most consistent or crucial input in the creative process, and therefore with providing the basis for their evident stylistic and thematic continuity. His selection of materials defines and shapes the contributions of others, producing a personal signature and reviving a purer notion of auteurism.

The definition and development of Weir's style during the Australian and American phases of his career have relied on the contexts and conditions within both industries. With a small pool of talent and technical personnel available during the revival, some continuity in casting and crew for Weir's Australian films was both desirable and inevitable. The personal vision realized by the director and his collaborators in these productions is sustained through their continued work on the American films. Weir's signature as identified in his first feature films (a predisposition to mysticism, openendedness and significantly detailed mise-en-scène) gave him an art-film reputation in keeping with the aspirations of the Australian national cinema that also was well suited to the director-driven and genre-based American cinema of the 1980s. However, in both phases of his career, Weir's films are distinguished from those of his peers by their fertile union of art-film style, genre structures, and auteurist consistencies.

Weir's output and experience provide a marked contrast with the Australian directors who followed him to America. Weir was the first of the revival's filmmakers to be offered a Hollywood contract,[32] but other acclaimed Australian filmmakers continued this trend, with most choosing to live as well as work in America. Of these, Gillian Armstrong so far has not enjoyed as great a commercial or critical acclaim for her American productions. Fred Schepisi gained success with popular American productions (*Roxanne* [1987], *The Russia House* [1990]), adaptations from drama (*Plenty* [1985]), and Australian subject matter made in Australia with an American star (*A Cry in the Dark* [1988]) and remains one of the most consistent and adept filmmakers to have made the transition from Australia to Hollywood. Bruce Beresford's films have had a mixed reception: While being held responsible for his failures (*King David* [1985]), he has not always received credit for his successes. Beresford's journeyman work on *Driving Miss Daisy* (1989) received more publicity and many more Academy Awards and nominations than his direction and writing of *Breaker Morant* (1979), the film voted the best of the Australian revival in a poll of Australian critics and film industry personnel in 1984.[33] Although all of the highest ranking Australian filmmakers listed were pursuing their careers in Hollywood by 1984, Weir's work overshadowed the poll, gaining more votes for more films (seven titles in all) than Beresford, Schepisi, or Armstrong, and later migrants like George Miller or Philip Noyce.

Weir's enduring popularity in Australia has been consolidated by the American experience, whereas his contemporaries have enjoyed mixed fortunes in Hollywood. The vagaries of Hollywood appear to have damaged Weir less and rewarded him more than his contemporaries. While the departures from expectation in *Mosquito Coast* were not welcomed by the viewing public in the same way as those of *Witness*, the consistency of Weir's films suggests the likely survival and continued autonomy of his niche within the American film industry. Weir's individuality in expression, his uniting of the poles of art and genre film and American and European concepts of authorship, and the openness of his films to personal interpretation, seem attuned to contemporary sociological and cinematic circumstances:

> The shift of emphasis from the frame of the genre film to the creator of the genre film mirrors and accelerates a cultural shift from placing the weight of responsibility on society to placing it on the individual. The anxieties about impotence and failure reflect the search for myths of individual responsibility that can survive the collapse of the social forms outside the films.[34]

The difficulties facing characters within Weir's films, like those of their readers outside them, arise from their relationship to the conventions of film and society. Making and reading film either can follow patterns of genre and narrative conformity or diverge into auteurist, interpretative freedom. Emphasis upon the individual making the film or the character beset within its diegesis must be accompanied by a consideration of the individual reading it. Tension between filmmaker and industry, film text and convention, and reader and expectation within the Weir canon reflects and elucidates the director's constant theme of the individual confronting an authoritative establishment or an enigmatic or illusory world.

From an analysis of both phases of Weir's career, we can detect the persistence of artistic individualism alongside entertaining narrative: the dualism of a European auteurist cinema with classical genre contexts in Australia, and genre films, adapting previous patterns, belying a Hollywood auteurist signature in America. The examination of this stylistically unified and geographically divided canon of work, with its limits based in authorship and its findings in structure, necessitates a parallel analysis of genre staples and their occurrences as structures and a discussion of instances of genre subversion that prompts the use of other forms of criticism, such as literary adaptation, film as dream, and psychoanalysis. That these critical methods prove useful or indeed unavoidable when analyzing material of this complexity underlines the frailty of auteurism as a concept in film evaluation but promotes its strength as a premise for alternative analysis and the demarcation of fertile textual territory.

Notes

1. David Bordwell, *Narration in the Fiction Film* (London: Methuen, 1985), p. 62.

2. David Bordwell, Janet Staiger, and Kristin Thompson, *The Classical Hollywood Cinema: Film Style and Mode of Production to 1960* (London: Routledge, 1985), p. 78.

3. Elizabeth Jacka, "Critical Positions," in *The Imaginary Industry: Australian Film in the Late '80s*, eds. Susan Dermody and Elizabeth Jacka (North Ryde, N.S.W.: AFTRS, 1988), p. 74.

4. Mitsuhiro Yoshimoto, *Kurosawa: Film Studies and Japanese Cinema* (Durham, N.C.: Duke University Press, 2000), p. 61.

5. Andrew Tudor, *Theories of Film* (London: Secker & Warburg, 1973), p. 145.

6. Stuart Kaminsky, *American Film Genres*, 2nd ed. (Chicago: Nelson Hall, 1985), pp. 5–6.

7. Susan Dermody and Elizabeth Jacka, *The Screening of Australia Vol. I: Anatomy of a Film Industry* (Sydney: Currency, 1987), p. 35. See also Franz Kuna and Petra Strohmaier,

"Reluctant Admiration: Australian Films of the 1970s and Their Critics" in *Twin Peeks: Australian and New Zealand Feature Films*, ed. Deb Verhoeven (Melbourne: Damned Publishing, 1999), pp. 139–148.

8. For detailed consideration of the industrial and contextual history of Australian cinema, see Andrew Pike and Ross Cooper, *Australian Cinema 1900–1977*, 2nd ed. (Melbourne: Oxford University Press, 1980/1999).

9. Sue Mathews, *35mm Dreams: Conversations with Five Directors About the Australian Film Revival* (Melbourne: Penguin, 1984), pp. 76–78.

10. Interview with the author, June 1993.

11. Mathews, *35mm Dreams*, p. 81.

12. William C. Siska, "The Art Film," in *Handbook of American Film Genres*, ed. Wes D. Gehring (London: Greenwood Press, 1988), p. 364. See also Tino Balio, "The Art Film Market in the New Hollywood," in *Hollywood and Europe: Economics, Culture, National Identity, 1945–95*,

eds. Geoffrey Nowell-Smith and Steven Ricci (London: BFI, 1998), pp. 63–73.

13. Interview with the author, June 1993.

14. Mathews, *35mm Dreams*, p. 108.

15. Ian Jarvie, "National Cinema: A theoretical assessment," in *Cinema and Nation*, eds. Mette Hjort and Scott Mackenzie (London: Routledge, 2000), p. 81.

16. Interview with the author, June 1993.

17. Bordwell et al., *Classical Hollywood Cinema*, p. 373.

18. Bordwell, *Narration*, p .232.

19. Thomas Elsaesser, "American Friends: Hollywood Echoes in New German Cinema," in *Hollywood and Europe*, eds. Nowell-Smith and Ricci, p. 154.

20. Ulf Hedetoft, "Contemporary Cinema: Between Cultural Globalisation and National Interpretation" in Cinema and Nation, eds. Hjort and Mackenzie, p. 282.

21. Interview with the author, June 1993.

22. *Ibid.*

23. David Stratton, *The Last New*

Wave: The Australian Film Revival (London: Angus & Robertson, 1980), p. 67.

24. Brian McFarlane and Geoff Mayer, *New Australian Cinema: Sources and Parallels in American and British Film* (Cambridge: Cambridge University Press, 1992), p. 15.

25. *Ibid.*, p. 136.

26. V. F. Perkins, "The Atlantic Divide," in *Popular European Cinema*, eds. Richard Dyer and Ginette Vincendeau (London: Routledge, 1992), p. 195.

27. Interview with the author, June 1993.

28. *Ibid.*

29. Stratton, *Last New Wave*, p. 70.

30. Interview with the author, June 1993.

31. Michael Bliss, "Keeping a Sense of Wonder," *Film Quarterly, 53* (1999), pp. 2–11 (p .4).

32. Stratton, *Last New Wave*, p. 57.

33. "The Top Ten Films," *Cinema Papers*, 44/45 (1984), pp. 62–65.

34. Leo Braudy, *The World in a Frame: What We See in Films* (London: University of Chicago Press, 1984), p. 174.

Chapter One

Michael (1971), Homesdale (1971), and The Cars That Ate Paris (1974)

Peter Weir's first feature film, *The Cars That Ate Paris*, was a logical development from his work in short and experimental films. Its themes—of the dangers of conformity within an authoritarian establishment and the difficulty of individual action—and its tone of black humor in portraying a bizarre threat beneath everyday existence, show a development from the narratives of *Michael* and *Homesdale*, also written by Weir, and preview the artistic and commercial success of *Picnic at Hanging Rock* (1975).

Stylistically, *Cars* shares elements with Weir's previous shorter films, such as composition and framing and use of soundtrack music. While these elements recur throughout the filmmaker's entire body of work, the narrative and style of all three films reveal them also to be films of their times. The youth rebellion of *Michael* is rooted in contemporary alternative culture and Weir's own experience of the 1960s. The allegory of *Homesdale* provides a critique of Australia's past cultural inheritance from Britain and its closer ties with America in the postwar period. The style of *Cars* combines tropes from European and American cinema, suggesting the western in its setting and recent French film in its editing. As well as helping to define Weir's mode of expression, *Cars* also inspired other fantasy and horror films made in Australia and coincided with contemporary American science-fiction films.

Weir had begun his film career eight years earlier, making two short comedy films for a social club's Christmas revue while working as a stage hand at ATN 7 Television in Sydney. His experience of Flower Power and anti–Vietnam War marches in Europe during the 1960s had given him the desire to work in the entertainment industry, as well as the material background to *Michael*. Weir's revue films were well received, and although still employed as a stage hand, he began to direct and edit film sequences for "The Mavis Bramston Show", a topical satirical program.[1] This gave him invaluable experience prior to embarking on his filmmaking career.

In 1969, Weir left ATN 7 to join the Commonwealth Film Unit, an organization in the forefront of the campaign for a new Australian film industry and home for a pool of local talent. With no film training or production infrastructure in Australia at that time, the CFU provided a haven for aspiring filmmakers such as Donald Crombie and Michael Thornhill. Thornhill's first feature, *Between Wars* (1974), and Crombie's *Caddie* (1976) give an indication of the variety of styles spawned by the CFU. Thornhill's film is an examination of Australian society and politics and the antithesis of Weir's combination of lyricism and documentary in *Gallipoli* (1981), whereas Crombie's film exemplifies the simplification and prettification of the period film movement inaugurated by Weir's atypical *Picnic*.

Weir gained more practical experience with the CFU before being offered the chance to direct. The first prestigious project launched by the unit was *Three to Go* (1971), which consisted of three short films focusing on the problems of Australian youth. The individual segments were scripted and directed by three of the CFU's leading lights: Peter Weir (*Michael*), Brian Hannant (*Judy*), and Oliver Howes (*Toula*). The critical response to the film provided valuable encouragement to the individual filmmakers and the indigenous film industry:

> These case studies transcended their functional purpose to become the first major landmark in the new wave of enthusiasm and energy that swept the Commonwealth Film Unit during the 1960s. *Michael* opened the trilogy flamboyantly with a film-within-a-film depicting Sydney under siege from young revolutionaries . . . and the scene seemed to be a symbol of the film's sympathy for the rebelliousness of youth and of the new spirit then felt to be storming the barricades at the Film Unit.[2]

In an interview, Weir recalled these formative years and the awakening to cultural and political change, particularly in regard to

American (and subsequent Australian) military involvement in Vietnam:

> The war unleashed energy and conflict, passion. You always have to look at movements in society, to look at any sudden movements in the arts. You never get a sudden rash of painters, opera singers, dancers, or filmmakers just like that from nowhere. In this case it coincided with this great movement that I had become aware of overseas. Phrases were coined like "do your own thing," "the alternative society"— they've become clichés, but they had power then—and then there was the daily bombardment of songs.[3]

In addition to the groundswell of the youth movement defying established authority, there is also the sense of the comparatively young Australian nation, personified by its younger generation, beginning to oppose the imposition of foreign cultural and societal mores. Opposition to parental control in *Michael* becomes emblematic of Australian opposition to structures of control modeled on those of the British Empire (the public school ethos of *Homesdale*, and the Victorian ladies' college in *Picnic*). The suspicion of establishment control first seen in the family situation in *Michael*, and developed further in the figures of the manager in *Homesdale* and the mayor in *Cars*, emerges as a dominant theme in Weir's work, persisting in the colleges of *Picnic* and *Dead Poets Society* (1989), the families and societies of *The Last Wave* (1977) and *Witness* (1985), the commanders in *Gallipoli*, and the television producer Christof in *The Truman Show* (1998). The situation of the individual protagonist in Weir's pictures suggests that integration into society always entails a loss of personality and authority, and the choice between conventional and unconventional communities is never a clear-cut decision between liberty and security.

Australia's alignment with America in Vietnam became a prominent contemporary example of the former country's submission to another colonial power. The movement for Australian film called for cultural distinction from the earlier dominance by British and American cinema. The impetus for Weir in *Michael* and other early films appears to be against the colonial mindset, the enduringly conformist postwar political climate, and the contemporary conservative atmosphere that had exchanged mimicry of

British patterns for adherence to American doctrine. Stylistically, *Michael* seems most closely related to recent European film, with its documentary footage, jump-cutting, and montage sequences. This self-conscious and reflexive style, contrasting the depiction of iconic popular culture with politically motivated discussion, recalls the committed social critique of Jean-Luc Godard's films of the previous decade, *Vivre Sa Vie* (1962), *Les Carabiniers* (1963), and *Weekend* (1967).

The apparent division between an establishment just emerging from the postwar influences of Britain and America and a younger generation drawing inspiration from the US antiwar movement finds expression in *Michael, Homesdale,* and *Cars* in their towns, institutions, and families riven with generational and ideological differences. This trio of early works shows Weir in touch with contemporary social and artistic movements, with the tone and content of his writing attuned to the iconoclasm of both the younger generation and the nascent Australian film industry. At the same time, his direction gained depth and proficiency from observation of contemporary foreign examples coming from both the popular and art cinema schools, in the course of creating a personal cinematic idiom.

Michael opens with documentary footage of civil war in Sydney, with a street battle fought between student guerrillas and the army similar to the war scenes of *Les Carabiniers*. Mistaken for a dream sequence accredited to the central character by some critics,[4] this opening is crucial in that it not only outlines the film's agenda of struggle for emancipation but also illustrates its tendency to shift unpredictably between styles and modes of narration. As pop music fades in to replace the noise of the fighting, the film cuts from the battle to the foyer of a cinema, where Michael and his fiancée Judy look at a poster for the movie *Rebellion* with the line, "*Rebellion*—Could it happen here?" The view of the poster links with shots of newsstands from the earlier scenes, with newspaper headlines exclaiming, "Rebellion: Militia Called In," and "Weapons Seized in Sydney," which are answered by a banner draped over a burned-out bus carrying the slogan "Resist—Revolt—Reform." These proclamations serve as narrative shorthand and as representations of the dogma of the two sides in the conflict. Both the authorities and the groups opposing them seem obliged to categorize events and doctrines, thereby gaining sway over minds in the contest for control. That both camps use the same method and strident tone is the first indication that the writer-director does not fully espouse either cause.

The next sequence is preceded by a rapid montage of images, including faces and guns from the film, still photos and cultural icons, and the words "YOUTH" and "QUAKE." This is followed by a close-up of the screen of an old-fashioned television, where a woman playing an organ introduces a panel discussion show called "Youth Quake." The panel, consisting of middle-aged men and women, is seen in front of a set bearing photos of Jimi Hendrix, James Dean, and John Lennon, providing a link with the rush of references seen in the montage. The panel is headed by Neville Trantor, who explains that the program will look at "some very perplexing problems" concerning the youth of today, with illustrations from "film clips of interviews with young people."

When he introduces the "first film clip," the film cuts again to a close-up of an unframed photo of a young man—Michael. As the camera pans over other framed family photos on a mantelpiece, the voice of Michael's mother expresses her fear of youthful rebellion, feeling that a breakdown in family life is to blame. The inclusion of photographs in these scenes again defines the opposing sides of the conflict: the younger generation—Michael and the icons of popular culture influencing him—and the home and family, the establishment with set notions of its own past (recorded in photos) and its present (presumed juvenile obedience). The repeated use made of photos and the ideological weight they are made to bear in Weir's films begins here with the image of Michael placed in a chronological, familial context, the background from which he attempts to break free.

Dissatisfied with family life, office routine, and his equally staid fiancée, Michael seeks a more challenging milieu, and so the most recent photo of him remains unframed. In *Picnic* and *The Year of Living Dangerously* (1982), the inclusion of photographs of principal characters implies a desire by society (in *Picnic*) or other individuals (in *Year*) to control or manipulate the lives of those contained in the frame. In most Weir films, the reductive rationalization of complicated events or characters suggested by the act of making and retaining a still (static and unchanging) image of them comes to represent the establishment's inability to control the unpredictability of events or the individuality of people. The frequent inclusion of still photos in Australian film narratives and an attendant overreliance on them as talismanic repositories of fact rather than subjective encapsulations of opinion is a notable feature of the revival. In Australian thrillers (such as Ken Hannam's *Summerfield* [1977]), horror films (Colin Eggleston's *Cassandra* [1986]), and comedies (Baz Luhrmann's *Strictly Ballroom* [1992]), the still photograph occupies a crucial role but has unpredictable value within narrative resolution. The containment of possible interpretations of personal or communal history as suggested by the preservation of photographs reflects the importance of the past in the definition of present identity (of the nation and the individual) in contemporary Australian film.

A similar pattern of imagery forms the basis of *The Night the Prowler* (Jim Sharman, 1978), in which an alleged assault upon a young woman in her suburban home throws her upbringing into question. The Bannister family's white weatherboard house is seen in the title sequence, followed by a sepia picture of a baby girl in a baby carriage. The father, overseas during World War II, is sent photos fortnightly of his growing daughter Felicity, but he fails completely to relate to her on his return. As she reaches adolescence, he gives her stilted lectures about remaining "clean and pure for the man who eventually puts all his faith in a girl." She is also seen framed in mirrors in the house, matching her parents' controlled image of her. At first ensconced in a virginal white bedroom, Felicity takes advantage of the rupture in the family caused by the "night" to change her lifestyle, dressing entirely in black leather, gaining a circle of alternative friends, and vandalizing the homes of other middle-class suburbanites.

Weir's film has little of Sharman's parabolic tone. While *The Night the Prowler* eschews linear narrative, flashing backward and forward through Felicity's experiences before reaching a conclusion of subjective enlightenment, *Michael* is at once more linear and less conclusive in structure. The film clips of Michael's experiences, although interrupted by and contrasted with the intrusions from the "Youth Quake" discussion, follow each other chronologically, and the particularities of his situation and the generalities of the debate offer only choices, not resolution.

As Michael leaves for work, another pop song rises on the soundtrack. The lyrics ("You led me along this path / And I don't know what else I can do") encapsulate the routine of family and working life mapped out for Michael, as we see him waiting at the bus stop with a group of identically dressed men, walking through a revolving door and past numbered work stations, and hanging up his suit jacket with those of his colleagues. Michael's journey is punctuated by more instances of shifts in mode, as he visualizes a scene from the opening film. He seems to see a sniper on a balcony in the city, but a subsequent cut to the same point of view shot reveals no one there.

Next he sees Neville Trantor filming in the street for "Youth Quake." Trantor coaches the young people with him: "Now I want you to look angry. Not so much angry, but aggressive, but above all be yourselves, all right?" Credibility is undermined further as he talks directly to the camera and makes mistakes with his lines, and later the camera focuses solely on his face and excludes the youths posed in the background. The camera's positioning alters constantly, first showing Michael watching the film crew setting up, next having Michael in the foreground at the left of the frame with Trantor and the youths, with their backs to us, facing their own camera in the background, and changing again to show the numerous takes from the recording cameraman's point of view. When Michael walks away, Trantor's commentary continues as a voiceover until Michael reaches the office. This sequence recalls the formal experimentation of Godard's films, such as talking heads expounding political viewpoints and actors posing together at the end of scenes in *Weekend*. In *Weekend*, Godard questions the conventions of the film medium as well as the condition of Western society; in *Michael*, Weir explores the cinema's expressive potential in a similarly reflexive fashion, employing a lighter touch with comparable social subject matter.

In the following scene, Michael is shopping with Judy, and the walls of the clothes boutique, covered in photos of models and stills from *Rebellion*, provoke another montage accompanied by more music. The portraits of Lennon, Hendrix, and Dean reappear, followed by a shot of a middle-aged woman looking to the left out of frame, and the last still of a naked girl. When this is replaced by the same shot of the middle-aged woman, we realize we have returned to the program panel. In addition to the humor of the woman appearing to look at the picture of the girl, the juxtaposition of the images underlines the insuperable distance that separates the members of the older generation forming the panel and the program's studio audience from the younger generation, influenced by the concatenation of audiovisual stimuli that, ironically, flank the "Youth Quake" scenes in montages and decorate the studio where the panel sits. This is reinforced by the panel's inability to answer the questions they are given, instead becoming divided between a despairing liberal conscience for and a disciplinarian reaction against the excesses of contemporary youth. The lack of suitable answers and guidance previews Michael's disappointment and aimlessness at the film's end.

Michael's position between the two factions is indicated by his youth on one hand and his respectable dress and unadventurous job on the other. Having obeyed the will of his family so far, he begins to sense new possibilities in the welter of pictures and sounds surrounding him. The next stage in his and the film's development is his initiation of independent thought and action. We see him leave work colleagues in a bar to strike up a conversation with Graeme (an actor from *Rebellion*) and his girlfriend Georgina. Instead of their words the soundtrack consists of another song, with the lyrics, "What do you want? / What do you need?" Graeme takes Michael to a lively youth group, where the possibilities of social change and the need for the "revolutionary overthrow of the power elite" are discussed. As with the panel of older experts, the younger speakers cannot reach a consensus on the right course of action, and the audience (including Michael) remains completely passive.

Among the cuts between the faces of the speakers and the audience, we see a shot of Neville Trantor, appearing to listen to the speeches, linking the different areas of debate as the montage sequence had done earlier. The spatial, generational, and ideological separation of the two locations of the debate (the studio set and the youth group) is overridden by the film's editing, showing us again that the problems are the same viewed from either position, and that Michael (and Trantor) seem to have their feet in both camps, being unable to side completely with either. Trantor's appearance here parallels Michael's presence at the filming in the street. Both observe without comment, seeming to accept the events at face value without prejudice beforehand or further consideration later. The nonaligned stance of the main protagonist is carried over into the film's undidactic form, which mocks the jargon of both the panel guests and the young speakers as well as their comparable inarticulateness.

Michael's marginalization continues in the next sequence, a home movie of a barbecue following the weekly visit to church. The awkwardness of his mother's introduction of Judy to her friends and Michael's restlessness during the meal prompt him to meet Graeme again. A new song starts when we see him invited in by Graeme, and again the music and lyrics stand in for unheard conversation: "I'll be home with them again." A rapid succession of shots links stills from *Rebellion* with a visit to a theater where Graeme is rehearsing, and among these images we see Michael's mother looking at a clock. This is the night of Judy's twenty-first birthday, and Michael not only arrives late but also invites Graeme and Georgina to join the party, to the annoyance of his own and Judy's parents.

The next morning, his mother demands an apology, and Michael leaves for work. Hammering drum music accompanies his walk to the office, and he pauses outside the dark frame of the revolving door, refusing to enter. (This pause before the door anticipates Truman's undermining of authority and disruption of routine in *The Truman Show*. In a virtually identical action, Truman—another male characterized by and controlled through his fabricated immaturity—turns away from the door to his office building when his suspicions about his environment are confirmed.) In the sunny street, Michael gazes at a recruitment advertisement ("Join a Young Team Going Places"), and its picture of young successful men and women combines with headlines from the newsstands ("Pop and Pot," "School Riots," "Student Wreckers," "Challenge to Government") in another montage. Again the strident, conflicting voices of the establishment and popular culture, vindicating moral indignation or vilifying staid conformity, are impressed upon the minds of Michael and the audience by this visual and verbal shorthand. The juxtaposition of these summaries again stresses the reductive nature of categorizations, in the form of slogans or framed images, whether they are used by those supporting or opposing the establishment.

The framing composition of the revolving door returns when Michael calls his boss from a phone booth. He is silhouetted in the booth, with the bright sunlight producing a sharp contrast between the darkness of the booth and surrounding shadows and a path of white light opening from the door of the booth to the left of the frame. This suggests a positive course for him to follow but also seems to limit him to only one way ahead. Michael spends his day with Graeme, putting his tie on a statue in the park and making fun of naval officers at the seaside as a song professes, "A change is not a sin / Just live your life the way you want / Try it today." These lighter scenes are replaced by awkwardness at Graeme's home when Michael is introduced to his circle of friends. When he reenters the house after an acrimonious phone call home to explain his whereabouts, he finds Graeme and the others laughing over his problems of going through "the big mum and dad thing." Michael is a small figure in the background, framed in the doorway and surrounded by the darkness of the passageway through to the room in the foreground, where the rest of the group is smoking and drinking.

This provides a visual representation of his limited options: He either must try to grow toward the light in order to join the group or retrace his steps homeward. Once more, Michael appears as an intermediate character, with a wealth of stimuli seeking his attention, but with the groups associated with these influences appearing as cliques more prone to assert authority than offer answers to the queries of youth.

At only thirty minutes' duration, *Michael* cannot be a full essay on the youth culture phenomenon or contemporary politics, but it does succeed in encapsulating some current issues and filmic styles. Both it and *Three to Go* earned praise on release, but *Michael* was "the embodiment in people's minds of the series and of the great leap forward which the [CFU] was taking."[5] The film's montage sequences provide epigrammatic links between its varying modes and stand as compact representations of the influences on the main protagonist rather than portrayals of his mental state. While the visual characteristics appear pertinent to the subject and the satire, the sound and music seem more attributable to the necessities of current working conditions. In an interview, Weir admitted,

In those days it was a substitute for dialogue. We didn't know how to write dialogue for Australians and the actors were frightened of saying it. . . . So I pulled a lot of tricks to have minimal dialogue in the picture [. . .] It was a case of the editor, Wayne Le Clos, helping me out of a lot of trouble. Even though I had reached a reasonable technical level and the film won the prizes of the day, I didn't really know what I was doing. I was always one step ahead of myself, just charging right on out there and letting the techniques come after me.[6]

Where songs stand for dialogue, their lyrics represent an early example of the purposeful use of music to reinforce imagery. Weir has refined this technique throughout his career, and its overt character in this film does not detract from other discernible stylistic elements, such as the restrictive framing toward the end of the film, a compositional feature he also used in *Wave*, *The Plumber* (1979), and *Green Card* (1990), or the photographs and the clock in the family home, which were to have a more profound significance in *Picnic* and *Dead Poets*. In responding to a rubric for discussion of youth culture, Weir and his collaborators produced a film in which the conspicuous but apt style of the time also furthered development of the director's own visual expression. The political and cultural resonance of the material motivates the adoption of a visual style that, in providing a rush of signals rather than an orderly assimilation of information, is ideally suited to the film's and the main protagonist's nonaligned stance.

As well as being a segment of a larger film, *Michael* rings true as an episode in a wider existence, as do the events of *Year*, *Witness*, *The Mosquito Coast* (1986), and *Dead Poets* in the lives of Guy Hamilton, John Book and Rachel Lapp, Charlie Fox, and the boys of Welton Academy, respectively. The open-endedness of Weir's films points to a dissatisfaction with pat resolutions that is visible from this first commercial work. The narrative of *Michael* is linear without being chronologically exact and does not offer resolution to insoluble problems of youth. Michael is a character with a past reduced to a collection of static family pictures, and a future as yet undecided. That final decisions are difficult if not impossible to reach in youth as well as age has been seen in the film's confused debates and in its lack of closure. We have seen images of Michael in the family home, but the most recent picture remains unframed, and the film's ending, with Michael walking away from Graeme's house into the night accompanied by a melancholy song, points to the difficulties of integration in either conservative or progressive cultures ("You've tried this game too many times / Hoping I'd play your way . . ."). The film's conflation of everyday events and the subjective experience of media stimuli succeeds in illustrating the dislocation between individuals and generations. Clarification of these issues is difficult, with the pronouncements of both sides being only the most strident voices in a polyphony of signals, and so the film's own articulation, and our interpretation of the maelstrom of meanings assaulting Michael, must also be problematic. The complex task of interpretation provides a fitting parallel to Michael's own difficult choices, and the film's eclecticism illustrates Weir's readiness to engage in formal experimentation in his chosen medium.

Homesdale opens with a triumphal song swearing loyalty to the eponymous institution, a hunting lodge that, a sign informs us, offers "Happiness in Hospice" and "A New Experiment in Togetherness." The lyrics of the opening song evoke the obedience and enthusiasm of a military academy or public school, where the inmates can be molded to suit the institutions of the establishment. The song's tone of black comedy and absurdity continues *Michael's* mockery of authoritative figures and prefigures the macabre comedy of *Cars*.

The film's opening is comparable to that of *Dead Poets*, in which the ceremonies of a new term at Welton Academy are enacted in the school chapel, with the ritual presentation of the Four Pillars (Discipline, Tradition, Honor, and Excellence) as the centerpiece of the proceedings. Weir's treatment of the methods and effects of authority in education develops from *Homesdale* (via *Picnic*) to *Dead Poets* eighteen years later. *Homesdale's* allegorical elements become finely honed in *Picnic's* period drama but can still be found in the melodramatic narrative of *Dead Poets*.

Homesdale's grandeur is contrasted with the lodge's overgrown grounds and its rusty iron gate. The establishment, which may be a holiday center, rest home, or mental institution, serves mixed parties of guests. Of the two groups seen in the film, all but one of the guests in each has stayed there at least once before. As the first group arrives by boat, we see its "new man," Mr. Malfry, (played by

Geoff Malone) taking pictures with his camera, which contains no film. The group members are subjected to a variety of "games" and ordeals, which are configured so that the lodge's staff can keep the guests at a constant disadvantage. At dinner, the manager shocks the assembled group with his recollections of cannibalism during the war as just part of a "job which had to be done." This prompts other anecdotes, like Mrs. Sharpe's remembrance of those who "didn't come back," and ex-soldier Mr. Vaughn's story of laughing hysterically at a fatally wounded friend. The manager treats national conflict as an edifying experience ("we had something to live for then, and something to talk about now"). Miss Greenoak inquires ghoulishly into his memories of police cases ("suicides, murders, road accidents . . ."), to which the manager replies, "nothing is an accident." He quotes the case of a man who killed four wives by faking road crashes and entertains the group with a brief, macabre dramatization, comprising a dummy corpse, a noose, and a motorcycle. (Weir himself seems to be the motorcyle rider in this tableau, and he also appears as a member of the Homesdale staff.)

In bathetic contrast, Mr. Malfry sadly relates the death of his dog, and Mr. Kevin (Grahame Bond) is described as having seen more death than anyone else because of his work as a butcher. In a similar pattern, a figure (presumably the manager) carrying a lamp and preceded by organ music and a choir singing "O God Our Help in Ages Past" visits all the guests (except Malfry) as they sleep and recalls their sins and fears. The accusing voice-over recounts Mrs. Sharpe's secrets about Buchenwald, Mr. Kevin's butchery, Miss Greenoak's lost youth and beauty, and Mr. Levy's guilt and fear of death. The figure's movements prefigure those of Mrs. Appleyard as she hides the evidence of Sara Waybourne's suicide in *Picnic*. The sequence ends with a shot of Mr. Malfry in bed, while two speakers in voice-over intone and repeat a ritual blessing: "Come and stay again, everlasting peace at Homesdale"—"Thank you, Father." (Hypocritical usage of religious ritual and terminology, in the service of the controlling establishment, recurs in *Cars* and *Dead Poets*.) Homesdale's atmosphere of domination and inculcation and the potential for both guilt and salvation within the establishment are maintained in this nightmarish progress and heightened the next day by the games and tests.

The next morning, the guests are coaxed into compromising

positions by the staff. The manager tells Mr. Malfry that as a new guest he must feel free to come to him with any little problem he may have, which can be their "little secret." Mr. Levy (James Lear) is led to believe that he has shot one of the stewards by accident but is reassured by another member of staff that this can be their "little secret." Having been kept constantly off-balance, the guests are dispatched onto the grounds on a treasure hunt. After a parodic sermon and benediction from the manager, they are sent forth into the "great bush of life" with "individual maps for individual treasure."

What the guests find in the wilderness is suggested by their treatment and characterization. Mr. Levy discovers a chest containing a framed photograph, identical to one hanging in his room. The photograph is of a Victorian family grouping, with the face of one child on its mother's knee ringed in black ink and all the other faces obscured by black crosses. At the bottom of the frame is a legend explaining, "Living = O, Deceased = X": The picture embodies the elderly man's guilt as a survivor and fear of his own death. Miss Greenoak, dressed in a child's sailor suit, meets a young man in doublet and hose, but when he turns toward her she discovers his face is horribly disfigured. At first she backs away in terror, but finally she approaches and embraces him. This may represent her recognition of the unpalatable truth that exists outside her romantic fantasies, and that she must accept both the ugliness of the world and her own aging. Mr. Vaughn, now in uniform, advances confidently through the undergrowth but then recoils from a large spider seen in close-up in its web, showing the personal phobias behind the soldier's professionalism. Mr. Malfry fails to find his treasure and falls into a concealed jungle trap. Just as the guests have been accused or incriminated during the night and disarmed by the staff during the day, so they are rewarded or victimized according to a strict plan in the course of the treasure hunt.

Mr. Malfry's victimization continues when the guests return. He is called before the manager and dressed down like a schoolboy, told he is "not pulling his weight," threatened with the cane ("it hurts me more than it does you"), and encouraged to do better with clichéd public school exhortations ("pull your socks up, head down and get into that scrum, pads on and out to the wicket"). At the evening revue, the guests' turns consist of mimicry and mockery of one another. When he is too shy to perform, Mr. Malfry is set upon by Mr. Vaughn and the attendants, and Mr. Kevin pretends to execute him with Mr. Vaughn's machete. Crushed by the experience, Mr Malfry is upbraided by the manager: "You stupid little man, why can't you join in? You'll have to leave in the morning!" This drives Mr. Malfry too far, and during the night he beheads Mr. Kevin with the machete. A rapid search of the lodge uncovers the murder weapon, and the manager finds Mr. Malfry sitting calmly in his office. This genuine act of violence, suggested early in the film by a parody of the shower scene from *Psycho* (Alfred Hitchcock, 1960), is the culmination of Mr. Malfry's psychological torment.

Following the manager's mockery of his grief at dinner, Mr. Malfry retires to his room and studies a framed photo of his dog. As he looks at it in close-up, the whines of a dog appear on the soundtrack. Like Mr. Levy, Mr. Malfry's ailment is centered on a photo; before the meal he studies the paintings and prints in the lodge, Dickensian caricatures suggestive of harsh discipline and corporal punishment. While none of the guests can expect to be "cured" by their therapy, only Mr. Malfry is victimized relentlessly by the manager, but this treatment proves to be a making as well as a breaking, when the epilogue shows him as a new member of the staff, welcoming the next party to the lodge, and in particular the new group's first-time guest. He is accepted into the ranks of the establishment, presumably since he has passed the last test by showing himself capable of violence when provoked. He has proved the most malleable of all the guests, just as the manager describes the new man Mr. Sinclair as "excellent in every way."

The authority in evidence in this fantasy is used not for peaceful regulation and order but for manipulation and abuse of weakness. By the end Mr. Malfry has learned to "join in" with a vengeance, not so much integrated as submerged in the established order's doctrines of cultured sadism. In showing the weakest member of the party enlisted as one of the guardians, Weir's antiauthoritarian allegory reinvokes the earnest question of "who guards the guards?" The other less suitable cases either have been rejected or acted as a controlled environment for the reeducation process. Mr. Malfry's empty camera comes to symbolize his formlessness and pliability at the hands of the manager, who can remake him in his chosen image.

The details of the lodge, the inclusion of close-ups of the disturbing pictures it contains, and the high-contrast monochromatic stock produce an expressionistic style reminiscent of *Dr. Stangelove or How I Learned to Stop Worrying and Love the Bomb* (Stanley Kubrick, 1964). Kubrick's influence on Weir is discernible in *Homesdale*'s portrayal of institutionalized madness, which closely resembles the anarchic parody of the U.S. Defense Council in *Dr. Strangelove* and the incompetence and ruthlessness of French generals in World War I in *Paths of Glory* (Stanley Kubrick, 1957). The president's war room and the generals' chateau are equally ornate, and Kubrick's tracking shots through both find parallels in Weir's camera stalking the lodge's corridors, stealing into the guests' rooms, and hunting down the murderer.

Homesdale's allegorical narrative shows the beginnings of thematic and stylistic features that find fuller expression in Weir's later films. Like Michael and Weir's other heroes, Mr. Malfry is pitted against an overweening and calculating authority, and the distasteful nature of his treatment is heightened by the final shock of his recruitment to further its cause. In place of *Michael*'s open ending, this bleak epilogue hints at the subversion of generic expectation seen in the later features. *Homesdale*'s music and editing, the meaning held in still photos and pictures, and the consistent theme of individuality set against a malevolent authority all look forward to *Cars* and to Weir's later Australian and American films. The manager's harsh discipline anticipates the rigors of Appleyard College and Welton Academy. The horrors to be found in the bush during the treasure hunt spring as much from human nature as from the wildlife, and this concept, expanded into the girls' exploration of Hanging Rock, is encapsulated in a near-identical shot in *Picnic* of a spider in its web. Unlike these later films, each with an historically specific setting, *Homesdale*'s contemporariness and dreamlike logic anticipates Weir's metaphysically questioning films, *Wave* and *Fearless* (1993).

Writing about *Homesdale* in retrospect, after the completion of Weir's first three features, Brian McFarlane noted,

> Weir satirizes here, without making them less unsettling, the oppressive forces that are at work endemically in his films. . . . Weir is not concerned here with straight-forward realism

(though later films show he is able to achieve this), but with the cinema's capacity for teasing reality out of a play of fanciful notions. He already knows a good deal about how to use the camera to create a horrifying moment or a grim joke, and it is clear how his background in experimental filmmaking will make itself felt in the formal demands of the full-length feature.[7]

Between the completion of *Homesdale* and the making of two documentaries (*Incredible Floridas*, 1972 and *Whatever Happened to Green Valley?*, 1973), Weir traveled to Europe and the Middle East, and some of his experiences formed the basis of the stories of his first feature films. Weir related the genesis of *Cars* to David Stratton:

> I was driving through France, and I'd been diverted off the road by some roadworks and I thought: Why did I follow those directions? I seemed to be wandering through some very strange little villages. Later I was in England and I saw a paper with the headline "Shotgun Shooting in East Cheam" and below, in a tiny paragraph, "15 Dead on M1," and I thought, "Well, if you're going to kill someone you kill them in a motorcar accident, not with a shotgun."[8]

Weir may also have been influenced by the highly regarded films of foreign directors who had worked in Australia in recent years. Two productions linked by critics are *Walkabout* (Nicolas Roeg, 1970) and *Wake in Fright* (Ted Kotcheff, 1971). Both films make use of the distinctive Australian landscape to analyze human society, but while Roeg's film becomes a parable of idyllic existence threatened by modern sophistication, Kotcheff's centers on a remote community in which futility and isolation prompt a descent into barbarism. The influence of these two films on Weir's first feature is not certain, although the influence of *Walkabout* is apparent in the lyrical evocation of the bush in *Picnic*. In contrast, the North American input in *Wake in Fright* from its Canadian director illustrates the application of generic motifs of the western to Australian cinema.

In *Cars* and *Wake in Fright*, a lone individual enters a secluded town and is brought down to its level of depravity and violence despite attempts to resist the attractions of the local lifestyle. In both films, the genre subverted is the western: The solitary strangers are singularly incapable of correcting the corrupt towns after the model of *Shane* (George Stevens, 1953). A purer interpretation of the western model applied to Australia is found in the scourging hero of the *Mad Max* trilogy (George Miller, 1979, 1981, 1985). Kotcheff's defamiliarizing gaze on small-town Australian life is comparable to Weir's stance as a foreigner when working in America in the next decade. His criticism of American society in *Witness* and *The Mosquito Coast* (1986) also hinges on subversion of the western genre and reappraisal of the role of the male hero.

The formula is also reworked in *Shame* (Steve Jodrell, 1987). Drawing on the same conventions, *Shame* recalls the title of Stevens's archetypal western and portrays the campaign of a lone female biker to defeat a gang of young rapists in a remote outback town. The feminist slant to this western narrative is increased by the barrister heroine's mastery of the motorcycle and her emblematic costume of black leather and white t-shirt, recalling that of Marlon Brando in *The Wild One* (Laslo Benedek, 1953). In *Cars*, the assumption of this iconic clothing by the local police sergeant is indicative of the moral inversion of Paris: Where the very appearance of Brando's character incited the town's folk to violent action against the biker gang, the thuggish demeanor of Paris's police betrays the town's institutionalization of violence, in its pragmatic economy based on engineered car crashes.

Weir's avowed openness to the creative input of cast and crew suggests other continuities between *Cars* and *Wake in Fright*. The crew assembled for the shooting of *Cars* was, in the estimation of producer Jim McElroy, the "nucleus"[9] of the most experienced technical personnel in Australia at that time, that had worked on most of the recent feature productions. Members of the crew included, in Weir's recollection, "Johnny McLean, who'd been camera operator on *Wake in Fright*," and others who "had worked with Tony Richardson on *Ned Kelly* or on *Walkabout* with Nick Roeg."[10] In this communal, creative atmosphere, some exchange of ideas may have occurred to influence Weir's film.

Cars begins, like *Michael*, with a film within a film. The precredit sequence, accompanied by simpering advertisement music, shows a white weatherboard house where a blonde girl dressed in white waits on the balcony. A white convertible arrives outside, and the girl joins a well-dressed young man in the car. They pass a friendly, waving drover with his flock of clean white sheep, visit an antique shop, and smile as they enjoy cans of Coca-Cola and Alpine Brand cigarettes, with the product names seen in close-up. A threatening tone enters the music, the car suddenly sheds a wheel, and the man loses control. He tries to correct the steering wheel with the hand that still clasps the cigarette packet, but the car careers off the road and overturns. The music ceases and, while the camera pans over the landscape, is replaced on the soundtrack by an eerie, billowing wind.

This dumb show suggests *Cars'* combination of art film, horror genre piece, and social satire. The diverse elements of this prologue (consumerism and car crashes reminiscent of Godard's *Weekend*, shifts in mode and reflexive mimicry of other media, and the tone of black humor) will be multiplied by the film proper, expanding the references to horror and western films, continuing the use of self-conscious editing techniques, and building on the director's anti-authoritarian themes.

Arthur Waldo (Terry Camilleri) enters Paris when the car he shares with his brother crashes on the steep road into town, leaving Arthur in the hospital and his brother dead. Arthur is welcomed into the community by the local doctor and is invited into the mayor's home while he recovers from the accident and tries to overcome his fear of cars. Gradually he realizes that Paris subsists on the spoils of crashes caused deliberately on the country roads. This revelation accompanies his deeper integration into the town's life, first as hospital orderly, next as parking officer, and finally as the mayor's adoptive son.

In *Wake in Fright*, a school teacher, passing through the rural community of Bundunyabba on his way to the coast for the holidays, is lured into the town's seedy life by a night of gambling, in which he loses all his earnings. Thereafter the locals lead him on a spree of drunken debauchery that ends in a brutal kangaroo hunt, despair, and attempted suicide. His fall from educated superiority is so swift that questions are raised not only about the mentality of the rural population but also about superficial divisions between classes and races.

Following the buildup during the credits to Arthur's accident, which is heralded by the horror-film–type music heard as soon as the car follows the sign off the highway to Paris, the shock of the crash is succeeded by "a quintessential Weir image: a deceptively sleepy little town surrounded by comfortable hills."[11] Gentle piano music accompanies this view of Paris nestling in the valley. Similar shots form the opening of *Shame*, as if this blank, innocuous landscape is incapable of harboring danger. The long shot of Paris is replaced by views of two men (Councillor Metcalf and an out-of-town insurance investigator) discussing the accident. Metcalf reenacts the crash with a toy car and a model of the hill road: "Impatient—travelling at an unsafe speed for these old country roads. Dark night, probably had a few beers with his evening meal . . . consequently, fails to take the bend, towing a heavy caravan— over he goes. Both killed instantly." The councillor's recourse to a model to prove his case is paralleled by the mayor's obsession with a model of the Paris of the future. Like the worm tub in *Mosquito Coast*, built as a prototype of the ice-making tower in the jungle, the architect's computer simulations in *Fearless*, and Christof's creation of Seahaven in *Truman*, the models that Weir's characters cling to show their need to believe in man-made rationalizations of the world rather than address their real environments (a Paris threatened by the youths' cars, a natural and moral jungle that refuses to conform to science or human will in *Mosquito Coast*, an engineer's design about to be undone by a lethal fault in another man-made mechanism in *Fearless*, and the producer's perfect set and manipulated protagonist in *Truman*).

The piano music returns as Arthur recovers in the white-painted hospital. Before discharging him, Dr. Midland asks if he can conduct some tests he has devised for crash victims. The test consists of Arthur saying what he sees in a series of black-and-white photographs the doctor shows him. After a chair, a dog, and a house, there is a picture of a car. Soon afterward, the doctor shows Arthur a shot of a car damaged in an accident, and he hesitates before saying, "Smash." The doctor replies, almost as a correction, "Accident." The next pictures are of a table, a cat, and a pen, but then a still of a dead body in a wrecked car makes Arthur close his eyes before saying, "Accident." The doctor quickens the pace through another series of everyday objects, and the last picture, suddenly in color, shows a corpse in a bloody car wreckage. Arthur hides his face in his hands as the doctor's hardening voice affirms, "Accident."

Control and inculcation begin with the interpretation of photographs, returning us to *Homesdale* and the manager's assertion that "nothing is an accident." In *Wake in Fright*, similar economy with the truth in Bundunyabba results in the numerous suicides being reported as accidental deaths. The doctor's manipulation of the truth of Arthur's accident and his domination of Arthur himself justify his conviction that he "should have been a professional photographer," a (re)maker of images and people.

On leaving the hospital, Arthur is met by the mayor of Paris (played by John Meillon), who has organized Arthur's brother's funeral. The assembled townsfolk stand around the hearse frozen and expressionless, recalling the dehumanized provincial population of *Invasion of the Body Snatchers* (Don Siegel, 1956) or the submissive, automaton women in *The Stepford Wives* (Bryan Forbes, 1975). In each film, the burden of secrecy and conformity characterizes the townsfolk as inhuman, whether they are simply people acting immorally for survival or are literally replaced by aliens or androids.

During the walk to the cemetery, an unusual shot shows the mayor and Arthur walking behind the hearse from within the car itself, their faces framed in its rear windows. This is the first stylistic indication of Arthur's submergence within the town and the car culture, followed later by shots through the windows of him trapped in his car when he is unable to leave the town and in the mayor's car when he rams and kills Darryl. As the framing in *Michael* marks out the young man's options, so frames in *Cars* show Arthur enmeshed in the Paris mentality.

At the graveside, while Charlie the village idiot looks on, the vicar's eulogy echoes the speeches of the manager at *Homesdale*. Again, religious belief and its practitioners are the dupes or willing tools of an establishment bound by double-think, giving Christian burial to its own victims. Tellingly, these articles of belief lead to the following scenes inside the monolithic town hall, where the mayor toys with a pristine scale model of the Paris of the future, while outside the wide and dusty streets evocative of the Wild West are suddenly filled with the cars of Paris's youth, decorated with spikes and shark's teeth.

A similar juxtaposition of the church, the town elders, and the disruption of the younger generation occurs later, when the cars

The Cars That Ate Paris (AUS 1974)
Picture from the Ronald Grant Archive

circle the town square, formed by a ring of white-painted stones with a field gun at its center. A series of cuts shows the middle-aged parents and younger children forming the congregation awaiting the arrival of the Reverend Mulray, driving to Paris in his own car, and Arthur, who watches the cars perform stunts in the street and then walks out of town to one of the fields of car wrecks, where he meets Charlie proudly displaying his collection of Jaguar crests. The western inheritance is apparent in the image of the beleaguered townsfolk huddled in the church while the outlaws rampage outside. The youths' lack of respect for the Sabbath is a reflection of their whole-hearted adoption of the doctrines of their elders. The car is an economic and totemic symbol, idolized and customized as an expression of power and individuality. In the secular graveyard, Charlie treasures the holiest of relics from those who drove before. All the elements of the mise-en-scène further the notion of the car underpinning this society and providing literal and spiritual sustenance, the past (the wrecks), the present (the vicar's transport) and the future (the youths' beweaponed vehicles) of Paris's devotion.

At the center is the town square, similar to the war memorial with its circling chain strung between artillery shells at the heart of the rural town in *Le Boucher* (Claude Chabrol, 1969). The reminder of a glorious history of institutionalized violence counterpoints the murderous events of the present: the butcher, an ex-soldier sickened by the slaughter in Algeria returning home as a psychopath in Chabrol's film, the long-term incorporation of violence in the day-to-day existence of Paris in Weir's. This is a fuller exposition of the iniquity of excusable violence in war first mooted in the after-dinner anecdotes of *Homesdale* and anticipates the portrayal of discipline in *Picnic*, *Gallipoli*, and *Dead Poets*.

Textual and technical characteristics from the earlier films can be found throughout *Cars*. The importance of the family unit is stressed in the relationship between Arthur and the mayor, who offers Arthur a permanent home as his adoptive son, provided he does not try to leave or tell the vicar his suspicions about his own and other accidents. Having seen Arthur speak to Reverend Mulray, the mayor pursues him through the undergrowth in his large, finned car. When he catches him, he makes his offer of a home and a job (as parking officer) as they stand on the hill overlooking the town. The filial conflict and the opposition of family against outsider and town against wilderness evoke the moral parables of the western, and especially the relationship between father and adoptive son in *Red River* (Howard Hawks, 1948). The hospitality of the patriarchal figurehead brooks no refusal. In parallel with the voraciousness of the town's dark economy, the town's first family absorbs all foundlings, and just as the mayor's wife has a secondhand fur coat, so she has secondhand children in Hilary and Jeanette, orphans from another crash.

Montage sequences reminiscent of *Michael* reveal the workings of the town, showing the pattern of a crash and its aftermath and the day-to-day running of the barter system. The first sequence begins with Arthur, retiring to bed, being disturbed by weird shouts and cries, in an echo of Mr. Malfry's uneasy night at *Homesdale*. In a series of cuts, we see the bandaged heads of two "veggies" (brain-damaged zombies from crashes or the doctor's experiments) framed in the frosted glass of a door in the hospital. The scene changes to the street outside, where the shouts still echo, and then to woods, where signal lanterns appear and the horror theme music recommences. A bell sounds in the local bar, and the patrons leave at once. We see a driver's view of the hill road through the windshield, and the music peaks as a blaze of lights ahead makes the driver scream and lose control. Next we see the doctor in his operating theater, preparing his instruments, as a voice shouts in terror. The doctor beckons to someone out of the frame, and shots of Arthur in bed are intercut with an injured man being manhandled into the operating theatre by an orderly and a nurse. A white Jaguar is pushed silently through the streets, and the horror film music is replaced with pumping mechanical sound as the citizens of Paris remove all the car's fittings and the doctor's patient is tied down. The car is dismantled under the gaze of headscarved women who resemble the *tricoteuses* of revolutionary France, evoking another period of institutionalized violence. The mayor is handed a car radio, which he hides inside his jacket; Charlie removes the car's crest, and in the hospital the nurses take the victim's watch and shoes. Elegiac harp and violin music accompanies the torching of the remains of the car. The next scene cuts abruptly to daylight, with white car skeletons littering the surrounding hills, their similarity to corpses accentuated by the buzzing of flies.

This sequence contrasts with the homespun atmosphere of the second montage, set to dreamy music, which begins with a mobile crane being maneuvered toward a wreck. We see a man working on a large white hood, a child sitting in a tire, and a grandmother polishing a chrome hubcap on an open porch. A notice asks for tires to "swap for food, clothing, milk, petrol, and oil," and in the local store a man brings in a parcel of clothes to exchange for groceries. These relaxed scenes of deranged domesticity clash with shots of a crippled gravedigger carrying armfuls of white crosses, the decorated cars ramming one another, the mayor with his model of the town's future, and scavengers picking over a scrap heap. The sequence ends with Charlie walking toward the camera carrying the huge white hood on his head, transformed into an inhuman shape by his burden.

The music and the homely images of the second montage contrast with the juxtaposition of debased human and mechanical surgery seen in the first, and in both the dark humor depends on the connection of Paris's literal murder and consumption to modern Western society's murder of animals for food and murder enacted in war and crime, and of contemporary moral myopia and pragmatism to Paris's solution to economic stagnation. Again, a possible model for these sequences can be found in *Weekend*, in which titles bearing ideological slogans, voice-overs reciting political tracts, and images of the slaughter and dismemberment of a pig link the iniquities of middle-class consumption and greed to cannibalism. Weir's sequences transmit a similar message without verbal address, relying on the meaningful clash of images and music to produce the desired ideological effect.

Arthur's association with the town is signaled visually as well as verbally. Like Mr. Malfry, he finds that there is only a short distance between imprisonment on the inside and guarding on the outside. In the capacity of parking officer, he is tasked with reining in the law-breaking of the younger elements, "cleaning up the town" and "making it a decent place for people to park," parodying the western hero's nobler aims. Framing highlights his position, as when Arthur's attempt to drive away is watched by the mayor through the window of the Voyager Insurance Co. (a legalized form of profit from the misfortune and fear of accidents), or when Arthur is seen through the mesh grilles of the cars that guard the roads out of town. The grilles hide the drivers from view, dehumanizing them and anthropomorphizing the cars themselves. After the mayor orders a youth's car destroyed for an attack on his house, the mayor's henchman Max warns that "the cars are upset over the burning," and in the climactic razing of the town, the vehicles roar like wild beasts in an echo of Mr. Malfry's articulate photograph.

Arthur's assimilation into the mayor's family puts him in an identical position to Michael, being relatively young in comparison with the powers that be, but not as young as the real counterculture of the cars. By siding with the authorities, he too becomes their enemy, prompting standoffs in the main street between the parking officer and the young drivers. The echoes of the western are strong here, with the youths dressed like characters from "spaghetti" westerns (such as the *Dollar* trilogy, Sergio Leone, 1964, 1965, 1966), and their encounters with Arthur marked by guitar and harmonica music reminiscent of *Once Upon a Time in the West* (Sergio Leone, 1968). However, Arthur's inability to gain the respect of the youths means such elements are included to bathetic effect. The lack of success of the outsider figure in his generic role as bringer of justice to the town is highlighted by Sergeant Cotter's intervention over the attack on the mayor's home. This reemphasizes the town's moral inversion and the film's wide generic reference, in the local law enforcer, dressed like the rebel of the biker movie, upbraiding the youths, dressed like western villains, for parking offenses while he supports the town's criminal economy.

The absorption process, begun with the photographic test and Arthur's framing with the mayor in the windows of the hearse (literally a car of death), is completed with the mayor's deal of adoption struck on the hill overlooking the town. Before this meeting, Arthur returns to the scene of his accident. He finds the probable source of the blinding lights in a derelict truck resembling a death's head. He looks at himself framed in the truck's rectangular wing mirror, which has been turned outward to reflect the headlights of oncoming cars. Although he intends to tell Reverend Mulray of this discovery, after the offer of sanctuary in return for silence, Arthur halts his investigation.

The frames that restrict him in these scenes, like those surrounding Michael and David Burton in *Wave*, show the limitations of choice in conformity, imposed externally by force or internally by social conditioning. By ignoring personal motives, Arthur becomes a trusted vassal, which distinguishes his violence in self-defense from Charlie's murder of Reverend Mulray, not as an aid to secrecy or favor to the mayor (who attacks him and calls him an "irreligious bastard") but simply so that he too can acquire a car. Charlie's act is a reminder of the car's tribal and totemic value. Like the division of a kill after a communal hunt, Charlie accuses the council of keeping the "best bits" of the car wrecks for themselves and poses possessively next to his own trophy.

When the cars attack the town, Arthur obeys the mayor's commands and overcomes his fear by starting his car and fighting back. Jump cuts exacerbate the violence of his repeated ramming, reversing, and ramming again to kill one of the cars. He smiles with relief at being able to drive once more. His earlier inability to drive has been mocked like the cowardice of the cowboy unwilling to draw, but unlike the western hero, Arthur's proof of manhood in an act of retributive violence does not cure the town's ills. He is confined to Paris not by the need to fulfill a heroic role but by his inability to move on, and this entrapment is the origin of his assimilation. He departs as a lone killer in a car rather than the savior of a corrupt society, previewing the solitary road warrior of *Mad Max*.

Cars' mix of horror, fantasy, and black comedy typifies Australian Gothic, a genre isolated by Susan Dermody and Elizabeth Jacka, who mark *Homesdale* as one of the earliest examples,[12] and provide a working definition of the species:

> They are in fact art films coming up into the feature category from the underground of experimental filmmaking, and from the sense of the marvellous in cartoon art, horror comics, and matinee serials. . . . Their hallmark is dark, inward comedy, in strong contrast to the loud and outward comedy of the contemporaneous Barry McKenzie films. . . . "Normality"—of the Australian suburban and small-town strain—is the hunting ground for Gothic comic hyperboles and motifs: the mix master; the front yard; the car, and the car crash; and the other things that litter the landscape of contained insanity. The normal is revealed as having a stubborn bias towards the perverse, the grotesque, the malevolent.[13]

While *Homesdale* acquired a cult following, *Cars* was not a commercial success, and it was left to later examples such as the *Mad Max* films to make significant returns at home and abroad. Weir drew comparisons between Miller's trilogy and *Cars* in an interview, with reference to a larger fictional context beyond the outlandishness of Paris, which recalls the revolutionary fantasy of *Rebellion*:

> I never took it as far as I wanted to, the feeling of a country in some sort of economic chaos. There were to be troops in the countryside, anarchy in the air, odd radio reports of massive road accidents, politicians being attacked, and so on—there was a whole subplot there. It's interesting when you look at *Mad Max* and *Mad Max 2*, because George Miller said the same thing: that in the first film he got done what he could, but in the second he was able to put in all the texture he'd wanted to in the first.[14]

This background is discernible in the radio reports that lead up to the first montage sequence. The ex-car radio in the bar relates the premier's address to the nation: "The future promises great things for us and our country. The light is at the end of the tunnel, but have you the strength to travel the short distance that remains?" The mayor repeats this speech verbatim at the Paris Pioneers Ball, turning the "short distance" into the town's determination to continue its work and close ranks before an external investigation into Mulray's death, and Arthur's return to driving.

From the bar, the scene changes to Sergeant Cotter's office, where we see him dress for a night on duty while the radio announces that the "state road toll reached an all-time high this weekend with eighty-two deaths, mostly in country areas." Finally, we see a yard of cars under dust covers, where a guard discovers Charlie scavenging for spares, while the radio continues ". . . the emergency measures taken by the prime minister. He specifically attacked the Third Riot Militia, comparing the PM's action to that of the president of a South American banana republic." This context of widespread disintegration also fits scenes in the credit sequence, in which Arthur and George drive past men manhandling a cow into the trunk of a car, stop in a small town where a group of people wait disconsolately outside the offices of the Commonwealth Rural Employment Scheme, and buy rationed petrol with coupons. Further information is seen in headlines at news stands: "Oil Price Rise"; "Currency Crisis"; "Opposition to New Laws."

Parallels can be found in *Mad Max* (1979), with a road sign bearing the highway's running total of fatal accidents, and in *Mad Max 2* (1981), where a prologue of documentary footage and a voice-over detail the collapse of civilized society. While outlining the context of societal breakdown, these elements also provoke comparison with the mayor's model of the unrealizable Paris of the future, the model landscape used to explain away Arthur's crash, and the doctor's manipulation of photographs. The use of "facts" in visual and verbal form by those in authority becomes a consistent feature of Weir's narratives, highlighting the reliance placed on scientific explanation and the inadequacies of such materials in defusing the doubt.

The wider, future contexts of *Cars* and the *Mad Max* trilogy (*Mad Max, Mad Max 2*, and *Mad Max Beyond Thunderdone* [1985]) highlight their allegorical elements and hint at their varying commercial success. The *Mad Max* films "work both artistically and at the box office . . . because though they are firmly genre-based, they mix and subvert and exceed their genres with such inventiveness."[15] The *Mad Max* cycle's principal genre (in common with *Wake in Fright* and *Shame*) is the western rather than science fiction, with defense of family in the first film, community in the second, and the nation's future (a colony of children) in the third, giving the lone hero successive moral tasks to prove his honor, even though he resembles the outlaws in appearance and skills. The desire for revenge, a recurrent western motif that provides the motivation in the first film, is replaced later by the heroic demands of solitary moral action. Max's similarity to the western hero extends to his alienation at the conclusion, in the first instance because of the loss of his family, and in the second and third as his violent role as a moral scourge denies him, like Ethan Edwards of *The Searchers* (John Ford, 1956), a place within the restored community. Max's usefulness to resurgent society resides in his difference from it, his taciturnity, and his use of violence to protect communities he cannot join. The division between the law and the lawless, with the hero placed apart from both groups, perpetuates the western's morally satisfying formula in a commercially successful form.

By contrast, *Cars'* adoption of western motifs highlights the town's immorality and the hero's inadequacy. The corruption of the council and the collusion of the townsfolk engender home-grown and self-destructive violence in the cars of the younger generation. The town can be cleansed only by complete annihilation. In this respect, *Cars* parallels the revisionist western *High Plains Drifter* (Clint Eastwood, 1972), itself a recapitulation of Sergio Leone's *Dollar* films. Arthur is a weak and guilty wanderer rather than a heroic nomad, closer to the western's civilized easterner who is transformed by experience in the lawless West, such as Ransom Stoddard in *The Man Who Shot Liberty Valance* (John Ford, 1962), than to the model of Shane or Max. Notably, the subversion of the western in contemporary American horror (*The Texas Chainsaw Massacre*, Tobe Hooper [1974]) also incorporates the depiction of a pervasive and ultimately unpurged corruption in the rural community.

Arthur is ushered into Paris because of the town's guilt-ridden hospitality and is integrated by his adoption and nepotistic appointment as parking officer. Because of his weakness (the inability to wield the modern weapon of the car) and through becoming part of the immoral town, he is doubly unable to save it. Riding out of town is more a resumption of a driving/killing role than the conclusion of heroic duty. With the razing of the town, Arthur and the other outlaw inhabitants of Paris seem set to migrate to other remote settlements. In direct opposition to the western formula, the actions of the outsider provoke an escalation of violence and result in the spread of lawlessness. This reversal of genre convention, with the film's allegorical portrayal of a society declining economically and morally, endows *Cars* with no melodramatic force or narrative closure, and, with a subsequently reduced commercial appeal, places the film in the art category already suggested by its use of music and editing. Combination of the clear morality of the western with the communal tensions of the biker movie leads to a questioning rather than a reaffirmation of society. Transplantation of a genre in *Mad Max* retains enough of the formula's moral and narrative elements for commercial viability, whereas *Cars'* contradiction of genre creates a polemic rather than popular text.

Confusion in the interpretation of *Cars* hampered the film's chances for box-office success. Upon its completion, it encountered difficulties in finding distribution, let alone an audience, because of its dissimilarity to successful Australian films to date:

> Reactions at the Sydney and Melbourne Film Festivals in June [1974] were vigorously divided, prefiguring the critical acclaim and commercial failure that occurred when the film opened. . . . Attempts were made to salvage the film commercially by changing distributors . . . and by changing the advertising campaign from horror movie to art film (in Canberra during the "Australia 75" arts festival), but neither succeeded.[16]

Meanwhile, the film's own allusiveness produced an unusual twist to the attempts to release it in America.[17] Stratton reveals how, after a breakdown in negotiations for a release through Roger Corman's New World Company, Paul Bartel was approached by Corman to direct *Death Race 2000* (1975):

> Corman first came to him with the idea of the cars themselves, and the rest of the plot was built around them. Bartel

himself never saw *The Cars That Ate Paris*, although he was aware that a print of the film was in Corman's offices.[18]

Death Race 2000 is more pure science fiction than *Cars*, and more exploitational in using armed vehicles in a sanctioned version of hit-and-run, but its picture of a police state using avid consumerism, television viewing, and violent sport to control the populace and to channel aggression unites themes and imagery from Weir's film and *Rollerball* (Norman Jewison, 1975). The institutionalization of violence in sport is comparable to the pragmatism of Paris's way of life in *Cars*, and in all three films a shadowy authority asserts the economic necessity of the status quo. Paris's mayor demands loyalty and effort for "the future"; *Rollerball's* "corporate society" uses games of death to divert citizens' attention away from their lack of rights and history; and in *Death Race 2000*, the moral minority that vows to end the race can achieve its aim only through multiple murder.

The fantasy of Jewison's film, the populism of Bartel's, and the allegory of Weir's comment on the violence, consumerism, and hypocrisy of contemporary society. While none is as consciously stylized nor as politically motivated as Godard's *Weekend*, their narrative form and genre structures make them more accessible as covert social commentary and successful as inspirations for other filmmakers. Drawing from the western and science-fiction genres, *Cars* reflects contemporary American films, such as *The Stepford Wives* and *Westworld* (Michael Crichton, 1973), and is itself re-reflected in later Australian films merging these genres (*Mad Max* and *Shame*).

Cars, *Homesdale*, and the Australian Gothic genre bridge the distinctive periods of science-fiction film, appearing after the American films of the 1950s betraying fear of dehumanization and conformity (Siegel's *Invasion of the Body Snatchers*, remade by Philip Kaufman in 1978), and before those of the 1970s portraying society gripped by technological conspiracy (*Coma* [Michael Crichton, 1977]). In their connection of popular film genres with a fantastic critique of popular culture, they epitomize the duality of the revival's early years, re-rendering Hollywood models with art-film techniques. As such, *Cars* is comparable to Godard's amalgamation of art-film style and B-movie material (the gangster

film in *A Bout de Souffle* [1959] and the science-fiction film and
film noir in *Alphaville* [1965]). This combination of generic modification and stylized composition emerges as Weir's characteristic
mode of cinematic expression.

Cars and other Australian Gothic films can be seen to represent
a development in socially conscious, hybridized horror/science-fic-
tion films that parallels contemporary American trends, and Australian Gothic horror has continued to emphasize the iniquity of
the family and establishment authority. Examples such as *Incident
at Raven's Gate* (Rolf de Heer, 1988) and *Body Melt* (Philip Bro-
phy, 1993) have perpetuated the portrayal of deviancy and corruption in rural isolation begun in *Wake in Fright*. Another notable
comparison is apparent in the work of David Cronenberg. His use
of the horror formula for both exploitation and social commentary
is visible in *Shivers* (1974), which like *Body Melt* echoes Weir's film
in opening with an ironic advertisement. Perhaps the ultimate expression of Cronenberg's (and, by extension, Weir's) critique of
consumerism, immorality, and the car in contemporary culture appears in *Crash* (1996).

In advancing the themes and developing the style seen previously in *Michael* and *Homesdale*, *Cars* revealed Weir's propensity
for reworking genre motifs that would come to prominence in his
later films and helped to establish a specific national genre in Australian Gothic. *Cars'* failure to find an audience did not impede
Weir's progress to his next, more prestigious production, *Picnic at
Hanging Rock*. The social satire incorporated in *Michael*, *Homesdale*
and *Cars* at the level of comedy or horror becomes refined in *Picnic* by a more pervasive symbolism, derived from its novel base and
other artistic sources. Weir's next two films, *Wave* and *The Plumber*,
are a postscript to *Michael*, with successful white middle-class families being faced with bizarre threats to their cloistered existences,
as if that generation's youthful wish for an alternative to life within
society's constraints has returned when they have become, like
Arthur and Mr. Malfry, upholders of the order.

Picnic would prove to be a greater commercial and critical success than *Cars*, and even more important to the foundation of the
succeeding Australian genre, the "period" film. Assuming the look
as well as the technical style of the European art film, *Picnic* is
unique among Weir's films in not subverting an American genre

model. However in inaugurating the Australian "AFC" (Australian Film Commission) genre, it united the revival's twin ambitions of commercial success and cultural respectability.

Notes

1. Sue Mathews, *35mm Dreams: Conversations with Five Directors About the Australian Film Revival* (Melbourne: Penguin, 1984), p. 82.

2. Andrew Pike and Ross Cooper, *Australian Film 1900–1977* (Melbourne: Oxford University Press, 1980), pp. 327–328.

3. Mathews, *35mm Dreams*, p. 84.

4. Graham Shirley and Brian Adams, *Australian Cinema: The First Eighty Years*, rev. ed. (Sydney: Currency, 1989), p. 266; David Stratton, *The Last New Wave: The Australian Film Revival* (London: Angus & Robertson, 1980), p. 59; Don Shiach, *The Films of Peter Weir* (London: Letts, 1993), p. 22.

5. Richard Brennan, "Peter Weir—Profile," *Cinema Papers*, 1 (1974), pp. 16–17.

6. Mathews *35mm Dreams*, pp. 86–87.

7. Brian McFarlane, "The Films of Peter Weir," *Cinema Papers*, 26 (1980), Special Supplement, pp. 1–24 (p.6.).

8. Stratton, *Last New Wave*, p. 62.

9. Gordon Glenn and Scott Murray, "Production Report—*The Cars That Ate Paris*," *Cinema Papers*, 1 (1974), pp. 18–26 (p. 21).

10. Mathews, *35mm Dreams*, p. 91.

11. McFarlane, "Films of Peter Weir," p. 8.

12. Susan Dermody and Elizabeth Jacka, *The Screening of Australia Vol. I: Anatomy of a Film Industry* (Sydney: Currency, 1987), pp. 171–172.

13. Susan Dermody and Elizabeth Jacka, *The Screening of Australia Vol. II: Anatomy of a National Cinema* (Sydney: Currency, 1988), p. 51.

14. Mathews, *35mm Dreams*, p. 92.

15. Elizabeth Jacka, "Critical Positions," in *The Imaginary Industry: Australian Film in the Late '80s*, eds. Susan Dermody and Elizabeth Jacka (North Ryde, N.S.W.: AFTRS, 1988), p. 77.

16. Pike and Cooper, *Australian Film*, p. 354.

17. Subsequently, a shorter, substantially reedited but no more successful version of the film, entitled *The Cars That Ate People*, was distributed in America. See Michael Dempsey, "Inexplicable Feelings: An Interview with Peter Weir," *Film Quarterly, 33* (1980), pp. 2–11.

18. Stratton, *Last New Wave*, p. 64.

Chapter Two

Picnic at Hanging Rock (1975/1998)

More than twenty-five years after its release, *Picnic at Hanging Rock* remains the film with which Peter Weir's name is most closely associated and maintains its place as one of the keystones of the Australian film revival. It can be credited with establishing Weir's name outside Australia and with broadcasting that country's national cinematic renaissance. These achievements came through recognition of the film as a quality production, both as art and entertainment. David Stratton has traced the film's lengthy gestation, through the initial interest of producer Pat Lovell, her recruitment of Weir and screenwriter Cliff Green, and the involvement of the McElroy twins.[1] *Picnic* earned praise for its period recreation, and it helped to establish some of the elements of Weir's style and vision: the amalgamation of the normal and abnormal; collisions between society and individuals, and between societies and external forces; visual hallmarks of bleached, pale lighting, soft-focused nostalgic haze, and meticulous art direction; and powerful usage of soundtrack and music, reinforcing or undermining the image with conspicuous or incongruous sound.

Assessing the film after nearly thirty years is difficult given the concentration of critical attention it received on release. It has not remained sacrosanct as one of the first Australian features to enjoy widespread success. Brian McFarlane has since commented on *Picnic*'s "euphoric overvaluation at the time of its release,"[2] and its visual style and inconclusive narrative have been frequent targets of criticism. However, the status of *Picnic* and its director within Australian film history were reconfirmed by the release of the director's cut of the film in 1998, which used the original negative but incorporated a remastering of the complex soundtrack.

In being a literary adaptation, *Picnic* accords with other successful period films of the revival, such as *The Getting of Wisdom* (Bruce Beresford, 1977) and *My Brilliant Career* (Gillian Armstrong, 1979). The ubiquity of the period film as the mainstay of the Australian revival has led (retrospectively) to its definition as the "AFC genre," because such productions received financial support from the Australian Film Commission. This emphasis helped to establish a more decorous reputation for Australian cinema, after the notoriety of "ocker" comedies like *The Adventures of Barry McKenzie* (Bruce Beresford, 1972):

> The role of these films as quasi-official representatives of, rather than representations of, the nation did endow the industry with cultural and political legitimacy during those early difficult years . . . they possessed attributes which were the reverse of those commonly identified with the ocker films: they were tasteful and lyrical rather than brash and iconoclastic; reflective and artistic rather than physical and populist. While these attributes were just as misleading as those they replaced, they did create a "brand name" for Australian films, without which there was no chance of being marketed at all.[3]

Period films, whether adapted from novels (*Picnic* and *The Mango Tree* [Kevin Dobson, 1977]) or autobiographies (*The Getting of Wisdom*, *My Brilliant Career*, and *Caddie* [Donald Crombie, 1976]), shared high production values in re-creating Australia's past history, using canonical literary sources in validation of the country's cultural maturity. The AFC genre's brand of cinematic conservatism is more fully defined by Susan Dermody and Elizabeth Jacka:

> The closest thing to mise-en-scène are lyrical pans across picturesque landscapes or beautifully dressed interiors, giving brief, rapturous play to cinematography's recognition of what is our own. This includes not only distinctly beautiful place, but space, history, and cultural traditions. . . . The unconscious, the subjective, the marvellous, the disturbing, the cinematically literate: these are all off-limits to this tasteful, rather old-fashioned film storytelling.[4]

Paradoxically, Dermody's and Jacka's recognition of this trend toward a conventionalized and marketable Australian cinema, prompted by *Picnic*'s success, underlines how little Weir's film has in common with those that succeeded and imitated it. The novel's themes, in tune with the director's concerns, are the mystical resonances of events surrounding and characters experiencing the picnic disappearances, and the subjective interpretations of the incident are articulated by the film through cinematographic techniques. Despite the period setting, the themes of *Picnic* represent a logical progression from the Australian Gothic narratives of *Homesdale* (1971) and *The Cars That Ate Paris* (1974). While being credited with the inception of the AFC genre, *Picnic* represents both a developmental step in the career of its director, expanding on the treatment of institutional iniquity found in *Homesdale* and *Cars*, and a conscious artistic transformation of the Australian film. Faced with an insoluble mystery at the heart of the novel, Weir and his collaborators chose to concentrate on atmosphere in the adaptation, directing attention away from the lack of narrative closure by adopting the pacing and openness to individual interpretation of the European art film. This deliberate aesthetic choice proved crucial to the identification of Weir's own style and to the film's success:

> It did seem to me . . . the only way to approach it was to work in the style of a European film with the slower rhythms, with the lack of exciting developments that lead you to an expectation of a solution, but to try to develop within this approach something approaching the hypnotic, that is the rhythm of the film would lull you into another state and you would begin to go with the film and drop your expectations.[5]

Possible sources of inspiration for the art-cinema look, such as *L'Avventura* (Michelangelo Antonioni, 1960), *Elvira Madigan* (Bo Widerberg, 1967), and *The Go-Between* (Joseph Losey, 1970), have been identified by Don Shiach.[6] On close analysis, Widerberg's film appears to exert the greatest influence in terms of construction and cinematography. A title preceding the action asserts the drama's basis in fact and defuses suspense by revealing the ending. The doomed blonde heroine of *Elvira Madigan* is idolized by the same soft-focus, impressionistic shooting seen in Weir's film, and the editing of Widerberg's elegiac pastoral narrative uses similar freeze-framing and step-printing techniques to articulate the same themes of beauty, innocence, and mutability.

Where later period films united the settings of recent history and the received vision of Australia's colonial past with the aesthetics of unimaginative television drama, *Picnic*'s recourse to the mode of the foreign art film represented a different type of endeavor, courted a different type of audience, and criticized Australia's cultural dependence. *Picnic*'s deliberate disappointment of audience expectation, in its refusal to conclude its narrative or solve its mystery, is the clearest but by no means only indication of its reappraisal of conventional narrative form, which represents a formal parallel to its themes of individual, social, and national determination. Although it set in motion the trend of literary adaptation and period setting, *Picnic* in fact transcends its historical frame and transmutes its source text in its lyrical reinterpretation of social and cinematic structures. By transferring the motifs of Australian Gothic to a past setting and assuming the guise of a European art film in the subversion of narrative and the elevation of visual style, *Picnic* modified one Australian genre, adopted a foreign one, and prompted the evolution of a new Australian mode, the AFC genre.

The novel begins with a list of principal characters, with this disclaimer:

> Whether *Picnic at Hanging Rock* is fact or fiction, my readers must decide for themselves. As the fateful picnic took place in the year nineteen hundred, and all the characters who appear in this book are long since dead, it hardly seems important.[7]

This disingenuous attitude toward the credibility of the tale may seen pretentious or infuriating: The film compounds the crime by opening with an authoritative title and ending with a voice-over detailing the circumstances of Mrs. Appleyard's death and the unsuccessful searches of later years. The suggestion of a factual basis for the story is as good a selling point for the film as it was for the novel, but perhaps the definitive dating springs from a similar intention to that behind the specified period setting of *The Draughtsman's Contract* (Peter Greenaway, 1982). Use of a date ("August

1694") sufficiently removed in time allows considerable modification of manners and mores, of present or past times, to accommodate an allusive fantasy of the filmmaker's design. *The Piano* (Jane Campion, 1993), which offers a subversive reprise of the period film in a New Zealand setting, can also be seen to function in this way. Weir's, Greenaway's, and Campion's themes and treatments are clearly comparable, in portraying the threat to the individual posed by the social hierarchy, unjust distinctions of gender, race, and class, the potential for horror and violence behind the facade of mundaneness, and in their use of settings whose particularities are as irrelevant or misleading as they are apparent and emphasized.

In all three films, conspicuous art direction and costuming betray the artificiality of the narratives even as they purport to re-create a given setting. Just as the prevalence of design in these productions suggests the greater relevance of artistic detail, allusion, and symbolism, so it detracts from the importance of the historical environment:

> [*The Piano*] can be anchored neither to straightforward readings based on its main character's story world nor to the historical world of mid-Victorian colonialism—which is not to deny that both are presented with clarity. The film's themes are diffuse because its obvious symbolic riches coexist with a lack of hard information.[8]

Assuming the air of a period drama to transcend it in wider reference parallels these films' defiance of conventional narrative structure, as they create structures of meaning peculiar to themselves (flowers, visual and literary arts, and the opposition of Rock and College in *Picnic*, the "curriculum" for the draughtsman's drawings forming two "acts" of six sketches, with the thirteenth drawing as an epilogue or codicil in *The Draughtsman's Contract*, and the equation of arranged marriage and colonial occupation, the woman's body and bartered territory in *The Piano*). This heightening of style and obfuscation of narrative distances these films from conventional period drama:

> History, as we know, is always about already "completed" events; in the same way, the transparent film, with a narrative that purports to tell everything, rests upon a denial that anything is absent or anything has to be searched for.[9]

Picnic asserts the presence of the unknown and unattainable in its unclosed narrative. Rather than aspiring to tell all of a concluded action, it alludes to a wider artistic and sociological context by incorporating references that are worthy of interpretation in their own right as well as in the service of the inconclusive narrative. This narrative is not satisfactorily "completed" and so is unlike either "transparent" film or concluded history. In parallel with the quest for answers within its plot, it demands a deeper search for meaning from its viewers.

The period detail that delights audiences is one thing; the handling of a novel's confused time span is quite another, and Lindsay's novel revels in the distortion of tense. As the girls begin their ascent, we are given two alterations in the timescale by our omniscient reporter/author. Mike, watching only Miranda, "remembered afterwards" how she had called back to Edith.[10] When the girls come in sight of the Rock, tenses change again:

> Who can say how many or how few of its unfolding marvels *are* actually seen . . . by the four pairs of eyes *now* fixed in staring wonder at the Hanging Rock? *Does* Marion Quade note the horizontal ledges. . . . *Is* Edith aware of the hundreds of star-like flowers crushed under her trampling boots. . . . And Miranda . . . *does* she already feel herself more than a spectator agape at a holiday pantomime?[11]

Switching of the temporal perspective occurs frequently, as the narrator reveals the tangled affections of the young people called to the Rock. Irma loves Mike, Albert loves Irma, Mike loves Miranda: all love at first sight and all are disappointed, producing further twists of fate and tense:

> [Albert] had plenty of time to recover his mental equilibrium, since he knew, with absolute certainty, that he would never speak to Irma Leopold again.[12]
>
> Again she sees the flash of the creek, the wagonette under the blackwood trees and a fairhaired young man. . . . I knew even then . . . I have always known, that Mike is my beloved.[13]

The difficulty remains of transposing these shifting literary tenses into the visual medium, and varying filmic and editing techniques are used to replace or alter Lindsay's temporal distortions at crucial points in the film. When Miranda (played by Anne Lambert) opens the gate to the picnic grounds, a flurry of birds startles the horses of the drag, and the images of her enigmatic expression and the horses, and rapid pans following the birds against the trees, are overlaid for an effect beyond the capabilities of the written word. Eroticized slow-motion shots of Miranda leaping across the creek and floating up the slopes are associated with Mike's immediate perception and subsequent remembrance and hint at her later transmutation and idolization in the form of a white swan. Miranda's movement in slow motion is juxtaposed with the normal movement of the other girls within scenes showing their climb. Edith in "normal time" watches the three other girls in slow motion disappearing from sight on the Rock, and Mike (Dominic Guard) is also seen moving in slow motion during his solitary search. When Mike sleeps fitfully and deliriously near the summit, the soundtrack suggests that he hears a concatenation of voices and lines from earlier parts of the film, from scenes where he was not present and events of which he could not know. Further, the hysterical scenes at Irma's last visit to the College, related by Lindsay in a shocking present tense, are shown by a handheld camera caught within the crowd of crazed girls. A true convergence of the literary and cinematic methods is found when Edith remarks that the school party " 'might be the only living creatures in the whole world' . . . airily dismissing the entire animal kingdom at one stroke."[14] Lindsay includes a close-up description of the "teeming" wildlife among the "mountainous human shapes."

Weir's version consists of time-lapse views of ants scaling the celebration cake in Herculean but insignificant toil, which will be paralleled by the girls' ascent of the Rock and the many fruitless searches that succeed it. Green's script is faithful to the text, and Weir creates a collage of filmic tenses to match Lindsay's through time-lapse, slow motion, dislocated voice-over, and omnipotent revelation.

The inclusion and reappearance of images, visual motifs, and symbols make *Picnic* a rich viewing experience. Not only is it an art film, but it also consumes and imitates other arts, enlisting them to assist the viewer's interpretation. Perhaps predictably, some of the most clumsy or expressive images are derived directly from the novel: Miranda as the swan, forever just beyond Mike's reach; Irma recovered from the Rock, watched by Mike under veiling nets and a flower embroidered coverlet, "in a froth of muslin and lace . . . remind[ing] the young man of his sister's valentines."[15] As a vision of idealized romance that characterizes the novel's (if not the film's) notion of love, Irma (Karen Robson) comes to resemble a valentine's token when ripe for marriage, after miraculously maturing (although remaining immaculately "intact") on the Rock. As the sole survivor of the senior boarders, she is now the perfect example of Victorian desirability. She has displayed a coquettishness lacking in the erudite Marion or the ethereal Miranda, who by contrast is seen after her disappearance in pictures and portraits, analyzed in a newspaper photograph under a magnifying glass by Colonel Fitzhubert like a flower forever frozen, preserved at the moment of her loss. The swan associated with Miranda reappears as a small china ornament in the bedroom she shared with Sara, as a similar trinket Mike toys with during his police interview, and as a white bird on a glass used by Mrs. Appleyard (Rachel Roberts). The swan's freedom clashes with the regimented flock of white peahens on the College lawns, symbolizing the girls' confinement.

Flowers appear as symbols of love, purity, fecundity, or transience. The examples are legion: the flowers in Miranda's hand basin and in Irma's room; the rose Miranda hands to Mam'selle before breakfast; the blooms thrown over the party as they descend the school steps; the wall decoration around the top of Miranda's and Sara's room like a living tree bough (a flower design also features in Mrs. Appleyard's study, but its symmetrical pattern is quite unlike the fecund chaos seen elsewhere); the flower Miranda studies under a magnifying glass on the picnic; the daisies offered at her oval portrait shrine by Sara (Margaret Nelson); the drawer full of dried flowers rifled by Mrs. Appleyard when she clears Sara's belongings; and the white flower from a valentine pressed on the morning of the picnic.

The flowers raise (but do not necessarily explain) the issues of romantic ripening and sexual maturity detectable in the film, but they are by no means the only recurrent images. The appearance of white birds links with the costuming of the girls (a conscious choice on the part of Weir's wife Wendy to set the girls in "white against the natural landscape"[16]). Aberrations from this dress code become conspicuous: Miss McCraw's severe suit and veil, according with her "masculine intellect," echoed by Mrs. Appleyard's dress before the announcement of her death; the drab appearance of the junior mistress Miss Lumley; Mam'selle (Helen Morse), first seen in holiday white muslin like her pupils but later adopting more sober and mature hues; and the variations in Mrs. Appleyard's dress, from opulent colored gowns to mourning black like her monarch in the wake of the disappearances, to the cream-colored and flower-bedecked dress she wears for her last meal with Mam'selle, previewing her own imminent encounter with the Rock.

Costuming reinforces the series of changes undergone by principal characters, recognizing twists of fate in private and public fortune. In examining the fetishization of costuming (and especially corseting) in *Picnic*, Stella Bruzzi recognizes the importance of such eroticized clothing in the restatement of distance and difference between the objectified girls and their observers (particularly between Miranda and Mike, but also the girls and the cinematic spectator). The concealment and unobtainability of the girls are certainly central to the eroticism of the spectacle for Mike and the viewer, but it is an oversimplification to assert that "Weir only addresses a masculine erotic gaze."[17] The first image of Miranda waking on the morning of the picnic, presented as an almost static moment of erotic contemplation, is identified subsequently as the point of view of her roommate Sara. Similarly, Bruzzi concedes that corseting functioned as a female as much as a male fetishization, suggestive of an emergent and subversive (hetero- or homo-) sexuality rather than socially sanctioned constriction and conformity.[18]

Such emphasis on spectacle is established by the title sequence, which features recurrent use of mirrors in shot composition. Irma's face is seen in her dressing mirror while she sits with her back to the camera in her ornate boudoir. Blanche holds a dress against her body as she looks out of frame to the right, presumably at herself in another mirror, while another girl behind the camera but reflected in a large wardrobe mirror in the background reads Renaissance-style love poetry (an equivalent composition later shows Mam'selle in Irma's bedroom at the Fitzhuberts' home looking at Irma off-screen right, while we see her in a large mirror behind the French mistress). Mrs. Appleyard catches a horrified glimpse of herself in a dressing mirror in Sara's room when she removes evidence of the suicide.

These instances stress a sense of artificiallity, or rather of a falsehood under threat of revelation. The girls in the opening sequence are unnatural, since their education and prospective places in society are dictated by Victorian ideals remote from the experiences they will undergo, from their own romantic preconceptions and from the liberated conditions of modernity from which we view them. They are the forced flowers of their time, false constructs of society as much as they are artistic conceits of the film and novel. In this context, the shot of Mrs. Appleyard reveals the necessary narrative information of who is ransacking Sara's belongings and also shows the headmistress for what she has become with the College's misfortunes—a desperate woman pressured by the doctrines of society into attempting to preserve the school's and her own good name. The overdetermination of mirrors in this opening sequence recalls their presence in the prologue to *The Magnificent Ambersons* (Orson Welles, 1942). Mirrors are used to frame and therefore distance the affected styles of the past modeled by Eugene Morgan in his youth. The defamiliarized fashions are viewed with an affectionate if ironic nostalgia, but society's insistence on the observance of manners and appearance becomes a theme of crucial, tragic import as the narrative progresses. The significance of this prologue only emerges gradually. Eugene, who is seen initially as a slavish follower of fashion, becomes a symbol of the burgeoning modernity that challenges the old-fashioned obsession with appearances, and yet also the victim of another (younger) man's obsessive devotion to outmoded standards.

The most accomplished of *Picnic*'s mirror compositions shows Miranda twice in one shot, reflected in a large square mirror and an oval mirror in her room on the morning of the picnic. Later, we see just the oval mirror with her reflection, as she tells Sara to "love someone else" since she won't be there "much longer," and the shape of the image previews the scenes of Sara's devotion to Miranda's small oval portrait. This conspicuous framing suggests the many levels on which Miranda is perceived (as headgirl, senior boarder, most beautiful of the party, sole protector of Sara, an unearthly and too perfectly loving being to inhabit the College's confines) and how she is already going beyond these labels, to live for herself through her personal secrets and literally secreting herself when she leaves the College and its doctrines behind.

One of the objects Mrs. Appleyard is careful to remove from the bedroom is the book Sara has been seen reading earlier. Its pictures include details of Botticelli's paintings, first seen in Mam'selle's book during the picnic when she compares Miranda to a "Botticelli angel." This allusion to the visual arts links with the Renaissance poetry of the opening sequence, and other features of the art direction and design of the College's interiors illustrate the breadth of the film's reference. Cherubic figures on the large staircase seen on the morning of the picnic give their own mute comment on the contradictions of the school. The statuettes become framed between Sara and Miss Lumley when the latter stops Sara on the way to breakfast, remarking that neither of them will be allowed to go on the picnic. These figurines suggest the College's (and the Victorians') pretensions in copying classical, imperial predecessors, at least in the areas of government, control, art, and longevity. The two figures also relate to Sara and Dora Lumley as details within if not ornaments to that society; one is accommodated in a lowly, functional role, and the other will no doubt follow her into similarly humiliating employment. The statuettes are juxtaposed with the flower-draped figure honoring St. Valentine. The figure carries a bow and may symbolize Pan or Cupid, pagan gods of nature and love.

Paintings and pictures within the College encourage further analysis. In Miranda's room, a picture shows a child led by the hand by an angel. This may illustrate the love between Sara and Miranda, give a divine explanation for the girls' disappearance, or preview Sara's escape and salvation through suicide. Mrs. Appleyard's study contains a portrait of Victoria and the Union Jack, and several severe sepia portraits that seem to judge her actions. Another portrait of the Queen is seen in Sara's classroom, and Colonel Fitzhubert's study, decorated with Egyptian artefacts, reinforces the imperial legacy. Such representations expand until the film assumes the look of other art forms, with costuming and setting of the picnic scenes reminding Ross Gibson of "Manet-like tableaux."[19] Yet, as with Weir's filmic tenses matching Lindsay's, the film also finds its own idiom with which to represent the conflict between Rock and College, human nature and wild nature.

Gibson's comparison can be seen to be correct in spirit but inaccurate in detail, since the artistic model *Picnic* seeks to imitate is that of Australian rather than French Impressionism. As in the case of *Witness* (1985), Weir and his collaborators looked at certain paintings as a basis for art direction, lighting, and composition (seventeenth-century Flemish works for *Witness*, the Heidelberg School for *Picnic*). Drawing inspiration from nineteenth-century Australian painters, themselves influenced by European Impressionism, Weir and his director of photography Russell Boyd were able to depict the opposition of human order and the natural landscape and to illustrate another major theme of the film (transposition of European [British] culture to the Australian environment) through the evocation of an Australian adaptation of a foreign style.[20] Australian artists' adoption of Impressionism parallels Weir's conscious decision to craft *Picnic* within the style of the European art film, but in both cases the model is integrated with the nature and nation of Australia.

Graeme Turner remarks on the similarities between Frederick McCubbin's painting *Lost* (1886) and *Picnic*'s art direction.[21] The painting's colors and content (a child lost in the bush and almost swallowed from sight by the vegetation) are a likely source of inspiration for film and novel alike. However, *Picnic*'s allusions to works of the Heidelberg School can be detected before the excursion takes place. Long shots of the bush and plains in the opening titles resemble landscapes by Arthur Streeton (such as *Still Glides the Stream and Shall Forever Glide*, 1890), which encapsulate the color, expanse, and timelessness of the country. These scenes' pastel shading, recording of the morning mist, and disorientating shifts in perception and focus recall the Impressionists' attempts to capture nature on canvas. Similarly, the girls' first view of the Rock through the trees from their carriage recalls Tom Roberts's *Australian Landscape* (1920). The wonder that the landscape inspires in the schoolgirls at once suggests the mystery of life beyond the College's confines and the imperviousness of nature to the presence or practices of mankind. The contradiction of the threat or welcome that the Rock represents to those who are drawn to it lies at the heart of the narrative's mystery. To those left behind, the missing picnickers are irretrievably lost, and the failure of the searches strikes at the foundations of a self-confident society. To those that vanish, the enlightenment and independence of the leaving represent the revocation of the ties of a constricting societal system, based on a culture more alien to the natural landscape and human nature than the Rock itself. The investiture of the bush with foreign culture is visible in other paintings from the Heidelberg School, amounting to

> a deliberate attempt to equip a new nation with a mythology of spirits that belong uniquely to the Australian landscape. . . . Streeton's *Bush Idyll* [1896] shows fairies airborne amongst the gum trees, and at the same time Sydney Long begins to populate the bush with European demigods.[22]

Daniel Thomas sees this odd mix of cultural dependence and independent artistic expression as inextricably linked with the climate of nascent nationalism in late nineteenth-century Australia:

> The political nationalism of the eighties and nineties accounts for the emergence of heat and sunshine as an Australian symbolism, for Australian outback workers as realist mythology-figures, and for European demigods in Australian landscapes as fantasy mythology-figures. The Australian reception of some aspects of modern French art, Impressionism in the eighties, Symbolism in the nineties, also helps account for the look of the paintings.[23]

The period of Australian Impressionism accords politically and artistically with the milieu of *Picnic*, poised between the centenary of British settlement in 1888 and the federation of the colonized states in 1901. The transmutation of styles in the search for a national art at the turn of the twentieth century is reinvoked in the setting (1900), subject (indigenous and imported culture), and style (Impressionist and Symbolist) of *Picnic*, itself a cultural vehicle for a new national art form that imitates and innovates.

The portrayal of the Rock evokes parallels with literary as well as visual arts. It is a place of contradictions, arid and dead as well as lush and verdant, and its counterpart is the similarly daunting edifice of the College. Both Rock and College symbolize states of mind and body (free opposed to liberated, secure versus endangered), and both have dark and labyrinthine interiors, intimating their sexual and psychological significance. The growths, caves, and high mounds of the Rock recall the sexual motifs of Spenser's

Faerie Queene. The story of Belphoebe and Amoret in Book III, Canto 6 tells how the twins were separated at birth, the former being raised as a huntress by Diana and the latter becoming the adoptive child of Venus. Their ignorance of each other when in close proximity and their varying upbringing (one made for toil, the other for love) parallel the situation of the orphans Albert and Sara, acolyte of the College's Venus. Canto 6, verses 43 to 50 relate to the "Garden of Adonis," which "takes its form from that of the female sexual organs."[24] There Adonis, the lover of Venus, is kept free from death, safe from the ravages of mortality that afflict the rest of the garden. Michael Leslie interprets Amoret's captivity in the Castle of Busyrane and her lover Scudamore's attempts to rescue her as a further sexual allegory: "The Castle has no gate, but that fiery porch denies Scudamore entry; and Spenser seems to be drawing an analogy between the Castle of Busyrane and the female body."[25] The female knight Britomart enters the castle with ease, and one is reminded of the image of Mike prostrate on the Rock before a steep and beckoning oval passage that Albert (representative of the less romantically inclined but earthier and sexually liberated lower classes) scales without difficulty. While images of the girls prone before the towering pillars of the Rock stress its phallic symbolism, such connections with Spenser's text underline the Rock's characterization as a focal point for female sexuality, in dominant as well as submissive roles.

Mam'selle's reflection on Botticelli and Miranda initially appears misleading, as the detail she looks at before drawing the comparison comes from *The Birth of Venus* (1485). Suggesting that Miranda is the goddess of love is very different from admitting her likeness to an angel, but the indivisibility of sacred and secular love, the pagan goddess of love and the Madonna, is evident in their close facial resemblance in Botticelli's work. Perhaps faithfulness to the novel produces the anomaly between "angel" and "Venus," but through chance or intention Botticelli's Venus provides an interesting subtext to the film's narrative and imagery. Forming a triptych with *Primavera* and *Pallas and the Centaur, The Birth of Venus* sheds new light on the film's interpretation.

Miranda's dual position as figurehead of the school and an other-worldly character soon to escape restraint is comparable to Venus's standing in Botticelli's work. She is free-willed as well as dutiful, loving as well as obedient, a young woman responding to nature as well as a schoolgirl living under restriction. The eye is drawn to Miranda in Weir's picture as it is to Venus in Botticelli's. Her calmly dominating presence persists in newspapers, police notices, and Sara's portrait. Venus also appears in *Primavera*, but in that painting the emphasis has shifted:

> Ovid . . . relates how Chloris, a nymph of the fields, was chased by Zephyr and, on his touch, changed into the more splendid Flora, nymph of flowers. . . . The flowers issuing from the mouth of Chloris melt into the dress of Flora [Primavera] which in turn melts into the flowers of the meadow.[26]

The classical narrative indicates how the girls' lives are influenced by other, unseen forms of male authority (the patriarchs of Victorianism, the dreamed-of lovers of Valentine romance) and how they will eventually grow both in maturity and independence (vanishing into wild nature after expressing the free will of human nature). Chloris's transformation is translated pictorially into Weir's superimpositions, when Miranda's face merges with the foliage or the towering faces of the Rock.

The third painting, *Pallas and the Centaur*, stands in contrast to the others, linked in style rather than in content, but its modern interpretation fits *Picnic*'s preoccupations:

> Pallas, the goddess of wisdom, has been through the ages a personification of intellect and man's rational faculties. The centaur, on the other hand, a composite of man and beast, often symbolized the baser sensual passions. The painting is thus . . . a moral allegory celebrating the superiority of rational thought over sensuality.[27]

If we accept this reading, the doctrines of Appleyard College were never before so epigrammatically represented. The reverie of Renaissance poetry and the classical moral order of contemporary visual art both find their way into the art direction of *Picnic* and epitomize the opposing forces influencing the College's students: control of the body and constraint of the mind in preparation for societal roles, and romantic urges, ironically encouraged by classical study, that defy the dominant patriarchal order.

The girls and staff of Appleyard College inhabit the roles intended for Victorian womanhood. Differences between Australian and English upper classes are not explored: What is shown is an English aristocracy in temporary residence (the Fitzhuberts and their nephew) and an English bourgeoisie (Mrs. Appleyard and her values), with the pupils reflecting the spectrum of social fortune, from Irma's millions to Sara's orphanage upbringing. Native Australians (the College servants and the inhabitants of Woodend) come only from the lower end of the scale. Lindsay's position seems to equate with that of the insecure, middle-class Mrs. Appleyard—enviously admiring of the true aristocracy and alternately scornful and patronizing toward the lower class:

> Whether the Headmistress had any previous experience in the educational field, was never divulged. It was unnecessary. With her high-piled greying pompadour and ample bosom, as rigidly controlled as her private ambitions . . . the stately stranger looked precisely what parents expected of an English Headmistress.[28]

The values that can mock Mrs. Appleyard's aspirations can idolize Mike's inherent superiority to Albert (an attitude the film does not embrace) and can then be contradicted by Edith's statement: "My mamma didn't want me to do senior mathematics. She says a girl's place is in the home."[29] Whatever schooling Appleyard College provides (needlework and dance before mathematics, poetry half-remembered by Irma and not remembered at all by Sara, whose own verse is discounted) will be unnecessary; neither Irma the heiress nor Edith the dunce has need of education. Marion Quade is the only intellectual pupil, a favorite and younger version of Greta McCraw, and notably both are lost on the Rock. Clearly the disappearances are not only to be read in terms of sexual maturation and release.

An analysis of those who vanish or are otherwise affected by the Rock reveals that some traits of upbringing and background determine events. Greta McCraw, as an educated and unmarried middle-class woman, encounters something that will not surrender to her miracles of mathematics or any other system. Perhaps we should see her, like the pupils, as a victim of the system rather than its defender, and her escape as equally liberating. Her musing speech (not found in the novel) on the formation of the Rock is one of the most obvious indications of the currents of mental and physical repression in the school for staff and students alike: "Siliceous lava, forced up from deep down below . . ." If this is taken as evidence of sexual repression, other aspects of the film's approach to sexuality are as confused and class-ridden as the novel's. Lindsay has Mam'selle and Minnie both due to marry on Easter Monday[30] and Minnie actually pregnant by Irish Tom beforehand. The only remnant of this in the film is a glimpse of Mam'selle showing the seniors her engagement ring on the morning of the picnic.

However, the film occasionally heightens the sexual tensions and differences in class terms, contrasting Miranda's otherworldliness, Irma's arch comments, and the straightforward sexual satisfaction of Minnie and Tom. Mike, who is smitten by his visions of Miranda as she crosses the creek, is in fact the least changed by the Rock, retaining his vain, romantic longing and shunning the reality of Irma before him. He represents the repression and unreality of the girls' Valentine's Day wishes and the sexless society, which prizes the girls most highly in their virginal state.

Sandy Flitterman, in analyzing such point-of-view shots as the slow-motion views of Miranda, highlights the voyeurism of cinematic representation:

> Film viewing is structured on a system of voyeuristic pleasure. . . . The textual articulation of the desire of the filmmaker across the visual field dictates a specific position and function for the woman—as image and as lost object. . . . It is possible to consider the cinematic apparatus as defining an institutional site in which male appropriation of the scopic drive defines the woman irrefutably as the image-object of the look.[31]

The camera makes Mike's view of the girls an erotic dream to be shared with the viewer, but the young man himself arguably does not fully understand their attraction. That they should have such freedom and know how to exploit it are likewise mysteries to him. An eroticized image of a woman, created by a male and reflecting a male-orientated institution (Victorian society or the cinema), is lost, distanced physically from the voyeur and understood only on the level of image. The male and the camera lose sight of the females when they leave the restriction of the societal construct.

Picnic at Hanging Rock   Anne Lambert   (AUS 1975)
Picture from the Ronald Grant Archive

Laura Mulvey states that the appearance of the female object-image in mainstream cinema "tends to work against the development of a story line, to freeze the action in moments of erotic contemplation."[32] *Picnic*'s art-film narrative effectively ends with Miranda's slow-motion leap, which begins her fetishization as the swan, prevents Mike's romantic development beyond idolization of her image, and defeats narrative closure by previewing the girls' slow-motion disappearance at the summit. The ideal Miranda does return, but only in a further idealized form, as a swan or as a work of art, recreated in a photograph or portrait. She refuses to accept her societal role, and so she is lost to that society. Such an interpretation justifies the preponderance of mirror shots, seeing women as framed, contained images, and in the case of the double mirror shot, suggesting Miranda's escape from the male gaze or even her mastery of it. This appreciation of the institutional bias of the male gaze on the female body and the subversive nature of female evasion or acquisition of the look anticipates Weir's representation of Amish patriarchal society in *Witness*.

The three senior boarders embody different aspects of the human, rather than simply female character. Irma's charity, Marion's reason, and Miranda's love are all merely varying responses to the same societal problems:

> "Poor little Sara," Irma said. "I don't believe she loves anyone in the world except you, Miranda."
> "I can't think why," Marion said.
> "She's an orphan," Miranda said gently.[33]

Miranda embodies all forms of given and received love, as adored child, desired lover, and venerated symbol of womanhood. Her presence in the bush with her three companions evokes another comparison with *Primavera* and the classical reflection of the trinity of faith, hope, and charity in Venus's attendant Graces. The Neoplatonic interpretation of the painting shows Venus's role in mediating love arising from nature onto a higher plane:

> She is Love, which both gives life and has the power to go beyond the physical world into the realm of the intellect and the ideal. The classical Venus has become Venus Humanitas, the arouser of the passions who also moderates them in a full and universal harmony. Like the Christian godhead she is expressed in a trinity, the triad of Graces, whom Seneca interpreted as the threefold aspects of liberalitas, or generous love (giving, receiving, and returning).[34]

Marion's learning, Irma's unthinking giving, and Edith's need for love are unified in Miranda's Venus, whose powerful and tolerant love is unsuited to her prospective societal environment. (These conceptualizations of love contrast with Sara's indomitable and enigmatic passion, epitomized by her association with the print of Lord Leighton's *Flaming June* in Mrs. Appleyard's study.) All three seek a different kind of beauty in the world and find it in one moment when all clocks stop on the Rock. The particularity of Lindsay's and Weir's setting (exactly February 14, exactly 1900, exactly noon when the watches stop) and the succeeding vagueness of perception (confusion in tense, lack of temporal certainty and factual evidence) point to the pricelessness and vulnerability of one incident that will explain and justify all that precedes and follows it.

The three are caught in a Keatsian frozen moment when truth and beauty equate, as suffocating and inescapable as the flower press seen among the morning's valentines. Mike is also trapped in his moment of gazing on Miranda, ever loving the ever fair, in an eternal summer that will not fade. Neither filmmaker nor novelist can show what such an individual and intimate experience could be, as the undergoing outstrips any later re-rendering. As such, the conventional narrative can never be closed, and the task of completing the happy (liberation) or sad (incomprehension) endings falls to the viewer interpreting the wealth of imagery and intertextual reference.

Those females displaying qualities that cannot be accommodated within this society (thirst for knowledge and intellectual growth, universal and healing love, both attempts at spiritual transcendence rather than suppression of humanity) will not return from the Rock. Those embodying acceptable characteristics—unambitious homemaking in Edith, laudable but unthinking charity in Irma—are allowed to come back and assume positions in unassuming womanhood. There is room only for the giving and receiving of certain types of love within Victorian society. With no likelihood of receiving charity or love, Sara eventually follows Marion and Miranda, choosing the ultimate in independent action by taking her own life rather than returning to the orphanage.

Sara is at the bottom of the social order as the youngest and poorest boarder, a ward with a negligent guardian, and as such she represents the worst aspects of Victorian sexuality, which both Lindsay and Green treat with circumspection. Minnie mentions to Tom that the less fortunate pupils are "orphans, or wards, or—y'know," and Lindsay includes Mrs. Appleyard's thought that Sara's discreet and faceless guardian is "obviously a gentleman."[35] Tom jokes about Jack the Ripper as another Victorian mystery, but the school and its precepts repress more than sexuality, and the film's strength is that it explores more of these denials than Lindsay's novel and discusses individual and national determination rather than sexual or class subjugation alone.

Victorian society as portrayed in *Picnic* is obsessed with unchanging standards. The duration of the Queen's reign and the unsetting sun of the Empire epitomize the security of stasis. These principles form the basis of the school's system and find equally significant expression in the motionlessness of the Fitzhuberts on their picnic and the incongruity of the governor's garden party. The Britishness of the aristocracy is constantly in view: the school's reputation for English literature, embodied in Mrs. Appleyard's reproof to Sara that "Mrs. Felicia Hemans is considered one of the finest of *our English* poets" (my emphasis); Miss Lumley's playing of *Men of Harlech* in the "Temple of Callisthenics"; and Lindsay's comment on the garden party guests ("Pleasant comfortable people for whom the current Boer War was the most catastrophic event since the Flood, and Queen Victoria's approaching Jubilee a world-shattering occasion."[36]). The buffet, string quartet, and national anthem appear worse than incongruous in this landscape, especially after the unexplained disappearances.

Amid the imposed Victoriana, an opposing Australian quality emerges. The College servants are too few and too similar to their British counterparts. The Australian pupils are likewise tainted, but are still young enough to rebel, and, aside from Sara, the rebellion takes the form of escape into an impenetrable natural landscape that similarly refuses to conform to human rule. The natural environment becomes the symbol of resistance, the Rock being its focal point, and a center for youthful Australian resistance to elderly imported English values.

Shots of the Rock and its inscrutable faces that echo the searchers' shouts are accompanied by bizarre intrusions of sound and music. Much of the nightmarish atmosphere is attributable to the weirdness of the noise heard in scenes on the Rock. Weir reveals

> With the soundtrack I used white noise, or sounds that were inaudible to the human ear, but were constantly there on the track. I've used earthquakes a lot, for example, slowed down or sometimes mixed with something else. I've had comments from people on both *Picnic* and *Last Wave* saying that there were odd moments during the film when they felt a strange disassociation from time and place. Those technical tricks contributed to that.[37]

These sounds strengthen the sinister threat of the environment and contrast with the harmonies of the soundtrack music, which is characterized by two styles. One is Gheorghe Zamphir's panpipes, giving a lilting, primordial mystery to some natural passages, and the other is Beethoven's Fifth Piano Concerto, "The Emperor." These two pieces can be associated with the presence of the wild beside the measured beauties of civilization, but where they actually appear can be surprising. The panpipes accompany the opening and continue through all the scenes of the girls' Valentine's Day preparations. What is stressed may be a natural but unfledged emotion (half-comprehended love tokens), but there is also the crucial image of the pressed flower, emphasizing timelessness or time halted more than the repression of natural urges. The panpipes also appear with the opening of the gate to the picnic grounds and during the girls' ascent, more clearly associated with resurgent nature and release. An ultimately conclusive example comes when the pipes return when Mike and Irma meet and walk through the Fitzhuberts' gardens. They come to sit on a rockery, eerily decorated with faces carved in the stone (one old and mustached, another rounded and infantile). The music seems to herald a return to the wild but in fact suggests that Irma's maturation on the Rock now prompts a real rather than imagined love, in this case sanctioned by society as an admirable match. However, Mike remains obsessed with his mythologized vision of Miranda, and cannot return her love.

The "Emperor" music, rather than asserting the primacy of Victorian order, conveys more of an elegiac tone for Victorian society's vulnerable state. Its melancholic strains are next to images of the fruitless police search, the adoration of the rescued Irma by Sergeant Bumpher and Doctor McKenzie, and the final scenes with the voice-over leaving the mystery unsolved. It suggests that the stalwart values are in retreat, and the final pensive scenes indicate the capitulation of a social construct soon to pass into history. Notably, the same piece is used to articulate a comparable loss and regret in *Immortal Beloved* (Bernard Rose, 1994).

Symbolic use of music and other arts in the development of character and society also occurs in other Australian period films, notably *The Getting of Wisdom* and *My Brilliant Career*. In the former, the initially naive heroine Laura conforms to the rules of a pretentious, English-style boarding school to gain a music scholarship, choosing to express her rebelliousness covertly through her playing. This mode of self-expression, in the absence of other meaningful channels in a male-dominated society, can also been seen in the behavior of Ada, the heroine of *The Piano*. Sybylla, the heroine of *My Brilliant Career*, uses literary skills to make her way in the world, turning down the man she loves to avoid financial dependence and submersion in marriage. Her autobiography forms the basis of the film's narrative, with her control of both, through unconventional behavior and appearance and the act of transcribing her deeds and opinions, amounting to a subversion of conventional narrative comparable to *Picnic*:

> Most of us are used to the filmic convention of representing young women as ugly ducklings, only to have them turn into swans in the final reel. Sybylla's "plainness," however, is resolutely maintained throughout the film. . . . By not compromising on Sybylla's look, the film avoids the illogicality of exploiting the spectacle of the female, and earns the right to make its statements on its protagonist's plight.[38]

Sybylla's manuscript is sent away for publication, so even though she maintains a retired existence, her book gives her mental freedom and independence.

All three films, and their literary bases, evince a desire for self-determination, but in contrast to Laura's formulaic rite of passage, Sybylla and the College boarders defy convention. They break the rules of their diegetic social worlds while the films themselves challenge the conventions of cinema (in *My Brilliant Career* with a plain-looking and plain-speaking heroine, and in *Picnic* with a complex play of visual tenses and allusions to distract from narrative irresolution). Both films stretch the boundaries of the AFC genre in their filmic styles and their critical reception, *Picnic* being hailed as the first Australian art film and *My Brilliant Career* as a feminist text.

Other films approaching the themes of adolescence, society, and nature in conflict are marked by formal experimentation and skillful usage of music and image. *Walkabout* (Nicolas Roeg, 1970) uses disorientating sound to portray the fusion of ancient and modern. Aboriginal music merges with radio static and school elocution lessons, and a view around a brick wall leads into the deepest desert, accompanied by traffic noise. The treatment of the landscape, the clash of modern and ancient cultures, and experimentation with sound and vision in Roeg's film may have influenced both *Picnic* and *The Last Wave* (1977). *Is-Slottet* (Per Blom, 1987) depicts a secret, quasi-sexual compact between two schoolgirls, one of whom is lost in the ice palace of the title, a fantastic maze created by a frozen waterfall. Blom's film also features a disjointed timescale in memory and flashback, and it eschews all natural sound until the discovery of the surviving girl's secret and the simultaneous summer thaw and collapse of the ice palace. As in *Picnic*, there is a scene in a church, where the dubiety of a hymn's words provokes sadness and anger. The profound irony of "Rock of Ages . . . let me hide myself in thee" in *Picnic* summarizes the conflict between the rock of the establishment where one can hide in anonymity and the Rock existing both before and beyond it, which is its mortal foe.

One thorough search of the Rock should yield answers, but many searches only deepen the mystery. The establishment, like the novel reader or cinema viewer expecting conventional narrative closure, will be disappointed. *Picnic* may play upon the expectation of resolution, but it leaves this notion behind to attain a lyricism of imagery beyond narrative constraint, a contrasting convention of the art film. Society, embodied in Mrs. Appleyard, loses confidence when confronted with unexplained events. Her reminiscences of holidays in Bournemouth and memories of Miss McCraw hinge on unchanging conditions and dependability. Mutability is the unthinkable disaster that results in the collapse of the College, the headmistress, and the Empire. The ever-ticking clock in her study is halted like her life by the Rock's interruption of previously unshakeable control. (Miranda's resistance to such control has been encapsulated in her admission during the picnic that she no longer wears her watch, since she could not "stand it ticking above her heart.") What truly endures is nature and human nature; spontaneity and youth, nonconformity epitomized by the Rock and beckoning kindred spirits in the girls who shun a foreign (adult, masculine, and English) authority. The step-printed repetition of the pan over the picnic group that concluded the film offers only a return to an equally opaque and revelatory moment. Narrative ceases without conclusion, and time is halted in an erotic contemplation that remains unconsummated. The ultimate focus and preference of the film rests on a visual stylization (which nonetheless encapsulates its debate about time, beauty, and change) that arguably goes beyond art-film constructions to attain a parametricality of narrative[39]—an inseparability of style and meaning.

The concentration of *Picnic*'s narrative upon the halting of time and preservation of perfection makes the subsequent revision of the film in a director's cut all the more ironic. Weir's decision to revise an earlier work is fascinating in the light of earlier comments, in which he expressed the view that films were "utilitarian devices, consumer items that were used up within the year of their manufacture."[40] (The decision to proceed with the director's cut may have been taken at the same time as Weir was sponsoring the work of the National Film and Sound Archive in Australia, including the funding and provision of pristine prints of his own early films.[41]) The subsequent reediting of the film is also unusual, inasmuch as the running time of the new version is nearly identical to that of the original. Instead of simply adding to the existing cut, the director's cut omits several scenes and shortens other sequences to accommodate other, previously unseen footage. Like the director's cut of *Bladerunner* (Ridley Scott, 1982/1991), the 1998 version of *Picnic* appears as an alternative to rather than a restoration (except in terms of image and sound quality) or expansion of the original release.

The first omission in the director's cut occurs soon after the credit sequence. Shots of Mam'selle musing over her valentine on the landing, being met by the seniors, and walking around to the staircase are removed, resulting in a straight cut to Miss Lumley upbraiding the pupils descending the stairs. The following long take of the girls at breakfast is also shortened. More substantial abridgments occur later in the film. Nearly four minutes are cut from the period of Irma's convalescence with the Fitzhuberts, including the scenes of her meeting with Albert and Mike, the walk to carved rockery with Mike and Mam'selle, the short dialogue scene between Albert and Mike in Albert's loft room, and Mike's and Irma's trip on the punt. Consequently, the film cuts from Mike's vision of Miranda as the swan in the garden to the photos of the missing members of the party posted on a notice board. The order in which the photos of Miranda, Marion, and Miss McCraw are seen is also altered from the original, with Miranda's portrait now appearing first. This is followed by an exterior shot of the church and the school party exiting after the service (with the absence of scenes inside the church, "Rock of Ages" is removed from the soundtrack). The last significant cuts occur near the film's end, on the night of Sara's suicide. The crash of breaking glass, accompanying an exterior shot of the College in the original, is deleted, as are the scenes of Mrs. Appleyard rifling Sara's room.

The counterbalancing additions to the film appear equally intriguing. The largest single addition comes after the church sequence and consists of six shots showing a photographer attempting to get pictures of the girls outside the College and being chased away by the headmistress. An additional shot–reverse shot series is inserted in the picnic sequence, when Albert observes Mike crossing the creek and going after the girls. Albert's apparent suspicion in the original version is allayed by a second shot in which he looks after Mike, then shrugs and collects his coat from a tree. The potential for doubt over Mike's motives, and for Albert's suspecting him of wrongdoing, is removed by this addition. A later shot of Albert awake in bed, musing over the events, is also defused in this way, by the removal from the soundtrack of his recollection of Mike's comment that he is just going to "stretch his legs" before they leave the picnic grounds.

The alterations to the film's ending also appear to be prompted by the need to extend scenes between Albert and Mike, as the removal of Mrs. Appleyard's visit to Sara's room is compensated by additional dialogue between the young men. In the new version, Albert's description of his dream about Sara is introduced by Albert asking, "You still thinking about that bloody rock?" to which Mike replies, "I can't help it. It comes back every night in dreams." While clearly intended to smooth the deliberately jarring transition between night and day (a cut from Mrs. Appleyard catching sight of herself in the mirror to the young men chatting in the loft, which existed in the original version), this alteration restresses their kinship (previewing the mateship of the delicate, fair Archy and dark, earthy Frank in *Gallipoli* [1981]) and reemphasizes the relevance of dreams (anticipating *Wave*).

Accounting for and interpreting these changes represents a formidable challenge, given the canonical status of the original text. The abbreviation of certain shots on the morning of the picnic reduces the languor, and gently increases the anticipation, of the film's exposition. A tauter pace here works to exacerbate the subversion of narrative resolution later. Conversely, the slight diminution of the visible relationship between Mam'selle and the senior boarders is replaced by an increased emphasis upon the budding mateship between Mike and Albert. The deletion of their scenes with Irma creates space for this and removes the romantic distraction for both Mike and the viewer, albeit at the expense of Irma's presence and enigmatic silence in the film's later stages.

The removal of significant parts of the sequence detailing Sara's suicide and the addition of the photographer appear to be the most remarkable changes. The silence that hides Sara's fall in the director's cut transforms her death into an incorporeal, transcendent change, almost as unfathomable as the disappearances on the Rock, without compromising the recognition of Mrs. Appleyard's fear and culpability. In a film using conspicuous, disconcerting sound (the remastering of the director's cut also incorporates an upgrading to Dolby 5.1 Surround), this reduction to silence exhibits a maturer distillation of effect compared with the original. Similarly, the addition of the photographer, while connecting with the establishment's futile attempts at rationalization of events (recalling the newspapers and journalistic reports of *Michael* (1971) and *Cars* and previewing those of *Wave*), also anticipates the voyeurism and prurience of the audience in *The Truman Show* (1998).

In this light, the overall decision to create the director's cut and the specifics of its difference from the original text further illuminate the director's canon as a continuum, reemphasizing the Gothic and mystical intensities of the 1970s features and the scrutiny of masculinity, nationality, and contemporary society seen in the later films. Just as Weir's films of the 1990s (*Fearless* [1993] and *Truman*) embody a return to the themes and style of those of the 1970s, so the director's cut of *Picnic* can be read as a parallel rather than an improvement upon Weir's breakthrough film.

In *Picnic*, the Hanging Rock represents forces as ancient as the land and as young as the schoolgirls, not simply sexuality but individuality and—arguably, in the uniqueness of the natural landscape—national character. *Picnic* shows society in conflict with nature, even as the film confronts conventional narrative form and challenges audience expectation. It is a methodologically rebellious film about individual rebellion, a nonconformist's view of conformity that succeeded ironically in pleasing the establishment of a traditionally conservative industry, the cinema. Critic of Weir's woolliness, in attempting a poetry of images in opposition to narrative, essentially misapprehend the film, its novel base, and the timing of its production. Both the film's and the novel's factual statements at beginning and end provide a credible setting for the conceptual play of repression and release that they enclose.

Yet contrary to the authority of fact, we have the insertion of Miranda's voice at the very beginning of the film, intoning, "What we see and what we seem are but a dream—a dream within a dream." Even though it concentrates on the subjective and the unconscious, *Picnic's* dream of inscrutable rebellion against the rule of an unnatural order becomes exterior and public while retaining the images, associations, and elliptical quality of the mind. This painterly, enigmatic, and highly successful film put its director at the forefront of the Australian revival, displaying his ability to balance elements of narrative, music, and visual allusion:

> *Picnic's* excellence is typical of the classics of the fantasy genre, such as Carl Dreyer's *Vampyr* and Jacques Tourneur's *I Walked With a Zombie*—films as much, if not more, about themselves and their shifting, disorientating relationship with the audience as about a world full of mysterious events.[42]

This comparison with both European and American films based in psychological horror, the apparent extremes of auteurist and genre cinema, heralded Weir's assimilation into Hollywood while retaining his thematic and stylistic hallmarks. *Picnic* may have set in motion the cycle of period films that gave Australian film a known but unremarkable international name, but for Weir it represented a significant step forward in personal ability and popular renown, which would aid his access to an international career and audience.

Notes

1. David Stratton, *The Last New Wave: The Australian Film Revival* (London: Angus & Robertson, 1980), pp. 68–69.

2. Brian McFarlane, *Words and Images: Australian Novels into Film* (Richmond, Victoria: Heinemann, 1983), p. 45.

3. Graeme Turner, "Art Directing History," in *The Australian Screen*, eds. Albert Moran and Tom O'Regan (Harmondsworth: Penguin, 1989), pp. 113–114.

4. Susan Dermody and Elizabeth Jacka, *The Screening Of Australia Vol. II: Anatomy of a National Cinema* (Sydney: Currency, 1988), p. 34. Comparable criticisms of the conservative ideological and commercial purposes of "heritage" films made in the French film industry can be found in *French Cinema in the 1990s: Continuity and Difference*, ed. Phil Powrie (Oxford: Oxford University Press, 1999).

5. Interview with the author, June 1993.

6 Don Shiach, *The Films of Peter Weir* (London: Letts, 1993), pp. 39–40, 51.

7. Joan Lindsay, *Picnic at Hanging Rock* (London: Penguin, 1970), p. 6.

8. John Izod, "The Piano, the Animus and Colonial Experience," in *Jane Campion's The Piano*, ed. Harriet Margolis (Cambridge: Cambridge University Press, 2000), p. 86.

9. Christian Metz, "History/Discourse: A Note on Two Voyeurisms," in *Theories of Authorship*, ed. John Caughie (London: Routledge & Kegan Paul, 1981), p. 226.

10. Lindsay, *Picnic*, p. 29.

11. *Ibid.*, pp. 29–30 (my emphases).

12. *Ibid.*, p.120.

13. *Ibid.*, p. 129.

14. *Ibid.*, pp. 20–21.

15. *Ibid.*, p. 116.

16. Interview with the author, June 1993.

17. Stella Bruzzi, *Undressing Cinema: Clothing and Identity in the Movies* (London: Routledge, 1997), p. 43.

18. *Ibid.*, pp. 44–5.

19. Ross Gibson, "Camera Natura: Landscape in Australian Feature Films," *Framework*, 22/23 (1983), pp. 47–51 (p. 50).

20. "Picnic at Hanging Rock was a coming of age for all of us. From the start I felt we had to capture the 'Tom Roberts' light of the Australian countryside." Russell Boyd, quoted in an advertisement for Kodak films that used a still from *Picnic*, in *Cinema Papers*, 10 (1976), center pages.

21. Graeme Turner, *National Fictions: Literature, Film, and the Construction of Australian Narrative* (London: Allen & Unwin, 1986), p. 27.

22. Daniel Thomas, *Outlines of Australian Art: The Joseph Brown Collection*, expanded ed. (Melbourne: Macmillan, 1980), pp. 28–29.

23. *Ibid.*, p. 29.

24. Michael Leslie, "Edmund Spenser: Art and *The Faerie Queen*," *Proceedings of the British Academy*, 76 (1990), pp. 73–107 (p. 87).

25. *Ibid.*, p.83.

26. L. D. Ettinger and H. S. Ettinger, *Botticelli* (London: Thomas & Hudson, 1976), p. 129.

27. *Ibid.*, pp. 130–131.

28. Lindsay, *Picnic*, p. 9.

29. *Ibid.*, p. 58.

30. *Ibid.*, p. 134.

31. Sandy Flitterman, "Woman, Desire and the Look: Feminism and the Enunciative Apparatus of the Cinema," in *Theories*, ed. Caughie, pp. 243–244.

32. Laura Mulvey, "Visual Pleasure and Narrative Cinema," *Screen, 16* (1975), pp. 6–18, (p. 11).

33. Lindsay, *Picnic*, p. 33.

34. Umberto Baldini, *Primavera* (London: Sidgwick & Jackson, 1986), p. 90.

35. Lindsay, *Picnic*, p. 60.

36. *Ibid.*, p. 73.

37. Sue Mathews, *35mm Dreams: Conversations with Five Directors About the Australian Film Revival* (Melbourne: Penguin, 1984), p. 95.

38. Turner, "Art Directory History," pp. 110–111.

39. David Bordwell, *Narration in the Fiction Film* (London: Routledge, 1988), pp. 274–310.

40. Interview with the author, June 1993.

41. Paul Kalina, "Designing Visions: Peter Weir and *The Truman Show,*" *Cinema Papers, 127* (1998), pp. 18–22, 56 (p. 56).

42. Adrian Martin, "Fantasy," in *The New Australian Cinema,* ed. Scott Murray (Melbourne: Thomas Nelson, 1980), pp. 99–102.

Chapter Three

The Last Wave (1977) and The Plumber (1979)

> A vast gap is opened up between knowledge (as scientific investigation and rational enquiry) and gnosis (a knowledge of ultimate truths, a kind of spiritual wisdom), and it is in this gap that the modern fantastic is situated.[1]

The insistence of *Picnic at Hanging Rock* (1975) on Gothicism belies its period-film gentility and emphasizes the thematic consistencies it shares with *Homesdale* (1971) and *The Cars That Ate Paris* (1974). It also anticipates the union of art-film narration, social criticism, and the examination of contemporary existential crises that distinguishes Peter Weir's films of the 1990s. Stylistically, however, *Picnic* is closest to *The Last Wave*; despite their differences in setting, these films also share a depiction of an uncanny subversion of bourgeois values, which is accompanied and articulated by the eschewal of conventional narrative construction. In both of these films (and subsequently in *Fearless* [1993] and *The Truman Show* [1998]), doubts over the reliability and objectivity of perception and narration compel protagonists and viewers alike to question the structure, motivation, and durability of social and cinematic conventions.

In the wake of the success of *Picnic*, Weir's next feature film was at once a more ambitious production, with a budget twice that of *Picnic*, and a more personal one, with elements of the script derived from the director's own experience. The growth of the budget, caused by the special effects required for storm sequences, forced producers Hal and Jim McElroy to seek overseas funding before shooting began (circumstances that presage the more commercially conscious Australian film industry of the 1980s). A distribution agreement with United Artists provided more than half the required financing, with the South Australia Film Corporation and the Australian Film Commission guaranteeing to honor any cost overruns.[2] To recoup the investment, the film needed an international appeal, involving non-Australian personnel such as the Hollywood-based Romanian writer Petru Popescu and the American star Richard Chamberlain to play the lead role of David Burton.

In an interview, Weir said the idea behind his script for *Wave* sprang from an occurrence during a visit to Tunisia in 1971:

> I wanted to go to Tunisia because after Pompeii, the next best preserved Roman city is there. So we were driving there, and stopped for a walk, and I was suddenly seized with this strange feeling I was going to find something; I even saw what I was going to see. And there it was, on the ground, a carving of a child's head. I brought it home and thought about it for ages afterwards. What was that experience? Why did I see the head in my mind before I saw it in actuality? And then I started to think, what if a very rational person—a lawyer, say—had had the same experience? How would he cope with it?[3]

This incident, allied to conversations with the Aboriginal actor David Gulpilil, formed the basis of Weir's narrative.

The McElroy twins were apprehensive that the film's subject matter might lessen its international appeal. The preconception that narrative film should have universal appeal despite specific Australian content (extensive reference to Aboriginal lore) appears to have been uppermost in the minds of the McElroy brothers since their collaboration with Weir on *Cars*. The commercial failure of Weir's first feature may have prompted the producers to seek the widest possible audience for *Wave* and to downplay its cultural specificity.[4] This in turn may have provoked some of the discontent within the Aboriginal community caused by the film's content, despite the casting of Gulpilil and the cooperation of the Aboriginal Cultural Foundation in the production. Although Weir and his collaborators had taken great care to forestall criticism of their handling of tribal lore, the location shooting was picketed by Aboriginal groups. In interview, Weir revealed the extent of the assistance received from the respected tribal elder Nandjiwarra Amagula, who appeared in the film as Charlie:

> In accepting to do the film, he accepted the principle of recreating a lost Sydney tribe and their symbols, and tokens. Initially we made the naive request to use some of his tribal symbols to which he said absolutely not, nor should we use any existing tribal symbols, nor should we use any of our collected paintings and drawings of the vanished Sydney tribe. So Goran Warff, the art director, created a fictional series of symbols and Nandji approved them.[5]

Such care in defusing the racial and cultural tension inherent in the treatment of Aboriginal heritage indicates that Weir's screenplay concentrates instead on the irruption of the bizarre into mundane existence, continuing themes seen in *Cars* and *Picnic*. Jack Clancy sees *Wave* as a more successful social commentary than either of the preceding features because it mixes *Picnic's* fantasy narrative with *Cars'* contemporary setting:

> Where *The Last Wave* represents a development beyond *Picnic* is precisely where we find the echoes of *The Cars That Ate Paris*, because the neat allegory of *Cars* enabled Weir to touch on matters of immediate social concern—the dominant place of the motor car in Australian life, and the obsessions, fetishes, and neuroses that surround it.
>
> In *The Last Wave*, two contemporary issues force their way into our consciousness through all the teasing mystery—the place of Aboriginal culture in a materialist, rationalist, Christian culture, and an uneasy sense (again an echo of *Picnic*) of a physical and spiritual environment violated by that materialist, rationalist, white culture.[6]

The marked difference between the upper-middle-class Burtons and the lower-class Aborigines represents an opposition similar to that between the Rock and the College in *Picnic*, with a foreign culture intruding on the Australian domain. Combining the social commentary and alienation of Australian Gothic with the science-fiction film's personal or national apocalypse endows *Wave* with an art-film style for the depiction of genre material. *Cars'* genre awareness and European editing meld with *Picnic's* symbolism and the allegory of *Homesdale* in *Wave's* uncanny, unclosed narrative.

Weir's subsequent project, the made-for-television movie *The Plumber*, appears to be the antithesis of *Wave*, having a small budget, no major stars, a crew lacking all of the director's usual technical collaborators, and a limited theatrical release. Weir was contracted to make three films for the South Australia Film Corporation, which, like other state film boards, made small numbers of films for television. The narrative for Weir's script for *The Plumber* was again taken from life, drawing on the experience of friends besieged by an uninvited plumber. Despite its modest budget, three-week shooting schedule, and exclusively Australian cast, the film was well received at the Sydney Film Festival and was later screened in Los Angeles, adding to Weir's growing reputation in America.[7]

The Plumber's unassuming beginnings belie its importance within the director's work. It previews *Green Card* (1990) in its subject matter (a middle-class woman threatened by a stranger in her own home) and in its strictly commercial crafting (a narrowly conceived thriller as opposed to the later romantic comedy). It links *Wave*'s supernatural threat to the Burton household to *Green-Card*'s humorous disruption of a middle-class home through its stylistic similarity to both feature films. Constricting door and window frames within the filmic frame suggest the ignorance or prejudice of the white Anglo-Saxon mentality and its constraints on perception.

Jill's deceitful response to the intrusion of the loud, lower-class plumber Max reveals contemporary social inequality in a thriller rather than in fantasy mode. The conventional thriller heroine, whose courage and resourcefulness aid her struggle against the murderous male, is here transformed into a dissatisfied female academic who resorts to criminal deception against a class enemy whose threat appears purely psychological. Like the natural forces of *Wave*, Max's activities are directed against the middle-class property and home, with the dwelling symbolizing Jill's mental as well as physical well-being. Jill's safety within the confines of her university flat becomes reliant on Max's confinement in prison; her defense of property accrued through her studies and marriage relies ironically on accusing Max of theft.

While the threats to the middle-class white culture and the protective reactions to them differ between *The Plumber* and

Wave, the films share a cynical portrayal of bourgeois society. The hollowness and iniquity of imported culture seen in *Picnic* become the arrogance and vulnerability of the middle class seen in *The Plumber*, and the ignorance and barrenness of all modern Western life in *Wave*. The debate passes from the subject of nationalism versus colonialism in *Picnic*, to spiritualism and existentialism in *Wave*, and finally, in a preview of *Green Card*, to passion against conservatism in *The Plumber*. While describing *The Plumber* as an uncharacteristic "Pinteresque black comedy" when seen against Weir's other films of the 1970s, M. Kinder identifies its equation of several nested conflicts that connect the director's work:

> [Weir] cultivates the reading of this encounter on many dif-
> ferent levels—not merely as a sexual struggle between a
> swaggering macho bully and a timid, uptight woman, but also
> as a class struggle between the underprivileged working class
> and the snobbish, educated bourgeoisie; between the instinc-
> tive world of sexuality, improvisation, and charm and the aca-
> demic world of reason, science and law; between the sixties
> counter culture . . . and the seventies establishment.[8]

The mystical atmosphere Weir creates in *Wave* around the increasingly threatening weather and David Burton's gradual discovery of his destiny owes much to *Picnic*, in its evocation of the timeless landscape in the desert prologue and later in the slow-motion, time-lapse photography and unnerving sound effects. The juxtaposition of domesticity, Aboriginal and non-Aboriginal law, and relentless and uncontrollable weather in *Wave* recalls the portrayal of a natural threat to narrow provincial life in *The Birds* (Alfred Hitchcock, 1963). The sterility of human existence seems to conjure a mortal and metaphysical threat out of disregarded nature. Since the danger that the birds and the storms represent cannot be rationalized or averted, questions are directed instead toward the content and complacency of human life. The task of rationalizing bizarre events that confronts the unremarkable protagonists of both films is similar to the interpretative acts of their viewers. Both groups lose the stability of their normal environments, and this loss of security prompts a reexamination of their previous safe and ignorant existences: living in the modern urban setting, and viewing linear narrative film. In style and construction as much as in theme, then, both Weir's and Hitchcock's films enter the art-film category despite their genre derivation.

Considering the range of *Wave*'s themes (Aboriginal belief, the influence of ancient cultures on modern man, the significance of dreams), we can see not only the difficulty of combining such ideas into a strong storyline but also the potential for the same material to raise questions of social and spiritual harmony, individual and communal perception, subjectivity, and isolation. The inadequacies of *Wave* on the level of narrative clarity are its strengths on many other levels of allusiveness and on its examination of the nature of cinematic representation. In contrast, the compact thriller narrative of *The Plumber*, evoking *Homesdale*'s absurd dark comedy and Hitchcock's atmosphere of danger in domestic life (signaled by parodies of the shower scene from *Psycho* (1960) in both films[9]), produces a comparable analysis of empty suburban life and social inequality. Its genre source is similar to that of *Wave* but its linear narrative integrates Weir's stylistic and thematic features without the earlier film's dislocation and lack of closure. Where *Wave* weds Weir's visual style and abiding themes to horror material and art-film technique, *The Plumber*'s thriller format bases the same concerns in a controlled, commercial production.

In addition to the stylistic similarities between *Wave* and *Picnic*, a common theme is evident in the threat posed to human society by unbridled nature. The recurrent images of water in use by and under the control of humanity (garden sprinklers, water fountains in the street, hose pipes in the desert, dripping taps in the pathology lab) are set against other forms of the same element over which man has no mastery (ferocious rain and hail storms, overflowing baths, and the ultimate tidal wave). The apparent danger to the human (white) establishment posed by these phenomena indicates the genre debt, as in the case of *Cars*, to 1950s American science-fiction film. The staples of this genre (the perversion of nature, the invasion or control of the human body or mind, and apocalyptic disaster) are transposed into a context combining the superficial order of modern society and pervasiveness of ancient mythology. As such, *Wave* combines some characteristics from the broad category of science-fiction and horror films and some from 1970s disaster movies with the style and social critique of the European art film. The judgmental and punitive aspects of the disaster movie, especially in its subdivision of the "natural attack"[10] upon human society, can also be seen to influence the amalgamation of art and genre film sources in *Wave*.

Science and magic often equate in science-fiction films, and humanity's victory, though reliant on technology, is attributable to teamwork and communal responsibility in the politico-military and scientific establishment. The attraction of the portrayal of natural or supernatural catastrophes in science-fiction films resides in the illusion that "one can participate in the fantasy of living through one's own death and more, the death of cities, the destruction of humanity itself."[11] However, in *Wave*, these themes are altered significantly: David Burton is at best on the fringes of the establishment and becomes alienated altogether when he becomes involved in the Aborigines' case; the wider community, though suffering under the bizarre weather, has no answer to it beyond impotent categorizing of effects (hail never having been recorded in the desert before) and theorizing about cause (pollution is the agreed source of the black rain); the church, a safe refuge and sure foundation in American films (*War of the Worlds* [Byron Haskin, 1953]), is equally discredited for its narrow-mindedness (the church where David's stepfather preaches is seen in long shot, surrounded by foliage in a composition reminiscent of the endangered Appleyard College); and the disaster is an attack on a specific individual (and his dwelling place), a personal revelation more important than the (perhaps only imagined) destruction of the city or world.

With the establishment unaware of or unconcerned by the intimations of disaster, the Burton family and its home are the prime targets for disruption. As in *The Birds*, mundane events are a necessary contrast to the unenvisaged horrors that engulf the suburban characters, but they also provoke an examination of the moral bankruptcy of the society under threat. The homes in *Wave* and *The Plumber* represent the establishment under siege, and, like the minds of their inhabitants, they are unable to withstand external and internal pressures.

Shot composition in and around the Burton house depicts the straitened circumstances of the emblematic white, Anglo-Saxon Protestant family. When David first arrives home, the camera pans across the darkened garden to the white-painted porch, lit as a narrow rectangle in the center of the frame where his daughter Sophie hides to surprise him. This format, constricting the family members to a limited area flanked by darkness, is repeated throughout the film. The family is squeezed into the center of the frame, seen through a doorway, when David rises from their meal to discover water running down the stairs. Annie (Olivia Hamnett) is seen frozen in the doorway to the dining room as David talks with Charlie about the nature of dreams. At the mortuary, when David examines Billy Corman's personal effects, he is restricted to a narrow band of the frame, glimpsed through doorways.

This composition is most striking in the dream sequences set inside the house. David is seen through the doorway while asleep at his desk in the study, and on waking looks through the frame of the door to where Chris (Gulpilil), previously just a silhouetted figure out in the garden, now appears in the next room, offering David a sacred stone. David is next seen asleep at his desk as before, revealing that all, rather than just certain parts of the sequence, has been a dream.[12] This association of the representation of the family with David's dream state indicates that the house symbolizes David's mind and the establishment of white society,

The Last Wave   David Gulpilil, Nandjiwarra Amagula,
Richard Chamberlain   (AUS 1977)
Picture from the Ronald Grant Archive

both under threat from natural and supernatural powers, like the College and headmistress in *Picnic*. The invasion of the house and David's mind, begun in the dream by Chris's entry (inside rather than outside the window), is exacerbated by David's inviting Chris, with Charlie, into the house for dinner. Annie has never met an Aboriginal before despite being a fourth-generation Australian (this sense of ingrained parochialism is first suggested by David's admission that he has never seen a yellow pepper before, when he is offered one by the Italian janitor at his office). Annie's apprehension accompanies the children's overt curiosity. Her trepidation at her husband's alignment with the Aborigines (earning the couple barbed remarks at a colleague's party) provides the motivation for a later sequence: Annie, at the desk in the study (framed in the same way as David during the dream), studies a book of Aboriginal art and myth and becomes aware of her husband standing in the next room, in the position previously occupied by Chris. She looks through the doorway at the intruder, as David did earlier, and the constricted composition suggests the fatally narrow perspective of the white family and establishment, and David's alignment with the disruptive powers of darkness. Annie has already been seen barring windows and locking doors against the natural and metaphorical storms that threaten the house. Soon she is persuaded to leave altogether, and the intrusion of nature into the home is completed when David, returning home convinced of the truth of his prophetic dreams, searches the rooms as the doors and windows are forced open by the storm.

In *The Plumber*, the same composition underlines the divisions of class and sensibility between Max (Ivor Kants) and Jill (Judy Morris). When Max first knocks at the door of the flat, Jill is seen isolated at the left of the frame, looking toward the source of the sound through the bedroom doorway. Opening the door to Max, Jill is marginalized again, looking hesitantly around the door at the right of the frame. When Jill checks up on Max to be sure he is really working on the plumbing, she is seen peeping around the door, peripheralized again on the left of the frame. Max's disconcerting presence causes arguments between Jill and her preoccupied husband Brian (Robert Coleby). During the evening they are observed in a small area of light in their kitchen at the left of the frame. As well as being confined by the surrounding darkness, their figures are blurred by the net curtains of the window that frames the image. This perspective equates with Max's point of view as he watches the couple from the walkway of the apartment block. The accompanying reverse shot, of Max's face obscured by the curtains and the reflections in the glass, suggests not only his menacing presence on the fringes of the family but also his lack of importance (other than through threatening behavior) in the lives of the middle-class couple. The next day, Max's shadow is seen on the window as Jill refuses to let him in.

When Jill begins her counterattack, the compositions indicate her assumption of power over Max. After she corrects his bad grammar, he sings a defiant song in her bathroom. Although again she looks in on him around the open door, he is seen enmeshed in his own scaffolding, squeezed into the confined frame of the doorway in a preview of his eventual imprisonment. The shots progress through a series in which the frame is shared equally between Jill on the left, looking around the door, and Max on the right, then continues with Jill on her own, stepping into the doorway to look directly at Max and the camera, and ends with Max on his own, trapped within the tiny area of light seen through the bathroom door after Jill has gone to the university authorities. Despite his Dylanesque song of freedom, Max is disempowered during this sequence, and after Jill vows to throw him out, he is pushed to the right of the frame, looking anxiously around the doorway of her study.

The shift of authority that is signaled by these compositions illustrates both Jill's resolution to repel the intruder to her home and the combination of thriller material (voyeurism and intangible menace) with notions of physical (lower-class) and intellectual (middle-class) superiority. Max's threat to Jill is physical in nature but is pursued psychologically. He dismisses her accusations of harassment as the product of a bored housewife's overactive imagination. Her education and academic abilities do not offer any assistance in this battle of wills, and finally she resorts to the (ab)use of the establishment's legal machinery. Ironically, assuming authority over Max and reassuming control of the home is portrayed as a revocation of status: She expects the power of the law to deal with Max, once her artifice has produced damning evidence. On the evening before Max's arrest, Brian returns to the flat to find Jill dressed in a black, high-necked dress. Classical music is playing in the apartment, and Jill appears almost as a cameo, with her costume, the lighting, and the music recalling Mrs. Appleyard in her study in *Picnic*. Her perjurious methods use the power of the establishment, while her dress confirms her inferior status within it (Brian's research work has always taken precedence over her thesis). Her manipulative remarks accentuate her pose as victim (and female) in need of institutionalized protection and provoke Brian to instigate Max's arrest. The devices used in *Picnic* to stress the obsolescence of the Victorian establishment resurface here to emphasize the perpetuation of prejudice, derived from the British class model, in modern Australia.

The visual techniques present in *Wave* and *The Plumber* are a further development of forms of representation first seen in *Michael* (1971). Cultural, generational, and social divides highlighted in *Michael* are reexamined: the gap between white European and Aboriginal culture in *Wave*, and between middle-class liberal and working classes in *The Plumber*. In *The Chant of Jimmie Blacksmith* (Fred Schepisi, 1978), Jimmie, an Aborigine raised in an outback mission, is seen in constricted compositions to illustrate his circumscribed position in white Australian society. A shot of Jimmie dining with the Reverend Neville and his wife before he leaves the mission to find work opens out to reveal the scene bounded on every side by a door frame. At each step, Jimmie meets suspicion and injustice and finds himself driven inexorably into violent action against his oppressors. The limitations upon human action or the predestined nature of events beyond the characters' control motivates such compositions.

This recurrent visual composition is found later in *Witness* (1985) and *Green Card*, and although it represents a stylistic continuity, its usage illustrates the films' genre distinctions. Constricted frames in *Michael* and *Cars* parallel their other stylistic features, such as montage sequences, in contemporary social commentary after the style of the *Nouvelle Vague*. *Wave*'s frames unite this societal observation with an analysis of subjective vision, symbolized by the filmic and photographic frames seen within it. In *Green Card*, the differences between comedic characters signaled by similar compositions also suggest racial, sexual, and ideological distinctions. In *Witness* and *The Plumber*, the frames of observation accord with the tropes of genre thriller material (surveillance, suspicion, and voyeurism) epitomized by *Rear Window* (Alfred Hitchcock, 1954). The model of L. B. Jeffries, Hitchcock's immobilized and impotent observer, is discernible in David Burton's viewing of unpredictable events through the frames of his house and mind. In *The Plumber*, these frames maintain and empower the characters' differences. While *Wave* and *The Plumber* originate from classic genre materials (the solitary intellectual male and lone heroine beset by unenvisaged events), their varying motivations for these compositions (suggesting art-film subjectivity in the former and thriller voyeurism in the latter) elucidate themes common to art film and genre film: the nature of individual existence, the unreliability of perception, and the difficult task of interpretation for those inside and outside the cinematic frame.

A similar restriction of space and vision and imbalance in composition is discernible in the films of Michael Mann, which also seek to address art-film concerns within the genre context (in Mann's case, within the crime thriller category). The experience and perceptions of Mann's protagonists (criminals and law enforcers in *Manhunter* [1986] and *Heat* [1995]) are articulated through idiosyncratic wide-screen compositions, which are divided by vertical lines and blocks of color and which isolate characters at the extreme edges of the frame. The investigative gaze of the FBI agent upon crime scenes, still photographs, and home movies in *Manhunter* is represented in an identical fashion to the vision and movements of the serial killer he seeks, just as the police lieutenant and the master criminal who is his quarry are seen to be equally alienated and peripheralized in their living spaces in *Heat*. Ironically, the activities of the FBI agent and the cop are directed toward the defense of the family and the domestic ideal while their obsessive commitment endangers and threatens to destroy their own familial existences. The comparability to the concerns and characteristics of Weir's films (in observation via frames, in the reliance on photographic reproduction in investigation, and in the interrogation of moral and philosophical standpoints through the representation of domestic space) is apparent in Mann's injection of art-film materials into genre formats. As in the case of Weir's films (especially *Wave* and *Witness*), Mann as writer-director exhibits the auteur's emphases in visual and thematic terms while successfully updating classical formulas.

The appearance and interpretation of photographs in *Wave* and *The Plumber* provide a parallel to *Cars*. A genealogical record of David's family is explained for the benefit of Charlie. Photographs are visible in frames on the walls of the home and are presented to Charlie in a family album. He ignores the faces of David's ancestors to concentrate on the texture of the prints and their backgrounds. The photos show the different meanings ascribed to images by Aborigines and non-Aborigines. Charlie studies the pictures closely, not to know about David's family, but to learn about David himself. The Aboriginal creed, that "the Law is more important than man," is the mirror image of a Western definition of good citizenship through career success (as also suggested in the portrayal of conflict between Aboriginal wishes to preserve and non-Aboriginal desires to exploit tribal land in *Where the Green Ants Dream* [Werner Herzog, 1984]). Eschewing material gain, the Aborigines categorize honorable behavior through upheld tradition—obedience to a no less implacable establishment. The resistance to establishment authority discernible in Weir's other films does not conflict with the film's liberal attitude toward the Aborigines. The apparent alienation of Billy Corman as an uninitiated tribal member, Chris Lee's victimization for revealing tribal secrets, and David's estrangement from white society without gaining the spiritual state of the Aborigines illustrate the director's suspicion of relentless establishment structures underpinning both Aboriginal and non-Aboriginal society. Western family-based society and the Aboriginal tribe are juxtaposed as alternative structures in which human activity is accommodated, pursuing mutually exclusive cultural and spiritual or realist and materialist aims.

In *The Plumber*, Brian's theories about the reemergence of kuru (brain damage and madness caused by cannibalism) in New Guinea and Jill's anthropological studies of the same region are reinforced by photographic evidence. Again, the photographic image is used to verify or explain unanticipated events, just as David and Annie are seen poring over a book of photos detailing the "fatal impact" of Western civilization on Aboriginal culture. Brian's words become an authoritative voice-over, accompanying filmed images of sick villagers that fill the frame as they are projected for his team: "Is this part of the larger story?" However, when Brian's ideas prejudice his promotion prospects, he orders his assistant to get rid of the collected evidence. A close-up shows the unwanted frame enlargements being disposed of in a bin marked "Paper Waste Only." When clouded with unpalatable opinion, even photographic evidence can be discounted by the scientific establishment.

Before Max's arrival, Jill recounts the story of her confrontation with a Beatu man. The incident seems comparable to the Aboriginal boy's courtship dance before the schoolgirl in *Walkabout* (Nicolas Roeg, 1970), and the cultural gap produces similar misunderstanding. A photo of the man is included in her draft thesis, and another resides on her desk. Close-ups of the man's face point to her unnerving experience and her failure to understand another's actions, and parallel her aggressive action later. The quasi-sexual threat of men from different cultures or classes (suggested by tribal fertility symbols in the flat and an illustration from the *Kama Sutra* in the bathroom that Max notices) produces a similar desire for self-defense.

The framing of objects and people (the views through the windshield of David's car, the windows of the house forming a screen for David's dreams, the restriction of composition within the family home, and the photos in albums or books) as a prerequisite to perception associated with David and the establishment suggests an attempt to limit, categorize, or contain an unacceptable breadth of events, perceptions or cultures. *Wave*'s stress on composition and interpretation previews the style and subject matter of *The Year of Living Dangerously* (1982). In *Year*, the recording and categorizing of events by journalists develop into a desire to control them, but this proves impossible when faced with bizarre happenings inspired by a non-Western culture. The perspective of the camera (itself an artefact of Western technology burdened with the conventions of Western art) on such events questions the reliability of narration.

The obstacles to interpretation in *Picnic* and *Wave* arise from the subjectivity of experience—we cannot understand the girls' experience on the Rock or be sure of the validity of David's dreams. Viewing and interpreting inside and outside the film frame have resonances in the real and fictional worlds, when viewers rely on the perspective of an individual character for narrative information. Subjective vision relayed through point-of-view shots reflects the interpretative acts of characters and audience and, with the cultural representations in *Wave*, *Year*, and *The Plumber*, deepens debate on society, cinema, and individual perceptions of both. By uniting these viewing acts, subjective vision suggests

> a reciprocal relationship between film and audience: a film not only immerses and absorbs an audience into its world, there is also a countercurrent where the spectator immerses the film into his (psychic) world, brought to the threshold of consciousness by the energy emanating from the viewing situation itself.[13]

Subjective narration can erode the suspension of disbelief (impeding "immersion" in the text) and heighten the uncanny atmosphere by paralleling our individual vision ("immersing" the film in our perception of the world and comparing it with our genre-informed reading of fantasy film). The camera's assumption of David's point of view necessitates that we assume the interpretative act he finds increasingly problematic. The frame's constriction in the Burton house (in the obscurity of dreams and the precision of photographs) parallels the limitation of the cinema screen, via which we observe the opaque drama.

In *The Plumber*, the camera's apparent objectivity (revealing Max spying on the flat) encompasses the characters' subjective views (shot/reverse shot points of view through frames between Max and Jill). It indicates their individual standpoints (Jill's reserve and trepidation, Max's extroversion and anger) with the thriller's inclusive and unblinking realism. The same frames indicate Jill's empowerment when Max is confined by them. The objective vision of Max trapped in the bathroom scaffolding after Jill has left the flat shows him caught in his own chaotic design, just as the framing device now signals his victimization by Jill. This constrictive framing of the characters shows both sides of the subjectively viewed drama (neither Jill nor Max can prove the injustice of their treatment); this "objectivity," including the characters' biased views, forces judgment of their actions upon the viewer. The unreliability of the visual narrators in both *The Plumber* and *Wave* demands a greater interpretative task of the external viewer.

Subjective vision and self-conscious technique facilitate analysis of the nature of perception and narration, relation and interpretation of events, in the art-film fantasy of *Wave* and the voyeuristic genre thriller of *The Plumber*. The psychological narratives of both films prompt the subjective view and their reflexive styling. When David, having followed Chris to Charlie's house, leaves his car to go to the door, the camera remains, watching him through the windshield stained by the black rain. It is unclear whether he enters the frame to gain authority over the narrative (which has sprung from his dreamed images in the first place), or whether this act signals a revocation of any presumed control over events. He becomes submerged in the diegesis, and is as powerless as the other characters. His approach to the heart of the mystery at once arouses an anticipation in the viewer for some explanation for the events witnessed so far; but David's transgression of the boundaries of the screen, entering the unpredictable (yet predestined) drama, and our view through the tarnished screen point to the artificiality of the construct we are watching, highlighting our mental submergence in a drama from which we remain separated.

Weir widens the divergence from conventional narrative by emphasizing that photography allows exact duplication. As an additional indication in the mise-en-scène of David's deteriorating mental state, certain scenes are rerun. As he drives around Sydney, the windshield frames the same pedestrians and the same bus, with its advertisement for Taronga Zoo (another framed representation of a constrained and categorized natural world). When he arrives home for the last time, his earlier arrival is recreated, with Sophie seen hiding in the porch before he enters (the slam of the door returns us to the "present"). Searching through the house, David follows the course the camera took earlier in the form of the intrusive dream sent by Charlie, in which the camera assumed the intruder's point of view.

Wave's repeated images link David's dreams of the Aboriginal figure, the worsening weather, and the apocalyptic wave he sees. The threatened city and the sacred caves beneath it connect the victim and the prophesy in the same way that David's psychological state is reflected in the condition of the family home. The frequent storms, recurrent dreams, and repeated scenes indicate the breakdown of the character, his social milieu, and the narrative portraying both. Similarly, *The Plumber*'s restrictive framing and repeated references to experiences in New Guinea (the ever-present photo of the Beatu man, Brian's controversial film) betray the emerging pattern. Jill reacts violently against both alien males, with compositional elements narrating the cycle. Her victimhood, symbolized by the constricting frame, becomes the subjection of the Beatu man in the photo frame and of Max within the flat. Both are shrunk and disempowered, the Beatu man reduced to an image and Max belittled by distance as Jill watches his arrest from the balcony.

Far from reassuring the viewer of the validity of these details since they can be recalled to sight, devices of repetition and dislocation in *Wave* and *The Plumber* undermine the reliability of David and Jill as narrators. David's confusion and Jill's anxiety bias narrative information when their perspectives are used, and conspicuous "objective" shots (Max in the frame of the bathroom, David seen through the tarnished windshield) merely underline the unconventional use of subjectivity in both films. David's perspective obscures rather than illuminates *Wave*'s unclosed horror/fantasy narrative, and *The Plumber*'s framing questions Jill's actions (and the beliefs that spawn them), producing ironic sympathy for Max. Jill repeats her aggressive behavior and retrenches her racial and social prejudices in a narrative that signals her unchanging stance through its restrictive framing and still photos, inverting conventional thriller roles of victim and aggressor. David is caught in a self-perpetuating pattern of narrative and cinematic logic (an ancient prophesy realized, an ancient race reborn, earlier scenes recapitulated, a second killing echoing the first), challenging a similar middle-class complacency. However, *Wave*'s recurring compositions also hint at a more extensive adaptation of Aboriginal culture than the film's Dreamtime references, in accepting the unity of past and present, reality and myth, and their innate, repeated patterning.

David's meeting with Dr. Whitburn provides the validation of his dreams and Chris's theories about his ancestry. She asserts that Aboriginal people believe "in two sorts of time, two parallel streams of activity" (everyday life and the Dreamtime), that "whatever happens in the Dreamtime establishes the values, symbols, and laws of Aboriginal society," and that some people can be in contact with the Dreamtime through their dreams. The connection of dreams to the Dreamtime is less direct than a translation of the term—and the film's appropriation of it—would suggest, yet the Dreamtime's significance to the maintenance of social regulation and the relevance of this structural basis to Weir's film provide another unanticipated connection between the mythology and the film. Like the adoption of Impressionist tones in *Picnic*, the Aboriginal imagery pervading *Wave* increases the film's reference beyond the confines of narrative.

The analogy of objective Dreamtime law to subjective dreaming experience suggests a second analogy—that of dream to film. Hugo Munsterberg declared that the new art of cinema needed to be appreciated "under entirely new mental life conditions."[14] The ability of film to represent simultaneous action and recollection or fantasy through editing techniques constitutes "an objectification of our memory function."[15] The inner, personal vision of a dream can be compared to the individual's viewing and interpretation of film, even though the latter is nominally a communal and public activity. *Wave*'s use of potentially exclusive Aboriginal reference and its deliberate confusion of objective narrative reality with subjective vision form a visual parallel to David's alienation from middle-class society and his attraction to the alternative Aboriginal spiritual life.

Again, the viewer's and the character's predicaments converge: Both are diverted from a conventional narrative (a murder and courtroom drama) by unexplained occurrences in their dream/film observation and Aboriginal images or references in the diegetic environment. David and Jill are diverted from their tasks of rationalization (legal practice and academia, respectively) by the intrusion of the unknown and the unexpected. These unanticipated happenings in middle-class life are conventional tropes of the horror and thriller genres (arcane knowledge comes to light, a violent threat is manifested in daily events), but they also represent continuities within Weir's work (the menace beneath mundanity in Paris in *Cars*, the disappearances in *Picnic*). Such disruption has a moral slant and encourages an allegorical interpretation after *The Birds* or *Homesdale*. *The Plumber* subverts its thriller base by questioning the characters' actions along class lines, undermining the moral justification for Jill's retaliation. *Wave* diverges from horror or science fiction in the main character's inability to intervene in predestined events. The genre modification visible in *Cars'* western motifs resurfaces in these films, with subversion of thriller and science-fiction tropes (the victim's culpability, the intellectual's impotence) being highlighted by the pervasiveness of subjectivity (the dubiety of information gleaned from framed perception) and related art-film techniques:

> Dreams, memories, hallucinations, daydreams, fantasies, and other mental activities can find embodiment in the image or on the soundtrack. Consequently, the behavior of the characters within the fabula world and the syuzhet's dramatization both focus on the character's problems of action. . . . Subjectivity can also justify the distension of time (slow-motion or freeze-frames) and manipulation of frequency, such as repetition of images.[16]

These films' dreamlike logic and cyclic narratives recall *Homesdale*'s allegorical satire and *Picnic*'s period fantasy, while their contemporary settings evoke the metaphorical social commentary of *Cars*. *The Plumber* and *Wave*, like *Picnic* before them, ask audiences to drop narrative and genre expectations and immerse themselves in referential and reflexive texts, akin to conventional film narration and to dream vision, but also as riven with subjective and exclusive elements as the experiences of their protagonists.

Wider artistic and cultural references in Weir's films range from *Picnic*'s adoption of nineteenth-century visual arts and Renaissance literature to *Cars*' reinterpretation of genre film tropes with art-film stylization. *Year* assumes the style of the *wayang kulit* (shadow play) and includes a welter of narrative techniques (voice-over, newspaper reports, secret documents, still photography) to show that the obstacles to narration on a personal level are the strengths of cinematic narrative and reference. In *The Plumber*, characters are defined and divided by their separate pursuits (Jill's unfinished research, Brian's career ambitions, Max's loud music). In *Wave*, the images and concepts of Aboriginal myth perform a similar function in widening the intertextual allusion, and, like Weir's preceding and succeeding films, it includes these potentially alienating elements to reinforce its narrative of personal experience and individual isolation.

Before or during his dreamed vision of Chris inside the house, David walks out onto his doorstep to view the storm and finds the garden overrun with frogs. The frog's place in Aboriginal myth, in relation to storms and winds, expands the meaning of their appearance. Charles Mountford records the story of Tiddalik, the largest frog in the world, who caused a drought by drinking all the water in the land, but when made to laugh flooded the parched earth with the water that flowed from his mouth.[17] Another myth relates how Quork-Quork, the Frog-woman, hops through the rain listening to the storms created by her children.[18] Transformation of beings from animal to human form and vice versa was common in the Dreamtime, another element found in the film, with Charlie's metamorphosis into an owl. In referring to these concepts, *Wave* gives them a logical motivation within the context of its fictional narration, with the visual repetitions and images reinforcing the cycles of the narrative. The strange appearance of the frogs coincides with the distortion of perception accompanying David's dream. Likewise, Charlie's power of metamorphosis allows him to observe and preempt David's actions. The dramatic motivation of such elements accords with the close linkage of Aboriginal myth to contemporary society:

> [T]he Dreaming is the law. But in the Dreaming, Ancestral Beings frequently broke the law, just as people do today. The Dreaming is thus the generative principle of the present, the logically prior dimension of the now, while also being a period in which the plants and animals were still women, men, and children.[19]

The form of double-think implied by the Aboriginals' lack of distinction between myth and reality, past and present, is hardly different from the leaps in perception undertaken regularly by dreamers—and cinema audiences. Conscious and unconscious viewing of diegetic or oneiric constructs highlights the individual nature of interpretation, based on the enlightening commerce between real and imaginary, personal and communal. Understanding of the real world is deepened, and its features are interrogated on the basis of their re-vision in dreams. Alternatively, dream images represent transactions with, and are only relevant in relation to, the conscious environment. Where myth, history, culture, and social organization merge in the Dreamtime, allusion, narrative, and reflexive questioning vie for attention in the white, technological cinematic dreams of *Wave*.

David's dreams, with the exception of the final vision of the apocalyptic wave, are seen by him and the viewer through the frames of his middle-class life: the doors and windows of his home and the windshield of his car. The rectangular frames are both a medium and a restriction (as seen in the reduction of the area the Burton family occupies as abnormal elements invade the house). The full potential of cinematic representation (in the dream sequences, time-lapse views of clouds forming over the city, the special effects furnishing the bizarre weather) is still constrained by the ubiquitous rectangular frame (David looks out of his car on his vision of the drowned city, the teacher in the desert school watches the fall of hail through the doorway). Aboriginal artists have never demanded symmetrical frames for their images, working instead on irregular surfaces (cave walls, tree bark, the human body itself[20]). In combining Western technical art and Aboriginal mythic representation, the film evokes a conflict of form to match that of ideology and belief.

> The camera is not a machine designed for expressing sublimity—either of the Romantic pantheistic kind or of the postmodernist, supra-systemic kind before which the cohesive, centralized self begins to disintegrate. The camera does not express inexpressibility. Quite the opposite. It is designed not to warp the perspectival codes which were installed in art practice during the Renaissance.[21]

Weir's attempts at elucidating the inexpressible are found in the irregular, unframed compositions: the jagged area of light and shadow seen in the title sequence, with Charlie painting on the rough surface of a cave wall underneath a great overhanging rock; the distorted overhead camera angles used during David's meeting with Charlie inside his bare room; and David's last unfettered vision of the approaching wave. Similar compositions in *Picnic* (as when the girls and Michael are seen from between narrow passages in the stone, and when a policeman with a megaphone is filmed from within a cave on the Rock, silhouetted within an irregular area of light) are redolent of the same impassive and alien observation. The camera's and the film's inability to represent the unknown (in this context, what is not white, Western, or adequately framed) is obvious in the attempts of this film, in addition to those of *Picnic* before and *Year* after, to do so. The same framing technique seen in *Michael*, *The Plumber*, and later in *Green Card* expresses a comparable narrow-mindedness, the inability or unwillingness to comprehend another's difference. What is represented, alluded to, and enlisted to aid in the narrative expression is a range of other forms of representative and narrative art. That these other arts can be consumed and quoted points to cinema's propensity for reflexivity. Allusive and unclosed texts such as *Picnic* and *Wave* place the responsibility for the creation of meaning in the hands of the viewers, as does the introduction of subjective vision to *The Plumber*'s generic material. What may appear as a modernist obfuscation of meaning and violation of convention is rather a postmodernist transcendence of narrative form and openness to free interpretation, with the difficulty of reading fragmenting the social and cinematic self.

The debt of *Wave* to American science-fiction film is evident in its evocation of the impending destruction of civilization. David Burton's prior knowledge of the danger and his powerlessness before it recall the heroes of the earlier American films, unable to convince a skeptical establishment of the threat and finding their sanity brought into question. The subjectivity of David's dreams and his alienation from the community mean that his home and his mind are most, if not solely, at risk. These circumstances are effectively the same as those pertaining to science-fiction films dealing with the fear of being "taken over" by an alien consciousness, such as *Invasion of the Body Snatchers* (Don Siegel, 1956). Protection of the home, when deprived of the possessed father, symbolizes defense of the establishment, an acceptable, conservative ideal but one prone to reversal:

> The theme of depersonalization . . . is a new allegory reflecting the age-old awareness of man that, sane, he is always perilously close to insanity and unreason. But . . . the image derives most of its power from a supplementary and historical anxiety, also not experienced consciously by most people, about the depersonalizing conditions of modern urban life.[22]

This can be taken as the basis for the quasi-science fictional narrative of *Cars*, the allegorical fantasy of *Picnic*, and the reflexive representation of familial and societal breakdown in *Wave* and *The*

Plumber. In the later films, defense of the home becomes a parodic possession and protection of the frame: Sublimity is unattainable in *Wave* and domesticity and class are restated in *The Plumber* via the restriction of internal framing, suggesting incommunicable individual experience in the former and insuperable conservatism in the latter.

David's legal career gives an interesting perspective to Weir's continuing representation of conflict between the individual and the wider community. David is the upholder and enunciator of established law, interpreting rules laid down by the authorities in connection with the narrated actions of others (another parallel to the film viewer's position). The start of his own investigation, entering as well as observing the narrative, suggests his dissatisfaction with unquestioning conformity. His efforts toward self-fullfilment mix the doctrines of both establishments, previewing John Book's combination of pacifism learned from the Amish and morally justified violence in keeping with the role of the generic western hero in *Witness.* David follows Chris to the cave to learn the full extent of the Mulkurul prophesy, but he also seeks to warn the (white) world of the impending danger. His murder of Charlie, like the execution of Billy, is precipitated by the contrary desires for secrecy and revelation. David's desire to tell the world is proof to Charlie that David is not the reincarnated Mulkurul, but a transgressor of the law rather than a keeper and living proof of traditional belief. David's willingness or ability to perform a prescribed role (as a professional and family man in one establishment, or as a prophetic and predestined figure in another) reinvokes the choice between conformity and freedom made by Miranda in *Picnic,* and looks forward to the dilemmas which face the heroes of Weir's American films.

For Jill and Brian, rationalization in the form of academic work is also interrupted. Jill's thesis is ignored by her husband and disrupted by the presence of Max and the Beatu man's picture, and Brian's pet theories are dismissed by the World Health Organization representatives. Emotion (her anxiety and his ambition) disrupts their ordered, unchallenged existence. Jill is forced into a less authoritative role by her desire to be rid of Max. Both the plumber and her husband ask testing questions. Max shows off his general knowledge by asking if she knows the height of the Cheops

Pyramid—"Four hundred and seventy feet!"—and Brian demands (rhetorically) if she knows the cost of his gift of the watch that she claims Max has stolen—"Four hundred and seventy dollars!" Jill's ignorance of both figures hides her manipulation of the situation to her advantage, prompting the forces of law to remove Max for good. Assuming the vulnerability of a weak female role (marked by her penultimate costuming evocative of *Picnic*) is a revocation of authority and avowal of ignorance that reinforce the patriarchal status quo and paradoxically complete her self-reliant thriller heroine role. Before her evening performance for Brian that provokes Max's arrest, Jill is seen looking into Max's car through its rear window, deciding where to plant the incriminating evidence. This framing of her image in the car's window and the last (freeze-frame) view of her on the balcony emphasize the persistence of prejudice and division and, as in *Green Card*, the liberal intellectual's reinforcement of discrimination.

Mythological imagery and stylistic composition in both *Wave* and *The Plumber* allow them to overcome the framing limitations of their genre bases and engage in analyses of subjective experience. *Wave*'s transgression of narrative convention and *The Plumber*'s linear structure indicate the protagonists' responses to their circumstances (David's unending quest for fact over suspicion, Jill's resort to external authority to "end" her story). Both the characters within and the readers of these texts are engaged in interpretation: of the context and of the significance of their roles and responsibilities in eclectic diegetic worlds depicted in allusive, postmodern texts:

> The law is not simply inherited, it is created anew as an abstraction that draws upon past precepts and their constructive elaboration. The child is a lawyer, interpreting received law; the adult becomes a legislator, proposing law, thus participating in the evolution of society and culture. The film viewer in this mode takes the film's ideas as a source for his own construction.[23]

The dilemmas of role and responsibility, action and morality that afflict David Burton come to haunt the heroes of Weir's later American films.

Compositional and thematic elements connect *Wave* to *The*

Plumber and to *Year* and *Michael*. Other stylistic similarities to the rest of the Weir canon are also present. The howling wind accompanying every view of the isolated tower block in *The Plumber* recalls the sound effects of *Picnic*, as does the climactic use of classical music juxtaposed with tribal music and chanting. Bruce Johnson and Gaye Poole, in discussing Weir's use of music as a key authorial signature, note Jill's use of the tribal music as "a weapon"[24] within the apartment, an interpretation borne out by the merging of diegetic and extra-diegetic sound, Max's shouts and the chants and drums, at the film's conclusion. Filming speeds, altered to considerable effect in *Picnic* along with slowed down or subliminal sound effects, are again changed subtly in *Wave*, as Weir noted in an interview:

> [W]ithin a dialogue scene I would shoot the character talking in the normal 24 frames a second, then I would shoot the character listening in 48 frames, or 32 frames. I would ask the character listening not to blink or make any extreme movement so that you didn't pick up the slow motion, then I'd intercut those reactions and you would get a stillness in the face of the listener.[25]

This technique is noticeable in David's hypnotic meeting with Charlie in Charlie's bare room. Weir returned to such experimental shooting in *Fearless*, a film that continued his examination of the nature of the hero and his deeds, which are defined and constrained by, and reflect upon, culture and society. Again, the hero's experience of ostracism is relayed through slow motion, dream vision, and disorientating sound.

The introspection and reflexivity of *Wave* warrant comparison with other filmic treatments of the condition of modern man and contemporary art. In the art-film tradition, these subjects have been addressed frequently, by such films as *Walkabout* (a self-conscious narrative, with the incongruity of the civilized individual marooned in the outback emphasized by disconnected urban sounds and images of the landscape), *8 1/2* (Federico Fellini, 1963) (incorporating dreams as part of the film's narration, impeding the viewer's formation of meaning even as its narrative illustrates the inability of the artist to create), *Weekend* (Jean-Luc Godard, 1967) (intensely self-aware and anti-illusionist in its attack on the bourgeois establishment), and *Persona* (Ingmar Bergman, 1966) (an arduous labor to create meaning despite a subjectivity advanced to the point of solipsism).

Like *Persona*, *Wave* repeats sequences and images to stress that film's power of exact replication does not ensure correct or meaningful interpretation. Similarities to *Persona* appear in the screens through which the dreams are viewed, comparable to the white expanse where the women's faces appear to the boy in the mortuary, and in David's discovery of a carved face resembling his own at the sacred cave. He gazes at the face, and both are seen in profile, reflecting the film's division of expression and meaning—narrative and dream, drama and myth, Western and Aboriginal. What significance David gleans from the face is unknown. Subsequently, he loses it in the sewers in the course of his escape, and the camera lingers on the face floating on the water after David, now reduced to just a shadow on the wall of the tunnel, hurries away. The face, like David's dream images, is still "adrift in the cosmos" of meanings, while David is nearing the end of his existence, with his and the film's version of catastrophe.

In adopting the recurrent feature of the rectangular screen as a site for meanings and perceptions of dubious authenticity, *Wave* provides an apt counterpoint to its own unwillingness or inability to perform the functions of narrative film. The breadth of its reference, like that found in *Picnic*, succeeds in integrating differing cultures and modes of representation and interpretation, and in so doing previews the similar combination of varying bodies of art in *Year*. The use of the same compositions in the contemporary *The Plumber* extends the amalgamation of genre and art-film materials initiated in *Cars*, turning a thriller into a polemical piece. The international appeal sought by the McElroys in *Wave*'s conventional horror material was attained by its art-film subjective vision and philosophical searching, while *The Plumber*'s commercial inception belies its revision of genre tropes, prefiguring the American films.

Where *Picnic* evokes the visual style of the European art film, *Wave* tackles areas of its philosophy, introducing challenging notions of representation, narrative, and subjectivity to Australian cinema. *Picnic* gave the Australian industry the period film, melding European aesthetics with a setting and subject worthy of a national cinema. *Wave* and *The Plumber* address the other filmic influence on Australian film, that of American genre. This, in concert with art-film subjectivity and reflexivity, produces a worthy updating of the horror movie in a postmodern amalgamation of cultural and cinematic ambiguity, and a metaphorical thriller that builds on the cultural observation of the director's earlier films.

In an interview, Weir revealed how the presence of the Aborigines on the set produced such a wealth of material for discussion that the talk between cast and crew continued long after the cameras stopped.[26] In Robert Winer's view, this interplay of ideas on the set is both "the strength of the film and part of the reason for its ultimate lack of artistic cohesion."[27] Weir concluded that *Wave*, initially growing out of personal experience and proving to be a focus for filmic debate, seems to have evoked more than it could realize:

> That began a period of years of reading and talking and eventually of film, an effort that to me was always a failure, because I captured so little of what I got to know over that period. . . . It's only two to three percent of what I knew. Maybe what I discovered was meant to be personal. Maybe it wasn't something I was meant to put in a film.[28]

The Last Wave represents an accordance between form and content, element and argument. The very inexpressibility of individual experience defines the time of its making; the incommunicable qualities that both *Picnic* and *Wave* strive to detail leave their narratives unclosed and their interpretations open. The downbeat, questionable closure of *The Plumber* previews the development of Weir's style and themes in Hollywood, where such modified genre motifs would allow the refinement of his artistic and commercial aspirations.

The characters and society observed in *Michael* have been updated, aged and jaded by absorption into the establishment. *Wave* shows the efforts of the generation of the 1960s to regain a spiritual transcendence of mundanity. *The Plumber* shows a similar conflict between the establishment and the forces bent on its overthrow, with a darker vision of the permanence and pervasiveness of prejudice that will be transformed again into *Dead Poets Society* (1989) and *Green Card*. Social observation and filmic philosophical debate, integrated within the conceit of period film, the psychological threat of the thriller, and the dislocation of fantasy and horror, are present in Weir's genre-grounded and artistically allusive films of the 1970s. Their propensity for reflexivity, in an analysis of the viewed and a criticism of the viewing, make them exemplars of postmodern cinema, and their societal observation, inside and outside the frame, is developed in the frames of history and myth in *Gallipoli* (1981) and *Year*.

Notes

1. Rosemary Jackson, *Fantasy—The Literature of Subversion* (London: Methuen, 1981), p. 101.

2. Scott Murray, "Hal and James McElroy—Producers," *Cinema Papers, 14* (1977), pp. 148–153 (p. 148).

3. David Stratton, *The Last New Wave: The Australian Film Revival* (London: Angus & Robertson, 1980), p. 75.

4. See comments by Jim McElroy in Murray, "Hal and James McElroy," p. 148. Similar comments by the producers, suggesting that *The Cars That Ate Paris* was "not a study of anything particularly Australian," were made in an earlier interview. See Gordon Glenn and Scott Murray, "Production Report: *The Cars That Ate Paris*," *Cinema Papers, 1* (1974), pp. 18–26 (p .22).

5. Sue Mathews, *35mm Dreams: Conversations with Five Directors About the Australian Film Revival* (Melbourne: Penguin, 1984), p. 98.

6. Jack Clancy, "*The Last Wave*," *Cinema Papers, 15* (1978), p. 259.

7. Stratton, *Last New Wave*, p. 80. See also Michael Dempsey, "Inexplicable Feelings: An Interview with Peter Weir," *Film Quarterly, 33* (1980), pp. 2–11 (p. 4).

8. M. Kinder, "*The Plumber*," *Film Quarterly, 33* (1980), pp. 17–21 (p. 18).

9. Weir commented on his meeting with Hitchcock and the allusion to *Psycho* in interview. See Kyla Ward, "Weir'd Tales," *Tabula Rasa, 2* (1994). (also at www.zip.com.au/kylaw/TabulaRasa/Issue2/PeterWeir.html).

10. Maurice Yacowar, "The Bug in the Rug: Notes on the Disaster Genre," in *Film Genre Reader*, ed. Barry K. Grant (Austin: Texas University Press, 1990), pp. 217–8.

11. Susan Sontag, "The Imagination of Disaster," in *Film Theory and Criticism*, 3rd ed., eds. Gerald Mast and Marshall Cohen (Oxford: Oxford University Press, 1985), p. 454.

12. Eberwein isolates Weir's use of what he terms the "retroactive mode" of dream representation in *The Last Wave*. See Robert T. Eberwein, *Film and the Dream Screen* (Princeton: Princeton University Press, 1984), p. 140.

13. Thomas Elsaesser, "Narrative Cinema and Audience-Oriented Aesthetics," in *Popular Television and Film: A Reader*, eds. Tony Bennett, Susan Boyd-Bowman, Colin Mercer, and Janet Woollacott (London: BFI, 1981), p. 271.

14. Hugo Munsterberg, *The Film—A Psychological Study* (New York: Dover, 1970), p. 17.

15. *Ibid.*, p. 41.

16. David Bordwell, *Narration in the Fiction Film* (London: Methuen, 1985), pp. 208–209.

17. Charles P. Mountford and Ainslie Roberts, *The Dreamtime: Australian Aboriginal Myths in Paintings* (Adelaide: Rigby, 1965), p. 38.

18. *Ibid.*, p.68.

19. Peter Sutton, *Dreamings: The Art of Aboriginal Australia* (London: Viking, 1989), pp. 15–16.

20. *Ibid.*, p.39.

21. Ross Gibson, "Camera Natura: Landscape in Australian Feature Films," *Framework*, 22/23 (1983), pp. 47–51, (p. 50).

22. Sontag "Imagination," pp. 463–464.

23. Robert Winer, "Witnessing and Bearing Witness: The Ontogeny of Encounter in the Films of Peter Weir," in *Images in Our Souls: Cavell, Psychoanalysis and Cinema*, eds. Joseph H. Smith and William Kerrigan (London: Johns Hopkins University Press, 1987), p. 92.

24. Bruce Johnson and Gaye Poole, "Sound and Author/Auteurship: Music in the Films of Peter Weir," in *Screen Scores: Studies in Contemporary Australian Film Music*, ed. Rebecca Coyle (Sydney: AFTRS, 1998), p. 132.

25. Mathews, *35mm Dreams*, p. 95.

26. *Ibid.*, p. 97.

27. Winer, "Witnessing," p. 90.

28. Pat McGilligan, "Under Weir . . . and Theroux," *Film Comment, 22* (1986), pp. 23–32 (p. 28).

Chapter Four

Gallipoli (1981) and The Year of Living Dangerously (1982)

Marking the end of Peter Weir's Australian work and presaging his move to Hollywood, *Gallipoli* and *The Year of Living Dangerously* enjoyed varying critical and commercial success. *Gallipoli* occupies an important place in Australia's film revival, in its Australian finance (from Rupert Murdoch and Robert Stigwood) and its patriotic subject matter:

> The combination of perhaps Australia's best known director, Peter Weir, with its most successful playwright, David Williamson, therefore seemed appropriate for an assault on what is, with the possible exception of the Ned Kelly legend, the biggest Australian story, standing at the heart of Australian mythology.[1]

Gallipoli also reunited Weir with the producer of *Picnic at Hanging Rock* (1975), Patricia Lovell.

Although the Australian roots of this production were much in evidence, the beginnings of American interest in Australian film and in Weir also were discernible in its release through Paramount and in MGM's subsequent funding of *Year*. The importance of both narratives to recent Australian history is notable, with *Gallipoli* elevating the blooding of the Australian military (in the service of the British Empire) to the level of myth and *Year* admitting Australian involvement or compliance in the overthrow of Indonesia's President Sukarno. The innocence of obedience to the mother country was erased by the experience of World War I. The events of *Gallipoli* contrast with the ignominy of Sukarno's fall and Australia's powerlessness to intervene in genocide. The definition of

Australian nationhood, in the context of a cultural heritage from other countries, lies behind the fictional re-creation of factual events in films of the revival.

These two films can be analyzed together because of their similarities in writing (through David Williamson's involvement in both projects), casting (Mel Gibson's roles in both helped to establish him as a star), their historical settings (Australia's most famous action in World War I and the fall of Sukarno regime in 1965), and their connection with different examples of genre cinema. For Susan Dermody and Elizabeth Jacka, *Gallipoli* (with *Breaker Morant* [Bruce Beresford, 1979]), represented a development and combination of the "period film" and the "male ensemble film," such as *Sunday Too Far Away* (Ken Hannam, 1974) and *The Odd Angry Shot* (Tom Jeffrey, 1979),[2] in which groups of exclusively male protagonists (sheep shearers in Hannam's film, soldiers in the Boer and Vietnam Wars in Beresford's and Jeffrey's) depend on one another as "mates." A similar, more lighthearted combination of patriotism, period film, and mateship narrative underpinned the commercial success of *The Dish* (Rob Sitch, 2000).

Like many AFC genre films, *Year* was adapted from Australian literature, but it also paralleled contemporary films focusing on the lives of correspondents abroad, such as *Under Fire* (Roger Spottiswoode, 1983), *The Killing Fields* (Roland Joffe, 1984), and *Salvador* (Oliver Stone, 1986). As well as these general genre sources, certain critics detected particular filmic bases for Weir's films: *Paths of Glory* (Stanley Kubrick, 1957) for *Gallipoli*[3], and *Casablanca* (Michael Curtiz, 1942) for *Year*.[4] Comparison with previous Weir films is suggested in their specific historical settings, recalling *Picnic*'s "Valentine's Day 1900." The particularity of the quasi-factual setting allows an allegorical or fantastic exploration of social mores and filmic narrative in an intricate, self-conscious play.

The scope of the two films reflected the aspirations of the revival (in *Gallipoli*'s culturally significant subject, recalling *Picnic*'s definition of Australian youth in opposition to imposed, elderly British culture) and Weir's directorial ambition (*Year*'s large-budget, American-backed adventure previewing *Witness* [1985]). However, their relationship to *Picnic*'s period fantasy, allusiveness, and narrative experimentation and the reflexive drama of observation and interpretation of *The Last Wave* (1977) places *Gallipoli* and *Year* in the stylistic and thematic structures of past and future Weir productions, mixing Australian and American genres with personal themes and expression.

Before making *Gallipoli*, Weir visited the Dardanelles, and, as with earlier films, his personal experience influenced his conception of the narrative as fact and myth and the distance between present experience and past event:

> [V]isiting that peninsula, where the battlefield is preserved and so forth, because of being a military zone still . . . you can wander in the trenches and you can pick stuff up, and there's no one around . . . you have one of those odd moments where you know that the history that was in the books did happen.[5]

This private consideration was fleshed out by interviews with survivors of the Australian Imperial Force, their recollections being incorporated into Weir's and Williamson's screenplay. From the veterans came the theme of lost innocence more commonly found in the poetry and novels produced by the survivors of other combatant countries. In a *Cineaste* interview, Weir commented:

> In our country, we had no Wilfred Owens, no Robert Graves, no Sassoon, no great war poets who could tell us about the lost generation. . . . It took us a great deal of research, including many conversations with these old veterans, to realize we did lose our own flower of a nation. It was, in fact, the only all-volunteer army in the First World War. A special kind of man went. Sure, they were adventurers, but a very simple kind. They weren't swashbucklers, but they were a kind of warrior class.[6]

This reference to a classical "warrior" caste illustrates the epic conception of Australia's participation in world conflict that Weir was developing. By concentrating on two young, competing, and complementary characters, much of the wider drama (scenes of planning in the British government, and the conscription debate in Australia[7]) was deleted to focus on the central relationship between Frank and Archie. Another justification for such omissions was the presumed acquaintance of the Australian audience with the historical background. Isolating the characters from their circumstances in a form of factual dramatic irony (by rendering them ignorant of the causes and horrors of the war) strengthens the sense of the lost generation's innocence and the growth of national awareness since the end of Imperial obedience.[8]

Gallipoli's structure consists of three segments set in different locations. The first two are identified by explanatory titles ("Western Australia, May 1915" and "Australian Training Camp, Cairo, July 1915"), but the final sequence at Gallipoli is untitled, as the build-up to and significance of the place and its name have dominated the film from the first appearance of its title. The presence of these titles recalls the opening of *Picnic* and previews the beginning of *Witness*. The three-act format may be expected from Williamson's theatrical background, but the use of the locating titles announces at once how far the characters travel and how little they or their environments alter. Archie (Mark Lee) is young, confident, and optimistic, Frank (Mel Gibson) more worldly, cynical, and scared, and in their progress from one desert to another nothing occurs to change their outlook (or their fates) significantly.

The elliptical nature of the drama—moving from Australian to African to Eurasian desert and being started, punctuated, and ended with footraces—reinforces the distance of the narrative events from the modern viewer first established with the titles, and suggests the ways in which this is an appraisal of history from a modern perspective. For example, Archie's newspaper cuttings of the campaign already appear yellowed by age and frayed by study, as if the events are mythologized within months of their occurrence. Similarly, Frank's skepticism and frustration with Archie's naivety give him the air of a late-twentieth-century observer, judging with hindsight the deluded innocence of those fighting for the Empire.

The reflexive nature of the titled sections is heightened by this internal observer/narrator figure, reminiscent of David Burton in *Wave*, and presaging Billy Kwan in *Year*. Dark-haired Frank, the survivor, returns home after blond Archie's death; and Dermody and Jacka remark on this and other similarities to *Picnic*:

> Weir stated that he "wanted to show the men entering the myth," but we never glimpse them outside of it. . . . It moves sacramentally from point to point through the chosen scenes of the legend like Stations of the Cross... It moves inevitably toward [Archie's] appointment with death until his image freezes in an image that rhymes beginning and end. . . .

[T]here is a sense of predestination, an element completely out of place in a film which purports to be historical. [Archie's] appointment with the highest honor is presented as something preternatural, equivalent to Miranda's appointment with the Rock: two ineffable transubstantiations of golden youth.[9]

Peter Fraser also notes *Gallipoli*'s biblical dimension but considers that while Archie's sacrifice "has no redemptive value in the context of the film," it gains in impact through "its undermining of the expectations usually generated in a Passion narrative."[10] Fraser suggests that Weir's film is powerful and tragic but not essentially religious, although its frame of reference is clearly scriptural. More precisely, the foregrounding of religious imagery and allusion suggests the symbiosis between religion and patriotism in the formation of national myth. While noting the reverential tone of Weir's treatment, Dermody and Jacka do not recognize this as an artificial staging and analysis of accepted history, but rather as a straightforward re-creation. The requiems of the soundtrack, from the titles onward, mourn a well-documented tragedy, the images being a "mere" representation of the nation's well-known loss. The ultimate slaughter comes as no surprise to the generals, informed spectators, or Frank. The inevitability of Archie's fate is as much due to his existence within a stage-managed, cyclic drama as it is to that drama's playing out of completed history. *Gallipoli*'s linear narrative relies on a theatrical and self-conscious structure, a reappraisal of completed but re-created events that have undergone a transformation into folklore and that are now dramatized in a form combining the historic and the poetic, the emotive and the reflexive.

Year's gestation was prolonged by differences of opinion between the studio and the writers, and between the writers themselves. Weir bought the rights to C. J. Koch's novel on its publication and worked on a screenplay with David Williamson and Koch himself. The finished film exhibits many Weir hallmarks: an expert usage of soundtrack music (Maurice Jarre's score foreshadowing his later work on *Witness* and *The Mosquito Coast* [1986]), a fascination with mysticism (the shadow play, or *wayang kulit*, a parabolic form of drama drawn from Indian myths), and myriad examples of alienated or isolated individuals set apart from societies or cultures. An insuperable distance separating all human beings is evident in the characters' relationships: President Sukarno is isolated from his people and abandoned by his supporters, and he alienates his country through his policy of *Konfrontasi*; the foreign journalists are under threat from a volatile populace, and their camaraderie is strained by rivalry; Guy Hamilton (Mel Gibson) is alone in his ambition and inexperience; and Billy Kwan (Linda Hunt) is utterly apart from all society, despite his association with the Western "journos" and the Eastern poor, because of the stigma of his mixed birth and dwarfism. Similarly, despite being part of a national and regional contingent, Archie and Frank are set apart from the other soldiers (including Frank's mates Billy, Barney, and Snowy) by their close friendship, and yet they are separated by their differing views and destinies. In both films, the uniqueness of personal perspective and experience (one of Weir's enduring themes) becomes a particularly bitter element in human interaction, all social groups being mere collections of incompatible personalities.

Year's form and content appear to converge. The novel's concentration on Billy Kwan's status as a "hybrid"[11] is notable, and contemporary criticism highlights the film's apparent genre uncertainty: "Peter Weir . . . .tries hard to maintain a balance between the sociopolitical elements of the film . . . and its Hollywood love story."[12] Billy talks of himself and Guy as "divided men," split between East and West and their implied mentalities, choosing between personal desires, professional duties, and preferred designs. The film exhibits similar paradoxes: politics and love, exotic, romantic settings with authentic poverty and unrest, commercial considerations and Weir's art-cinema reputation, the linking of the cinema's genre past (simplified main characters in Jill played by Sigourney Weaver and Guy, a conventional "happy ending") with the present in its focus on the lives of correspondents abroad.

Weir's film differs from contemporary productions in its mix of these and other elements, holding its genre, romantic, and individualistic concerns in delicate balance. Like the other novels Weir has helped to adapt to the screen, *Year* shifts between narrative tenses and points of view, giving us both the narrator "Cookie" and Billy's files as sources of information. The narrator's reminiscences of 1965, including excerpts from the files, are not only marked by hindsight and admissions of nostalgia for the past but also (in an echo of Joan Lindsay) are given the authority of historical fact. The variety of channels for narration and constraints of genre cinema look forward to *Witness*, but *Year*'s storytelling techniques differ from the later film because of its inclusion of the novel's reference to the *wayang* drama as a parallel to its own events. The visual medium is better suited to use this imagistic conceit: *Year*'s adoption of the device gives the film a metaphor for its own action and a basis for its representation, attaining a unity beyond that sought by critics of simple genre film, and a form of filmic expression unanticipated, and often not seen, by the same critics who would praise *Witness* for transcending genre limitations.

The interplay of fiction and history in *Gallipoli* has been examined by T. H. E. Travers, showing the film's debt to the official record of the Dardanelles campaign.[13] This account furnishes detailed information for the re-creation of the charge at the Battle of the Nek by the Tenth Light Horse on August 7, 1915 (the failure to synchronize watches leading to the premature halting of the artillery barrage, the mistaken sighting of marker flags in the enemy trenches, and vacillation at command level), and provides eyewitness accounts of how two brothers ran at the Turkish positions as "in a foot race."[14] Having removed the wider references to the period in successive drafts, Weir and Williamson concentrated instead on the two central characters and their relationship. This emphasis produces at once the most specific of cultural references (male "mateship") and the most unexpected neoclassical framework for allegorical narrative (isolated young male heroes). The two men symbolize differing attitudes to the war, to personal ambition, and to running, and how they run reflects how they live. The twin threads of the characterization, combining outback reliance with classical models of male endeavor, are related to the actual events and the mythologized maturation of the nation at Gallipoli.[15]

Mateship originates in the outback as a complex mix of rivalry and respect, loyalty and love. Archie's sacrifice is the apotheosis of "greater love" when he takes Frank's place in the line. Athleticism represents another borrowing from classical epic, with the origins of the Olympics in "the very exercises and dexterity necessary to a foot soldier in war."[16] The young Australians' place with the heroes of antiquity is first suggested by the episode of the race meeting, where Archie's (moral) victory and Frank's (financial) defeat are followed by the arrival of officers recruiting for the Light Horse. The crowd surrounds the huge wooden horse, and a young boy with a bugle clambers onto its back in an obvious classical allusion. Subsequently, Frank and Archie undergo shared trials (having to cross the desert before they can attempt to enlist, and both of them suffering the humiliation of rejection) and cement their relationship with races for fun in the Egyptian training grounds, climbing the pyramids to leave their names to posterity in the ancient stone, next to those of troops of Napoleon's *Grande Armée*.

Later, while members of the infantry play football at the base of the pyramids, Billy gazes in awe at the inscrutable face of the Sphinx. His earlier reflection that the Egyptian monuments represent "man's first attempt to beat death," ignored by Frank in the midst of his schemes to "beat the Vics," accentuates the gap between past achievement and current concerns, contemporary subjectivity and historical objectivity. The stature of the pyramids as witnesses to the sweep of men over the globe and the journey of nations through history was impressed on Weir during his own visit to Giza, when he discovered the name of a Portuguese sailor carved on the pyramids on each of three voyages in the fifteenth century.[17] This linkage from age to age, bonding men with landscape and landmark (in event and artefact), provides a key to the progress of the Australian heroes from analogous environments and erases differences between eras and nations.

Gallipoli stresses this correspondence in the minimal differences between its three sections, between Frank and the audience in their modern perspectives inside and outside the historical frame, and between the initially distinct personalities of Frank and Archie. While both have close ties to others before and after their first encounter (Archie's mentor Uncle Jack [Bill Kerr], Frank's mates), these acquaintances are all forsaken. Ostensibly, this separation is caused by Frank's refusal to fight (later replaced by his preference for the "class" of the Light Horse) and Archie's desire to copy Jack's youthful adventures, but implicitly they are always moving in unison toward their moment of shared destiny. Fate is predetermined by forces beyond the young men's control: the politics of imperialism within factual history; the stylization and patterning of national myth related to the history, and of the drama they inhabit derived from that myth; and the knowledge of the inevitable outcome of the expedition available to the viewer acquainted with history, myth, or both. Filmic and factual frames determine the characters' destinies.

Archie can affect and elevate Frank and save him from death by choosing the certain death that awaits him. The realities of the war are unknown, suppressed in their minds until the day of the attack, just as the camera deprives them and us of the sight of the infantry's charge at Lone Pine (in which Barney is killed, Snowy wounded, and Billy traumatized). Instead, only the sounds of slaughter intrude from offscreen, a distancing technique adopted for the concluding battle in *Kagemusha* (Akira Kurosawa, 1980). At the conclusion of *Gallipoli*, Frank, trapped in a communication trench, hears the whistles heralding the final charge. Innocence is lost on the battlefield so that worldliness and cynicism can survive to return to the homeland, to inculcate the legend. *Gallipoli* never loses sight of the modern resonances of the past event, to which it

Gallipoli   Mel Gibson, Mark Lee   (AUS 1981)
Picture from the Ronald Grant Archive

bears witness through Frank and which it represents rather than reproduces. Neither Frank nor the viewer sees the massacre of the last wave; instead, only Archie is seen running forward to immortality in filmic freeze-frame and national myth. The story's historical frame becomes stylized into mythic and filmic narrative, a derivation rather than a documentation of factual events. *Gallipoli* evokes history but eschews full reproduction by concentrating on Frank and Archie. Mateship is celebrated as an Australian institution, but the mateship of Billy, Barney, and Snowy is abandoned for their particular partnership. However, Archie and Frank are no more (or less) than characters. They personify national attitudes in a given era: Weir's attempt to pinpoint the type of men who went to the war becomes a mythic exploration of the country that produced them. *Gallipoli* begins in rural Australia, where

> knowledge is handed down in a definitely Socratic manner from master to apprentice, as [Archie's] old uncle trains him to sprint with an incantation. . . . Likewise, male bonding implies secrets and experiences shared, troths plighted, and eternal verities invoked unto a pact of irrevocable friendship.[18]

An analogy to the close friendships and "secrets" of *Picnic*'s schoolgirls is discernible, with Archie's unalterable destiny comparable to Miranda's apparent awareness of her fate. However, where the disappearance of the girls becomes a rebellious act against repression by older generations, in *Gallipoli* the young men of the outback, indoctrinated with Jack's readings from Kipling and revering the fledgling legends of Anzac, leave their native land to reaffirm the subordination of the colony within the Empire. The enactment of their duty in foreign but familiar lands leads to a new assertion of freedom in defiance of the old order, liberty again being dependent upon the mentality of the young, the influence of the landscape and heritage, and the loss of an emblematic generation from both the constraint of the establishment and the view of the camera.

Although the desert settings imply continuity, each part varies from its predecessor in content and tone (youthful aspiration, naive exuberance, foreboding melancholy). In each location, strictly limited scenes are played out, each geographically and historically located episode lending the frame of fact to the narrative's representation. The successive scenarios give specific stages to the men's odyssey of mind and distance; upbringing and rivalry give way to separation and preparation until the final maturation of fate. Archie and Frank are measured against each other, the Australian landscape, other Australian troops, and the war itself. While the second and third sections display painstaking period recreation, the first act's simplicity and blankness is crucial to building the theme of teaching and the innocence of the individuals and their land.

Archie's scenes with Jack, Frank's and Archie's trek across the desert, and the glimpse of Frank's father in Perth give clues to how the land gives rise to its people, or conversely, the people shape the land and one another. The opening scenes, although not necessarily pertinent to the representation of all the men of Anzac, are integral to the birth of the legend. In this portrayal of people and landscape—people as part of the landscape—Weir's pictorial composition best fits his national and individual emphases.

Jack and Archie are first seen in extreme close-up against the dawn sky. The featurelessness of the land to the horizon makes every aspect of their faces all the more prominent (Archie's smooth and rosily lit skin compared with Jack's rough, lined, and balding head). Essentially, Jack's lineaments *are* the land, reflecting its sunburned and sparsely covered soil, filling the frame and his nephew's thoughts at the dawn of his potential. Jack's contribution to Archie's cultivation is always stressed in this way. The house's dark interior, where Jack tends Archie's feet after the cross-country race, reintroduces the pale light as a metaphor for the young runner's gathering of physical and moral strength from the older man. Jack's abasement before his nephew, and the task itself, evoke the example of John the Baptist to the young Jesus.

As Archie walks around the darkened room, Jack's face looms very large in the foreground. They compare Archie's wish to run away to war with Jack's youthful adventures. The uncle dominates the frame, and Archie even occasionally vanishes from view behind his head, bearing its own map of world experience. Jack's reading of Mowgli's realization of manhood shows his knowledge of Archie's intentions. The camera pans over the room from intent children's faces to Jack in his chair, across the landscape of childhood, the gap between infancy and age that Jack's teachings to Archie (listening from the doorway to this last lesson) will now allow the younger man to cross. After the reading, Jack and Archie walk outside to gaze at the hills beyond the plains. Archie is given the world to explore, just as the ocean of opportunity opens before Charlie Fox at the end of *The Mosquito Coast*.

Frank is also introduced in extreme close-up, in a harsh daylight according to his earthy cynicism. While his mates read reports from the Dardanelles (reacting with an excitement distinct from Archie's reverent poring over similar cuttings by candlelight), Frank is unseen until the subject of enlisting is raised. Frank agrees to leave with them, but simply to escape the boredom of their work, and his decision to join up springs from a desire for advancement in the postwar world. Meeting his father in Perth, Frank outlines his plan to better himself: "keeping his head down" and definitely not fighting for the British Empire. The variance from Archie's background could not be greater: Frank finishes his father's sentences, seeing his advice as outmoded and the current situation as one from which to derive advantage, not adventure. The newspaper headlines that pursue Frank (read aloud by Billy and by men outside his lodgings after the race meeting) prompt only stirrings of guilt. The same words, kept by Archie in his volume *Every Boy's Book of Sport and Pastime* and seemingly already aged and honored as a model for emulation, provoke instead intimations of glory.

Frank's motives for enlisting are probably those he expresses to his father, allied to his affiliation to Archie if not to Archie's cause. Frank becomes devoted to Archie rather than to the Empire, and Archie's failure to explain the need to fight to the old man they meet in the desert is another source of humor in their relationship and a satirical comment on the young men's naivety. Although Frank's reasons for enlisting may not be as pure or simplistic as Archie's, the mates' undisciplined exploits in Cairo are no more than another form of youthful adventure. In mocking the caricatured British officers, Frank and his mates accord exactly with the stereotype of unabashed Australians, becoming national symbols and objects of satire themselves in the process. Their behavior sets them apart from their military and Imperial superiors, providing a link to the portrayal of Australian male groups in male ensemble and period films—the striking shearers of *Sunday Too Far Away*, the footballers of *The Club* (Bruce Beresford, 1980, from a play by David Williamson), the and soldiers fighting for foreign powers and dubious causes in *Breaker Morant* and *The Odd Angry Shot*.

The pervasive character of the "larrikin"—an anti-authoritarian, irresponsible male who, though awkward in the company of women, bonds fiercely with other men—is a feature of the Australian revival. Although distanced by decades of time, the contemporary, fictional, and comical Barry McKenzie and the historical, factual and tragic *Breaker Morant* embody the same traits of cheerful nonconformity and casual self-assurance, which can be transformed into a belligerent national pride when they encounter other cultures. Moral and muscular ascendency over Egyptian storekeepers and mockery of English officers are the two sides of the fledgling Australian national identity: aggression springing from a presumed superiority and almost self-defensive parody engendered by inherited, cultural inferiority. Behind this ubiquitous characterization of the Australian male is a definition of Australianness as being distinct from other nationalities, especially those that have exercised political and cultural control over the colony and its people.

When the final charge is ordered, Major Barton calls on his men's pride in their country to provide the justification for their sacrifice that the (British) military command cannot give. As the first from their country to go to war, the men from Western Australia must set an example for the new recruits and subsequent generations. A legend suited to the people and the land must return to their native country. The enemy, insofar as there is one, is the British military establishment, an organ of the Empire abusing the qualities of Australian manhood that, ironically, provides the motivation for recognition and exaggeration of those same national characteristics and their institutionalization in Australian literature and film.

The court martial of Harry "Breaker" Morant and his Australian comrades for uncompromising (but unofficially ratified) methods of prosecuting Boer guerrillas illustrates the sacrifice of the Australian male and parallels Weir's treatment of the Battle of the Nek. *Breaker Morant* reveals the prejudice of race rather than class at the core of the system's hypocrisy. Archie's innocence and obedience to the Empire's call is a reaffirmation of the colonial system, even as the character of Frank's uncommitted and modern observer prefigures the desire to relinquish colonial duty, turning submission into self-determination. However, Frank's part in the mythic cycle is as predestined as Archie's—he cannot alter the events of the past, reconstituted as a staged drama that inspires and is inspired by their mythic interpretation and importance. As a past and skeptical or modern and informed spectator, Frank's role is to bear witness to a change in Australian mentality, either from within the frame at the decisive moment in national history or reviewing that moment from the perspective of conversant, contemporary society.

The soldiers on trial in *Breaker Morant* voice a more explicit criticism of the class and race discrimination within the structures of colonial rule:

> Morant's suggestion that they are fighting on the wrong side—against "farmers" like themselves—is a critique of the system itself. To see a greater brotherhood between the Boers and the Australians than between the Australians and the English is to go beyond nationalism to a more political understanding of the social structure, and it is a perception that *Gallipoli*, in contrast, is unable to reproduce in its depiction of the classless Australians and their upperclass English officers.[19]

Both films address the archetype of the Australian (fighting) man—a consistent figure if not always a pure one, an honest and simple journeyman engaged in events stage-managed by others more adept in duplicity. They are celebrations of an idealized national type and requiems for the passing of a brand of innocence not peculiar to Australia at the turn of the twentieth century. Their return to the myth's point of origin, with the knowledge of the factual events and the hindrance of subsequent folkloric reinterpretation, requires the presence of a worldly yet idealistic observer figure: the defense counsel Major Thomas in *Breaker Morant*; Colonel Dax, defender of the mutineers in *Paths of Glory*; Harry the career soldier in *The Odd Angry Shot*, who knows Australians who fight in Vietnam will be "an embarrassment" to their country when they return; and Frank, the survivor of *Gallipoli*.

Criticism of Australian culture and a different type of hero's clashes with a conservative Australian establishment form the basis of *Between Wars* (Michael Thornhill, 1974). The central male character, Edward Trenbow, is the antithesis of the larrikin: a politically active and introverted doctor of the new science of psychology who suggests controversial treatment for shell-shocked patients of World War I, opposes his son's desire to join up for World War II, and earns the distrust of the authorities for his outspoken pacifism. The episodic and inconclusive narrative of Trenbow's life—"between wars" seen as completed and conclusive—emphasizes the minimal impact of the individual on major events of national history. The film's portrayal of restraint imposed by a conservative British-based establishment drains personal life of significance but better explains the necessity of the Anzac myth to national identity than Beresford's and Weir's films. However, in common with them, *Between Wars* demonstrates the supremacy of events, both factual and dramatic, over their participants. Notably, Thornhill's film frequently appears anti-illusionist in its depiction of the changing eras and locations (the Western Front, Britain, and Australia from the 1920s to the 1940s), thus emphasizing the contemporary perspective and relevance of its social and political critique.

Including an internal observer/narrator and recognizing perspectives outside the period frame, which offer potential for fantasy or allegory within factually based narrative, highlight the period film's contemporaneity in reinterpreting the distant and recent past. Such features also are discernible continuities within Weir's work in themes and cinematic style, which link *Picnic*'s temporal play to *Year*'s multilayered narration.

Frank and Archie are locked into an epic cycle that encompasses both the timelessness of their (national) innocence and the fixed span of their fate. Jack's watch—passed to Archie, used to cross the desert, and at last left stopped in the trench—is a motif (like *Picnic*'s Impressionist paintings and poetry) derived from other media, as Weir explained in an interview:

> [T]he whole desert in *Gallipoli* was represented in my own scrapbook by Salvador Dali—those desert landscapes with the huge clocks melting. I always saw Frank and Archie in one of those paintings, walking past one of those clocks.[20]

Time is stressed from the first timed run to the mistimed artillery barrage, and from Archie's race against the legend of Lasalles to his race into death and the making of his own legend. Shots of clocks and watches recall the ticking clock in Mrs. Appleyard's study and the watches stopped on the Rock in *Picnic*. The halting of time, dislocation of narrative, and freezing of life with a momentous event are reintroduced from *Picnic* to *Gallipoli* and are attributable as much to the film's modern (re)vision of events as to the subjective, experiential narrative.

In addition to the inspiration from Dali, other arts used to similar effect in *Picnic* play their part in the formation of Archie and the myth: the reading from Kipling's *Jungle Book*, the framed photo of Harry Lasalles in Archie's room, the newspaper reports eulogizing the Dardanelles campaign, and the juxtaposition of modern and classical soundtrack music. Recurrent musical connections, including the linkage of certain pieces to certain actions, underline the patterns of drama and destiny. Jean-Michel Jarre's *Oxygene* accompanies the crucial running sequences: Archie's challenge in the outback, Frank's and Archie's race to the old man during their desert crossing, their race to the pyramids, and Frank's attempt to halt the charge with dashes between the commanders. Juxtaposed with this startlingly modern music are poignant classical pieces. Jack Clancy isolates the particular significance of one passage to the theme of doomed male love:

> Weir has Major Barton . . . playing a recording, on a wind-up gramophone, of the duet from Bizet's *The Pearl Fishers*, usually known as "In the Depths of the Temple." Containing lines translatable as "I want to love you as a brother," and "Let us be united until death," it is generally recognized as one of the opera's great lyrical evocations of love between males.[21]

This inclusion reinforces *Gallipoli*'s theme of close male companionship and presages Billy Kwan's last hours of hopelessness in *Year* (he gazes at the accusing photographs of Jakarta's poor that decorate the walls of his home while listening to Strauss's "September"). The choice of classical music in these helpless and tragic situations recalls Victorian society's impotence in *Picnic*, accompanied by the elegiac "Emperor" symphony.

Albinoni's *Adagio for Strings and Organ* accompanies the opening titles, and its foreboding tone is the first indication of the young heroes' fate. As in the case of *Picnic*'s juxtaposition of Beethoven and the panpipes, Albinoni's *Adagio* and *Oxygene* form another "acoustic binary"[22] within Weir's work. The *Adagio* returns to replace the dance music of their last night in Cairo as the Australians sail in darkness to the nightmarishly lit coast of Gallipoli, a crossing to Hades reminiscent of *Death in Venice* (Luchino Visconti, 1971). This piece also accompanies the final shots in the trench and Frank's vain race with the orders to postpone the charge. Unlike the slaughter of the two previous waves, we do not see the soldiers fall but hear with Frank the whistles and gunfire offscreen before we see Archie racing on in silence to his death at the freeze-frame. Music and image connect the film's beginning and end, restressing the predetermined narrative—a modern recapitulation of known and completed history, reconstituted and reinjected with meaning in parabolic and reflexive form.

In addition to *Gallipoli*'s three-act, elliptical structure, archetypal characterization, and concentration on the relevance of time, key elements illustrate the film's modern perspective on past events. Not only is the narrative a reordering of national history in line with the communal myths descended from it, but also its structure and reference highlight its status as a reflexive and auteurist work. Central to many Weir films is the presence of an onscreen narrator or observer (Michael, Arthur Waldo, David Burton, Samuel Lapp, Charlie Fox, Max Klein, Truman Burbank) who is immersed and distanced from his diegetic environment by viewing and interpreting in parallel with the audience. Important individual scenes (such as David's search through his house at the conclusion of *Wave*) lay bare the conventions of representation, betray the patterning of an artistic consciousness in the work rather than an illusion of reality, and provide insight for viewer and character at the same crucial moment. Robert Winer isolates this revelatory moment in *Gallipoli*:

> [T]he boys strip down and dive into the water. This otherworldly space of Weir's is shattered when a shell breaks through and tears a boy's arm. These scenes and the fateful ending are confirmation that the world is not just a recipient of their adventurous spirit—it has an existence of its own, bearing consequences beyond their prediction.[23]

Within this timeless haven, the young soldiers marvel at relics of the battle (bottles and broken rifles), and, as with the newspapers quoted earlier, the tone is one of archaeological discovery rather than contemporary awareness. Temporarily removed from the historical frame, the details of the past are viewed with distant puzzlement before the soldiers are recalled to the diegetic environment. Similar moments, comparable in imagistic terms but varying considerably in meaning, are found in recent quasi-spiritual war films *The Thin Red Line* (Terrence Malick, 1998) and *Saving Private Ryan* (Steven Spielberg, 1998). In Malick's film, swimming encapsulates a temporary escape from war and duty, and, in an echo of Weir's film, the soldiers appear to regain a prelapsarian state. In Spielberg's film, the aural isolation created under water in the Omaha Beach sequence merely anticipates the deafness induced by shell-shock in the final battle scenes. In both instances, sound is subjectified in relation to one character, and the nominal distancing is not maintained: Men are killed by shrapnel even when under water, and the subjective muting of the climactic battle emphasizes the horror of the spectacle. Although both films share *Gallipoli*'s commitment to authentic period recreation, the visual realism of *Saving Private Ryan* departs emotionally and intellectually from the reflexive, contemplative representation of war and its meaning in Weir's and Malick's films.

Symbolic distances can be found throughout Weir's films (variances in age, outlook, and moral codes between Michael and his parents and between Arthur and the denizens of Paris, the philosophical and physical separation between Appleyard College and Hanging Rock, differences of class, race, and belief between David and the Aborigines), and in *Gallipoli* the gap is between past and present, historical fact and accepted legend, and documentary and stylized dramatic narrative. In retelling the myth not as fact but as dramatic as well as national construct, *Gallipoli* demonstrates the artificiality of both. As *Picnic* can be read as an allegory of nascent nationalism, a dream of individual and cultural self-determination within a dream of art cinema, so *Gallipoli* stands as a drama based on a myth derived from history, an art film dreamed from the residue of folklore and fact. *Year* extends this filmic counterbalance of art and fact, story and narrative, auteurism and genre cinema, with its adaptation of a historical novel.

In addition to the frames of historical incident and filmic representation, *Year* also incorporates the representational frame of the Indonesian shadow play, or *wayang kulit*. It is adopted in faithful transcription from Koch's novel, in common with the images of Joan Lindsay's *Picnic at Hanging Rock* reproduced in Weir's film. The *wayang* serves as a frame of reference for the direction of events and the destiny that encompasses the characters within fictional and factual worlds. Politicians seek to control history and make it tell their preferred story, and Billy Kwan manipulates circumstances to bring about his own designs, but both are subject to the unfolding of history and the whims of the novelist. Justification for Koch's frequent use of the *wayang* can be found in Sukarno's adoption of its politically apt allegories:

> One of [Sukarno's] characteristics as a public speaker was his ability to convey a point to an audience by an illustration taken from the *wayang*, the Javanese shadow play whose themes were drawn largely from the Indian epics, the *Ramayana* and the *Mahabharata*. He could rely on his Javanese and Sundanese audiences to know the *wayang* stories and to grasp the nuances of his argument without hesitation. Was this simply a matter of rhetorical skill? Was he simply concerned to clothe his ideas in an acceptable and dramatic form? Or did he himself move in the thought world of the *wayang*?[24]

The drama's appeal to other users is clear from its adoption by the story's disparate narrators: Koch's persona "Cookie," Billy Kwan, and Weir.

Wayang ornamentation is present in the film from the title sequence. The frame is filled with the *wayang* screen, centered on a bizarre head or mask, a symbolic rendition of the alien quality of Eastern culture from a Westerner's perspective. This enigmatic design is succeeded by the shadow puppets themselves, characters appearing from the left and right of the frame. Sounds of an audience are heard, cheering the entrance of their favorite characters. The next shot shows us the Jakarta night scene, with passersby moving in front of the *wayang* screen, lit conspicuously in the background. When the shadow play next fills the frame, and pedestrians continue to walk across it, we have the first and clearest indication of the film's thematic concentration on differences of seeing and perception, drama in art and reality (or rather drama in a range of artistic realities), and self-awareness of film as film.

Closer views of the puppets are afforded by glimpses of them in the Wayang Bar (Koch's setting for the association of the foreign journalists with the characters of the indigenous drama), and in Billy's bungalow. The puppets are there to be seen above and behind the correspondents at the bar at Guy's arrival and on later occasions. After nervous introductions to the regulars and under uncomfortable scrutiny from Billy, Guy is seen alone at the bar, with two puppets on the wall behind him as an index of the possibilities—hero or villain, success or failure, friend or betrayer—the circumstances offer him. A role is to be determined for him by fate, ambition, and Billy's intervention.

The linking of the *wayang* and contemporary events in Billy's mind is stressed by Koch[25] in a scene expanded by Weir. At his bungalow, Billy explains the drama's form and ideology to Guy. He chooses with symbolic selectivity the characters of Arjuna (the hero prince), Princess Srikandi, and Semar the Dwarf Squire. Billy's requisitioning of the *wayang* as a structure for his own manipulation of relationships at once affirms and denies the symbolic play's applicability to his life's (the novel's and film's) drama. His chosen conclusion (Guy and Jill together) is achieved in Koch's plot and Weir's happy ending, but the black-and-white nature of the immoral Sukarno regime (combining poverty and privilege, Communism and militarism) and the lurid reporting it inspires provoke Billy to an idealistic but pointless (Western) gesture that contradicts his leanings toward the (Eastern) *wayang*'s impartiality: "In the West, we want answers. Everything is either right or wrong, good or bad, but in the *wayang* no such final conclusions exist." In seeking, like Sukarno, to manipulate others, Billy forgets that he is a player in a larger drama in which his aspirations have led him to assume an overambitious role: "And do thy duty, even if it be humble, rather than another's, even if it be great. To die in one's duty is life: to live in another's is death."[26]

Once the pervasiveness of Koch's references to the shadow play is recognized as being part of the screenplay's fidelity, Weir's use of the *wayang* as a pattern for composition becomes conspicuous in important sequences. Guy is seen as a shadow on the window on his return to the Jakarta office after sending his first report. He is a solitary, framed, and inactive figure seen in shadow form at this point because of his failure to gain any introductions or interviews on his first day. His representation as a puppet without a role fits perfectly with what follows: Billy's unexpected arrival to offer Guy a meeting with the head of the Indonesian Communist Party (PKI). Later, Jill and Guy are seen as shadows against the same window as they kiss. This example gives more than a voyeuristic thrill. With Guy and Jill on the camera's side of the window (which becomes a lighted screen for them in the darkened room), we can see both of them as players within a larger (factual) drama than Billy's manufactured romance. They are seen in detail and not as silhouettes: Jill has come to tell Guy of the arms shipment that will bring civil war, and he must decide between loyalty to her love and the scoop of his career.

Silhouetting of the characters occurs throughout the film, and the *wayang* motif with which Koch characterizes all political and personal incident comes to dominate the narrative. In the drive from the airport to the hotel on Guy's first night, the camera shares his view through the car windshield, putting a frame around the bustle of oxen, pedestrians, and *betjak* taxis picked out in the headlights. When Billy and Guy encounter beggars as they leave the hotel, we again share Guy's view of the black, crippled figures emerging from the mist, and this shot is reversed to show the beggars silhouetted in the foreground while Billy and Guy appear as small, dark figures in the pool of light cast from the foyer.

With Billy's explanation of the *wayang*, the use of light and shadow becomes more evident. Billy shows his prized puppets to Guy and becomes a shadow player himself, a small, dark figure against the pale wall, manipulating each character who in turn throws his or her pale image on the "screen." When Guy joins him, unwittingly picking up the puppet of Semar the Dwarf, he squats down to Billy's level to make the shadow move. The sequence ends poignantly when Guy studies Billy's photo portrait of Jill. He stands with the framed picture in one hand and the puppet still held in the other, with the room's lighting throwing his and the objects' shadows on the wall behind him. The image contains representations of the three main characters, centred on Guy, who holds the picture and the puppet as unthinkingly as he damages the lives they symbolize. The scene suggests that Billy's assumption of control over the others' lives is a delusion, a misapprehension of scale between harmless puppeteering and a journalistic wish to influence as well as report events.

However, events in public and private life soon become unmanageable for all the players: Sukarno, the great "Puppet Master," loses control of the conflicting forces of the Left and Right; Billy finds himself mistaken in both his political hero and his personal friend; and Guy and Jill are arguably never in control of their relationship. The sense of futility in human action, which lacks the predictability of patterned drama, lends an artificiality to the performances. The scuffle between Guy and Curtis and Jill's affectionate movement of her foot to touch Ralph under the table, unseen by the other characters but revealed by the camera, take on the falseness and stylization of the gestures of the *wayang* puppets. Mel Gibson revealed that he saw Guy as a "journalist first, but also as a member of the audience,"[27] showing his awareness that in genre film, plot, characterization, and conclusion are as subject to formulaic inevitabilities as they are in myth. Like Frank in *Gallipoli*, Guy is as much an impotent observer as an active protagonist. Characters watch their fates unfold, with every act or omission accommodated by the conventions and the director's manipulation of them. However, in Weir's film, the characters oppose such narrative authority by constructing their own preferred plots.

The varying narration of the novel and its implication of numerous levels of control (or destiny beyond control) are transformed into a point of view associated with Billy's schemes. This precipitates anguish and disillusionment when Billy discovers that no amount of knowledge he assumes he has of others can be translated into mastery of their actions (nor can it be a substitute for self-knowledge). The photographer and image-maker suffers for his susceptibility to the written word (which eventually causes his death). His attempts to categorize the world through visual (photos) and written (files) media prove fruitless when opposed by fate. Billy's failure to control character and event, image and subject, is at the heart of the narrative of both film and novel. While studying his pain, both narrative forms evince a power of organization and omnipotence that Billy longs for, and the disparity in narrative authority between Billy and Cookie, or Billy and the camera, holds much of the attraction for viewers and readers of his story.

Koch's Billy revels in the historical and mythical associations of his appearance and its implications of greater knowledge—and Koch also takes greater license in revealing it: "We have a long history. Kings were especially fond of us: they liked to have their dwarf fools around; and we were the only ones allowed to tell the truth."[28] The assumption of wisdom leads to the wish or right to intervene in actual events. Billy's dwarfism and unabashed behavior encourage the belief that life's drama can be better managed by a wiser, other-worldly figure. The "magic" powers of his cameras and his files in detailing others' existences are the Western side of his urge to manage and act as match-maker. The Eastern side is reflected in his love of the inconclusive, conventionalized *wayang* and in his small-scale mission of mercy in the kampong, described in the mode of the shadow play: "You do whatever you can about the misery that's in front of you. Add your light to the sum of light."

Billy's status as a creator rather than a mere recorder of dramatic episodes may also spring from uncertainty about his origins and beliefs. He watches others who are seeking him when he fails to appear for prearranged meetings; in the film and the novel he dresses up as Sukarno; and he maneuvers Jill and Guy with a masochistic and voyeuristic fastidiousness. His motives for involvement with the people he cares about are unclear, but his appropriation of others and his plans for them are more decisive acts of narration than Koch's persona Cookie initially appears capable of performing.

Cookie—R. J. Cook—is portrayed as the "father confessor"[29] of the journalists of the Wayang Bar, as a justification for the intimate knowledge (otherwise unobtainable) that allows him to relate events from 1965 with authority. In Koch's novel it is Cookie, and not Jill, who rescues Billy's files after his death, and he uses them with circumspection to reinforce his own story. It is the rescue of the files and his awareness of them in the first place that prompt Cookie to document the story of Billy and Guy. His knowledge of the files' existence is a privilege prefiguring the status of narrator, whereas in the film both Guy and Jill, and perhaps others, are aware of Billy's endless, subjective cataloging.

Cookie's advantaged position, with the voice of Guy and the words of Billy at his disposal and the benefit of hindsight in ordering events, leads to some dislocation in narrative time. Tense in Chapter 5 shifts without warning between past (Cookie's recollection of Wally and others confiding in him) and present (the immediacy of events in Jakarta during February 1965). Later, such distortion is used to inform us of Guy's later life[30] and to describe the horrors of the coup. In the last chapters, Cookie's adoption of the *wayang* becomes most telling, combining present-tense narration with the *wayang*'s preordination. Cookie has grown into his role as narrator by the time the Communist coup takes place. His piecemeal revelations of Billy's files and his frequent resort to *wayang* images lead to his assumption, like Billy with his puppets and Sukarno with his political opponents, of the role of Dalang, the puppet master. Cookie visualizes the atrocities of the coup he did not witness[31], and in Chapters 23 and 24 uses the Dalang's intonation ("May silence prevail . . .") in his recital of the crucial incidents in the lives of Sukarno and Guy. Past and present are merged as the narrator's vision encompasses the dictator's personal and political life, with each episode conjured into the present with the formula "I see you . . ."[32] and then shifts to Guy's final attempt at glory in the heart of the unstable coup:

> Trespassing on the main arena of events, he remains quite ignorant of their nature and, like all of us, will remain so until long after they are over . . . [H]e walks an invisible grid, inside a story where things are not what they should be. They seldom are, in Java.[33]

The last days of Sukarno's rule are related in a style befitting his (and the narrator's) predilection for the *wayang*. Guy has imagined his life to have a preordained structure, Sukarno has terrorized his ministers with altered *wayang* performances containing allegories of their misdemeanors, and both (like the already murdered Billy) have wanted reality to match the reliability and moral certitude of a mannered drama. Cookie's success as a narrator in the novel and Billy's failure in the film are the result of the difficulty in amalgamating East and West. Koch's narrator combines the Western habits of judgmental recollection and desire for accuracy with Eastern imagination, capable of mythologizing the past. Billy's tragedy resides in his inability to separate his inherited Western morality from his acquired Eastern transcendence. As a character in the center of the film's action, and therefore demanding our sympathy as well as our attention for his status as narrator, Billy has lost the distance given by the passage of time, which in the novel allowed Cookie's hindsight to equate with the Dalang's neutral mastery. In any case, in the film even the narrator is observed and inherently is at the mercy of a higher, omnipotent commentator.

Billy remarks that he has a "quaint view"[34] of people and events from his physical and social position. Weir creates a parallel to Billy's prejudiced position, moving the camera and composing the frame with attention to his disadvantaged place in both Eastern and Western communities. As in *Witness*, the narrator's stature as well as his opinion color the visual storytelling, but this standpoint cannot be maintained without the intrusion of an external, more powerful narrative source—the camera itself.

Shot/reverse-shot combinations in Billy's meetings and conversations throughout the film emphasize his stature. In a subtle parallel to Billy's own methods of recording and commanding events, the film's narrrative structure (voice-overs, camera angles, editing, and composition) makes use of both word and image to tell its story about him, as well as utilizing Cookie's *wayang* references as a model for lighting and framing. In Guy's first appearance in the bar, Billy occupies an isolated corner position near the bottom of the frame. When he first addresses Guy, Guy looks around at his head height before looking down to Billy's level. The camera alternates between their respective points of view. Billy inhabits the same portion of the frame, behind and down to the left of Guy, when they wander out of the hotel into Jakarta on the same night. For the moment, Billy is still observing, and is only just beginning to direct Guy's thoughts. His voice-over values Guy's behavior ("last night I watched you walk back into childhood . . ."), with a hint of a recent past tense to match Koch's as the voice-over represents part of the notes made/being made/to be made in Guy's file. In Billy's bungalow, before he demonstrates the puppets to Guy, the positioning of the bar scene is replayed, with the notable punctuation of a medium-length shot of them both (Guy at the left, Billy on the right), emphasizing their difference in height. They are also set against a background of Billy's photos on the wall behind them, another example of the photographer's movement from objective observation to subjective intervention: "I don't care about the photos. I care about the content. I'm not very aesthetically minded."

When Billy starts to maneuver Guy in his own drama, both his position in the frame and the camera perspective are altered. Surprising Guy in the news office after his failed broadcast, Billy stands over and dominates Guy as he sits defeated at his desk. Billy's commanding role, in offering Guy the Aidit interview to make his name, is emphasized when he sits on the desk, looking down from the left side of the image to the smaller, lower figure of Guy on the right. However, although Guy is seen from Billy's perspective, Billy is observed from another, impartial point of view, his excitement and exasperation with Guy's caution seen in progressively closer close-ups. The camera announces its authority over all the characters, their being the basis of its narrative despite their efforts to influence one another. Even at the most decisive points in his direction of narrative and character, Billy is at the mercy of both Guy's unreliability and the camera's ascendency.

Thus, when Billy demonstrates the *wayang* puppets to Guy, he is another small, shadowy and inconstant figure in the harsh light. At the dance at Wally's bungalow (when Jill copies Guy's action, having to look down to discover Billy is her new partner), Billy is among the dancers, glimpsed through the mass of taller bodies as he watches his plan (Guy and Jill furtively catching each other's eye, bumping into each other while dancing with others) come to fruition. Later, he is all but ignored as the camera cuts between the faces of Ralph, Jill, and Guy during their gentle sparring exchanges. His marginalization here undermines the next scene, in which he addresses Jill's portrait: "So it begins." It seems he is admitting his powerlessness, as "it" has begun not because of but in spite of his management, and he abdicates his narrative authority as well as his affection for Jill.

Like Prospero from Shakespeare's *The Tempest* abandoning his books, Billy loses faith in his photos. They have served as metaphors for his obsession with Guy, Jill, Sukarno, and the peasant woman Ibu, but they prove incapable of bearing the meanings with which he burdens them. Billy cuts the image of Guy out of a photo, detaching him from his background, as his voice-over intones "we are divided men . . . we're not quite at home in the world," which merely underlines the fact that Guy is part of another, larger narrative than Billy's. Addressing Jill's photo rather than Jill herself evinces no control over her affections. Considering the pictures of Ibu and Sukarno side by side gives Billy only symbols of the country's ills, and, like the poster that enrages him after the death of Ibu's child, the pictures prompt him to a symbolic act to right them. Billy loses control of his preferred story line (when Guy chooses reporting over romance) and his own life, taken arbitrarily by Indonesian security men described ironically by Cookie as *wayang* characters.[35] His former hero Sukarno sweeps past the scene of his death and is seen for an instant looking confusedly from the window of his limousine. About to be ousted as puppet master, Sukarno also appears as an observer, not a protagonist. Both are lost when they try to perform more than their prescribed roles in the drama.

It is not simply the loss of Billy's viewpoint that demonstrates his decline from author to character but also the growth of other narrative angles to replace him. Jill and Guy take the initiative (ironically when Billy is observing them, having purposefully failed to show up for an appointment with Jill to throw her and Guy together) when they discuss Billy in his own bungalow. Their conversation begins on a personal level, with Guy probing for details of Jill's previous affairs (with them pushed to opposite sides of the frame), but it moves to Billy, his files, and his interest in Ibu. Guy and Jill not only analyze Billy's behavior but also steal his modes of expression, as first Jill and then Guy occupy the frame while the other talks offscreen as a voice-over of dubious authority.

Similarly, Billy's maddened frustration with Sukarno's negligence of his people is seen from the perspective of the other journalists in the Wayang Bar. He paces back and forth ranting about the regime's injustices while Wally and Curtis look on bemused. The camera shares their view, noting the oddness of his behavior in isolation from the "documentary footage" Billy has viewed or shot of Udin's funeral and a rice riot in the street. Billy's words do not have the effect on the journalists that the earlier pictures had on him, yet he uses words on his banner in his last attempt to impose his pattern on the wider narrative. By contrast, Guy gets the most emotive reaction to his reporting when he resorts to a visual metaphor: "The main point of Guy's story on the Lombok famine, interestingly, is an image—'a recurring nightmare image of the gaunt ribcages and sunken eyes of starving children'."[36]

Having taught Guy to "see" and told him to tell the stories "nobody wants to hear," Billy forgets his own lessons. He resorts to words, an admission of defeat for an image-maker commensurate with mistaking Guy for a "man of light," capable of honoring love and loyalties, and Sukarno for a conscientious leader. Three versions of 1965 meet on the night of Billy's death: Guy's life of reporting and the threat posed to it by his commitment to Jill; Billy's plans for Guy, Jill, and Indonesia as a whole; and the president's game of political posturing. With Billy's death, Sukarno's fall, and Jill's disappearance from the narrative, the only story to continue is Guy's—that of a reporter and romantic hero caught in circumstances he cannot control.

The attempts of journalists to translate or retell news "stories" they gather are inferior narrative efforts compared with those of the makers of the news. Eastern dualism and uncertainty are used, if not comprehended, in the rush to sell stories and boost reputations, with journalists merely decanting already potted histories. Telling acceptable stories appears difficult for Guy. He displeases the Australian Broadcasting Service with generalities and Jill with the melodramatic specificity of the Lombok report. For him, the arms shipment is not *a* story but *the* story because it will be his, told without Billy's help and verified with evidence other than Jill's intelligence information.

Guy files a story on the arms shipment in the film, something he does not do in the novel. For both Koch and Weir, Guy must be reduced from author to character for the narrative to end. His failure to find the arms shipment and his foolhardy schemes on the day of the coup are the novelist's way of humbling him, after Billy warns that his ambitions will drive Jill away. The film lets him post his story and promise to leave with Jill but denies him (and the viewer) sight of the biggest story, as if once his function as correspondent has been fulfilled, Guy must be diminished to a romantic hero for the happy ending to be reached. Similarly, Billy's story must be quashed for the fated events to occur. Billy falls through the hotel window, literally pushed through the frame used earlier to symbolize the artificiality of the film's and his construct of reality, as his symbolic, verbal attempt to topple Sukarno is an unintended and preemptive coup against the narrative lines of film and history. The fictional frame that vanishes when Billy is defenestrated is that of his intended story, which is undermined by his miscalculation of Guy, Sukarno, and the flow of events.

Guy becomes aware of the narrative beyond his ken when, in a parallel to *Gallipoli*, he dreams of Tiger Lily's true identity in an underwater sequence derived from an earlier interlude in the swimming pool. He realizes that she and his assistant Kumar are members of the PKI and that they could have killed him at any stage of his investigation into the arms shipment. This is suggested earlier, when Kumar watches Guy return to his car in the rearview mirror. Guy is framed within the image, being part of someone else's plans and a pawn in larger drama. Both Billy and Guy are forced to cede authority to greater stories and storytellers: the *wayang* destiny related by Cookie, and the genre romance told by the camera.

Year's evocation of classical Hollywood (the exotic romance of *Casablanca*, Guy's choice between work and love, and the rivalry of the journalists recalling the pressurized, exclusive male groups seen in the films of Howard Hawks) with a concomitant constraint on the potential of narrative and characterization is also seen in *LA Confidential* (Curtis Hanson, 1997). The motives and actions of the trio of detective heroes are predicted and controlled, explicitly in the prologue by a sleazy journalist, implicitly by their pernicious, patriarchal police chief, and ultimately by the conventions of film noir narrative, producing a highly qualified "happy ending."

Weir's film, like Koch's novel, offers a considerably simplified account of events preceding the coup attempt on September 30, 1965, with its amalgam of fact and fiction, recollection and supposition, relation and dramatization of actuality. It is debatable if a commercial film could be made from the many theories still surrounding the Sukarno regime and its demise.[37] However, the most contentious feature of Weir's film (with only slight variance from the novel) is its conclusion—"an ending to surpass bygone Hollywood at its silliest."[38] Other critics (who nonetheless continue to express dismay at *Year*'s not being a political or realistic film), detect American film history as the influence, explaining Koch's and Weir's simplification of the novel's ending:

He has only made period pieces . . . and above all uses the
sum of his skill to imitate the workmanship of American "B"
pictures of the '50s. . . . Into the Indonesia of Sukarno . . .
Peter Weir transposes all the narrative patterns of a romantic,
exotic, and unpretentious cinema, haunted no doubt by the
memory of *Casablanca*.[39]

Such analogies may not be mistaken, considering Sigourney
Weaver's memories of Weir's direction of the two stars: "Weir had
to teach the couple how to kiss for the screen by showing them
clips of Cary Grant and Ingrid Bergman from *Notorious*."[40] The director may well have encouraged an artificial, referential performance from his relatively inexperienced actors, coaxing them to
give imitative characterizations. This reemphasizes the self-conscious and intertextual tone of both *Gallipoli* and *Year*. Their place
within conventionalized canon (of genre film, and of Weir's work)
can be recognized through their period placing, thematic and visual stylization, and predetermined narratives, without failing to
notice the modern philosophical concerns framed in past (film and
national) history. The viewer informed by history for *Gallipoli* is
replaced by one formed by cinema and genre history in *Year*, with
the stylization of both (the three-act structure and *wayang* reference) highlighting prior knowledge and predestination of narrative
and character. Their modern frames are dictated by cinematic and
social history, with themes emerging from the myths of both.

In *Gallipoli* and *Year*, Weir continued the accommodation of, or
homage to, American genre cinema, while retaining his own distinctive traits of mysticism and visual poetry, which would be met
with greater acclaim in *Witness*. Where *The Cars That Ate Paris*
(1974), *Picnic*, and *Wave* combined Australian culture and genre
cinema with popular and high-art forms of America and Europe,
Gallipoli and *Year* show a development of *Picnic*'s interplay of reflexivity and fact, the awareness of *Cars* and *Wave* of American
genre cinema, and a further integration of recurrent stylistic features (music, editing, and art direction becoming art consumption
and quotation). These tendencies emphasize the continuities
within Weir's work, despite the popular belief that his characteristic style has faded with the predominance of narrative over atmosphere and of genre over art. Yet the director's art-film reputation
must be attributed as much to the reinvocation and reinterpreta-

tion of genre as to significant art direction, editing, sound, and narrative ambiguity.

Guy and Jill are molded and "directed" by Billy even as all three are constrained by genre, itself being transformed by Weir. Archie and Frank are impotent protagonists within a stylized and reflexive, modern and revisionist *syuzhet* rather than fully formed personalities within a historical *fabula*. Their embodiment of contemporary innocence and modern comprehension makes an understanding of the reasons behind the events within both the factual and diegetic contexts extremely difficult. This tendency in factually based films such as *Gallipoli* and *Year* makes the mystery of the quasi-historical *Picnic*, the amorality of the anti-western *Cars*, and the inconclusiveness of *Wave*'s subjectivity easier to accept as an openness to a plethora of meanings rather than an unwillingness to complete narrative.

Year adopts an Indonesian art form despite the fact that the journalists within the diegesis live isolated from the country and fail to understand it politically or culturally. In the end, all Guy can do is leave, returning to the West after filing his melodramatic, opinionated "stories":

> Unlike the moment of *Casablanca*, there is no stark choice to be made here between neutrality and commitment—only the recognition that these events offer no place for the Western loner to insert himself as hero.[41]

The legend of Gallipoli can only be approached by a modern audience through the popular perception of World War I in general and the campaign in particular. The musical tropes of Weir's film betray our contemporary knowledge of the past tragedy (Albinoni's *Adagio*), and the temporal distance over which we (re)view it (Jarre's *Oxygene*). The film's punctuation with titles giving dates and locations is only a form of stylization comparable to the rarefaction of history into myth. In *Year*, Weir takes the features of two art forms—the innocence and simplification of genre constructs from past cinema and the parables and symbolism of the *wayang*—and creates a visual polyglot, keeping both in view while eschewing an ultimate Western distinction or judgment. He produces a synthesis, balancing popular genre and art like Billy's "opposite intensities." The screenplay and visual conceits, mating the novelistic and historic sources, devotional *wayang* drama and classical cinema, and Weir's own mystical and humanistic concerns, are faithful to the auteurist development of genre film.

It is ironic that these two films, held up as examples of Weir's developing skill in cinematic narrative, should concentrate on the difficulty of relating and interpreting stories. The framing of these narratives within factual and cinematic history, as well as within the director's own stylistic structures, portrays the maturation of Weir's heterogeneous film idiom, combining the details of art film with the signs and settings of genre and the focus on story-based film with the laying bare of the problematic processes of narration. On the threshold of acceptance into Hollywood, Weir continued to familiarize himself with the heritage of generic cinema and defamiliarize its features within his own work.

Notes

1. Jack Clancy, "The Triumph of Mateship—The Failure of the Australian War Film Since 1970," *Overland, 105* (1986), pp. 4–10 (p. 7).

2. Susan Dermody and Elizabeth Jacka, *The Screening of Australia Vol. II: Anatomy of a National Cinema* (Sydney: Currency, 1988), p. 63.

3. Adrian Turner, "*Gallipoli,*" *Films and Filming, 327* (1981), p. 33.

4. Emmanuel Carrère, "*l'Annee des tous les dangers,*" *Positif, 269/270* (1983), pp. 116–117.

5. Interview with the author, June 1993.

6. Claudia Fonda-Bonardi and Peter Fonda-Bonardi, "The Birth of a Nation—An Interview with Peter Weir," *Cineaste, 11* (1982), pp. 41–42.

7. Sue Mathews, *35mm Dreams: Conversations with Five Directors About the Australian Film Revival* (Melbourne: Penguin, 1984), p. 102.

8. See Martin Crotty, "Making English Gentlemen from Australian Boys?: The Manly Ideal in Two Elite Protestant Schools of Victoria, 1875–1920," *Australian Studies, 13* (1998), pp. 44–67, for analysis of the indoctrination of Australian public schoolboys with the awareness of colonial duty prior to World War I.

9. Dermody and Jacka *Screening Vol. II*, pp. 159–163.

10. Peter Fraser, *Images of the Passion: The Sacramental Mode in Film* (Trowbridge: Flicks, 1998), p. 129.

11. C. J. Koch, *The Year of Living Dangerously,* (London: Grafton, 1986), p. 83.

12. Max Tessier, "*l'Annee des tous les dangers,*" *Revue du Cinema, 385* (1983), pp. 39–40 (author's translation).

13. T. H. E. Travers, "*Gallipoli*—Film and the Tradition of Australian History," *Film and History, 14* (1984), pp. 14–20 (pp. 16–17).

14. C. E. W. Bean, *The Story of Anzac, from the Outbreak of War to the End of the First Phase of the Gallipoli Campaign, May 4, 1915*, 2 vols., 3rd. ed. (Sydney: Angus and Robertson, 1934).

15. The parallel myth of the definition of New Zealand national identity through the abuse of the British military command and the sacrifices of the Dardanelles campaign is presented in *Chunuk Bair* (Dale G. Bradley, 1991).

16. Karen Jaehne, "*Gallipoli*," *Cineaste, 11* (1982), pp. 40–43 (p. 43).

17. Interview with the author, June 1993.

18. Jaehne, "*Gallipoli*," p. 40.

19. Graeme Turner, *National Fictions: Literature, Film and the Construction of Australian Narrative* (London: Allen & Unwin, 1986), pp. 115–117.

20. Mathews, *35mm Dreams*, p. 93.

21. Clancy, "Triumph of Mateship," p. 10.

22. Bruce Johnson and Gaye Poole, "Sound and Author/Auteurship: Music in the Films of Peter Weir," in *Screen Scores: Studies in Contemporary Australian Film Music*, ed. Rebecca Coyle (Sydney: AFTRS, 1998), p. 133.

23. Robert Winer, "Witnessing and Bearing Witness: The Ontogeny of Encounter in the Films of Peter Weir," in *Images in Our Souls: Cavell, Psychoanalysis and Cinema*, eds. Joseph H. Smith and William Kerrigan (London: Johns Hopkins University Press, 1987), p. 94.

24. J. D. Legge, *Sukarno, A Political Biography* (London: Allen Lane, 1972), pp. 11–12.

25. Koch, *Year*, pp. 81–83.

26. Juan Mascaró, (translator), *The Bhagavad Gita* (London: Penguin, 1962), Book III, verse 35, (p. 59).

27. M. Smith, "Mcl Gibson," *Cinema Papers, 42* (1983), pp. 12–17 (p. 16).

28. Koch, *Year*, pp. 94–95.

29. *Ibid.*, p.58.

30. *Ibid.*, p.42.

31. *Ibid.*, p.270.

32. *Ibid.*, pp.263–266.

33. *Ibid.*, pp.275–276.

34. *Ibid.*, p.83.

35. *Ibid.*, p.245.

36. J. R. MacBean, "Watching the Third World Watchers," *Film Quarterly, 37* (1984), pp. 1–13 (p. 10).

37. See Harold Crouch, *The Army and Politics in Indonesia* (London: Cornell University Press, 1978), pp. 107–112, 118–125.

38. Ivan Butler, "*The Year of Living Dangerously*," *Films and Filmmaking, 345* (1983), pp. 34–35, (p. 35).

39. Carrère "*l'Annee*," p. 116 (author's translation).

40. Robert Sellers, *Sigourney Weaver* (London: Robert Hale, 1992), p. 101.

41. Gary Hentzi, "Peter Weir and the Cinema of New Age Humanism," *Film Quarterly, 44* (1990), pp. 2–12 (p. 9).

Chapter Five

Witness (1985) and *The Mosquito Coast* (1986)

Witness marked Peter Weir's American feature debut. The film was made for Paramount, starred a major American actor (Harrison Ford), and emerged as a considerable commercial success, gaining eight Academy Award nominations. While the film that followed it, *The Mosquito Coast*, was a critical and commercial failure, many links can be traced between the two productions: The director came to work on *Witness* only after funding for the first attempt at filming *Mosquito Coast* fell through in 1984[1]; after playing the role of John Book in *Witness*, Harrison Ford worked with Weir again in the central role of Allie Fox in *Mosquito Coast*; and both films, being produced in the context of the commercial cinema, had to stand or fall on their viability as saleable entertainment. *Witness* was a clear success in this respect, combining the action and morality of the western and cop thriller with an effective melodrama, while *Mosquito Coast* failed to find an audience. Where the former film met audience expectations in the character of its hero and the particulars of genre entertainment, the latter frustrated the same expectations by subverting genre and altering the features it shared with the preceding film.

One of the attractions for Weir of the *Witness* production was that it represented the model of the Hollywood genre product, made by craftsmen under contract rather than artists through inspiration. His frustration at the failure to find financing for *Mosquito Coast* led him to instruct his American agent to forward him only scripts that had already been "green lit."[2] Accepting *Witness* in place of his own personal project entailed working on a ready-made film rather than a subject of choice and submitting to more external supervision than had been the case in Australia. Although this might have been expected to cramp the style of as individual director as Weir, in actuality it represented a milieu of filmmaking that greatly interested him, as Weir explained in an interview:

> On my first rewrite, I dismissed the melodrama, removed it even, and the producer brought me back to earth and back to realities. He spoke as a great American showman and therefore, for me, connected with the 1940s and the golden age of Hollywood. He kept saying "audience" and "Remember it's a thriller, and if you keep that in mind you'll construct a kind of hybrid between your style and the genre." . . . I came to realize that if the Fords and the Capras had had total control, they might have had shorter careers—and made less good films. Here on *Witness*, I was facing a genre film, something that one was very familiar with—go in quickly, do it with style and grace, collect your cheque, and leave.[3]

This statement reveals the duality in Weir's films in general and *Witness* in particular: the desire to work within a regimented environment, such as Hollywood, and to make conventional films for mass appeal, such as genre pieces, but to do so in an individualistic manner and to retain a great measure of control, evinced by the remark about his own "rewrite" of the screenplay. *Witness* emerges as a combination of general commercial and personal artistic intentions; although these varying influences can be discerned in other examples of Weir's work, the balance here appears particularly profitable, resulting in a film faithful to the rules of entertainment and his own stylistic patterning. Only in *Mosquito Coast*, where neither genre adherence nor Weir's identifiable style is much in evidence, did this tendency to subvert the conventions of popular cinema into a "hybrid" form bring critical and commercial failure.

As in the earlier Australian films, the first scenes of *Witness* mythologize the landscape and the community living on it. The wedding of the characters to their environment begins with the Amish rising out of the fields, and the linkage of men to land goes beyond symbiosis to embody unity and ethics. The costuming, the establishing shots of the arable landscape, and the views of homesteads and horse-drawn carriages all suggest the settings and atmosphere of the classical western, with its staples of gaining and guarding territory and the willpower of the community transforming desert into garden. However, as the families close in on the Lapp farm for the funeral gathering, a title states that this is "Pennsylvania 1984." The separation in distance and time from the Old West, that a genre-aware cinemagoer is able to span or ignore when faced with examples of Hollywood's western mythology, is extended by this defamiliarizing title. Not only is the West not in the geographical west, but it is also no longer old. The classic western usually portrays the East as the home of refinement, older values, and newer technologies, in contrast to the rawness and danger of life in the West:

> The subject of the classic western was the impact of the East upon the West and of the West upon Easterners. . . . [T]he institutions of civilization—church, school, marriage, family— were always threatened by the barbarism of the frontier, embodied in earlier, primitive versions of the myth in the Indian, or, later, and more meaningfully, in the outlaw or the unscrupulous rancher.[4]

Notions of authority in the family and society as the foundations of civilization form the backdrop to the narratives of both *Witness* and *Mosquito Coast*. As the generalities of the western, they are reinvoked as part of the director's recurrent interest in communal versus individual responsibility, to analyze personal perceptions of society as well as the peculiarities of American mythology.

In *Witness*, Pennsylvania harbors both the older, refined, and regimented communities of the Amish, resembling the Edenic half of the western myth, and, further east, the city of Philadelphia, where the frontier town ruled by gun law and aggressive individualism has been revived by modern urban decay. These apparent contradictions underline the status of the police thriller as inheritor of the western's patterns of morality play and Hollywood melodrama, with its "polarization of the world into moral absolutes"[5] through its establishment of opposing individuals, groups, environments, and ideologies. The new and reversed opposition of East and West also appears in the opening of *Mosquito Coast*, when Allie Fox (Harrison Ford) remarks that the migrant workers who have come to Hatfield from Honduras have swapped their jungle home for the more "murderous and foul" jungle of modern America.

In response to the decline of Western civilization, Allie as a Founding Father takes his family to a fresh frontier, where he embarks on the creation of a new New World, reducing the time required and magnifying the damage inflicted on the landscape through the pairing of old colonial work ethics and modern technology. The Amish sect's deliberate seclusion from modern American society coincides with Allie's rejection of that society's material and spiritual state. The forward-thinking, backward-moving families of both films, trading aspects of the twentieth century (consumerism, violence, societal breakup) for precepts of the nineteenth (abstinence, colonization, patriarchy), parallel their postmodern reappraisal of the western genre.

In the western, a force (either hostile natives or criminal cowboys) threatens the creation of the new Eden from the desert. These two films give an unexpected perspective on this myth, as one Eden drives out another, provoking a reexamination of the qualities of both. Philadelphia, the site of earlier aspirations for new existence (recalled in the name of the bar Happy Valley, where John Book and Carter [Brent Jennings] look for suspects), has decayed into indifference and disintegration, vice and violence. The Amish community appears to be an idyllic enclave of communal labor and shared reward, but when threatened by violence from without it exhibits its own form of aggression in unwavering patriarchal authority. Allie Fox's antipathy for Hatfield and Baltimore may seem understandable from a nationalist (imported goods) and humanist (urban chaos) perspective, and his improvements to existence in Jeronimo are miraculous, but the reversal of fortune that negates his efforts springs from his (ab)use of modern technology as well as his biblical pride. Weir's adherence to genre conventions in *Witness* (protection of society by an individual, who places communal needs above his own) allows for the introduction of personal style in the midst of modern setting and melodramatic structure (art direction in the representation of the Amish farms, and themes of isolation and individualism in the narrative). Conversely, the parabolic structure of *Mosquito Coast* (Allie, the Promethean man, rising before being humbled) and the near absence of Weir's style result in a morally pessimistic film, frustrating audience expectations through mismatched genre signals when the father/star and family do not win through. As an example of formal escapism by Weir (from genre ties and the conventions of his own established style)—like the imbalanced combination of old and new, and egalitarianism and authoritarianism, in the story of the Fox family's experiments in literal escapism—*Mosquito Coast* ends as an eccentric failure in terms of the American way and of saleable cinema.

Before the appearance of the thriller plot in Philadelphia, the introduction to the Amish community and the Lapp family illustrates the principles of the sect. The strength of the community in its grief for Jakob Lapp is shown in the scale and shared activity of the funeral gathering. These qualities are seen again in the mobilization of the whole parish in the barnraising. However, the negative side of the group identity can be seen in the sexual segregation of the event, when all the Amish are gathered to listen to the eulogy delivered by one of the male district elders. After this, a long moving-camera shot follows Daniel Hochleitner (Alexander Godunov) through the farmhouse. He talks to other farmers before presenting himself to Rachel (Kelly McGillis), recently widowed and being comforted by other women in a separate room. Her father-in-law Eli (Jan Rubes) favors Daniel's plan to marry her. The camera's preferential treatment of the elders, honoring the speech, and of Daniel, empowering him to seek out and address Rachel, is the first indication of the sexual division of the Amish community (a restrictive, Bible-based patriarchy) and the camera's association with specific, narrating characters.

Following scenes of the idyllic rural life, Eli takes Rachel and Samuel (Lukas Haas) to the railway station for their trip to Baltimore. Close-ups of the carriage and occupants give way to long shots of the carriage and landscape, flattening the perspective and reducing the free space around it, until it is hounded along the highway by cars and juggernauts seen from the same low-angle perspective used earlier for the line of Amish carriages coming to the farm. The first shot embodies the reclusive and inflexible order of the Amish (Eli looks through the front windows of the glassed-in carriage), the second that culture's anachronism and defenselessness before the morality and technology of the twentieth century. These perspectives are not linked to any specific character's point of view but fulfil the same function as the opening shots of *Picnic at Hanging Rock* (1975), establishing setting, era, and an

obscure threat in the environment with a metaphoric concise-
ness—a director-as-author's frontispiece.

Samuel's position within this sequence provides a clue to the
widening of the perspective. He is seen looking out of the open
back of the carriage, rather than through the barriers of glass. His
openness to new views and the witnessing of unenvisaged events
are signaled by this and the views of the spreading landscape.
These represent danger to the reclusive community but budding
potential to Samuel, like the expanse of ocean laid before Charlie
Fox (River Phoenix) at the conclusion of *Mosquito Coast*. As in *The
Last Wave* (1977) and *The Year of Living Dangerously* (1982), the
framing of events by and their being viewed through the doors and
windows of rooms and vehicles provide an analogy to the perception of the viewer. They illustrate the limitation of vision by institutional and ideological precepts affecting viewers and characters
alike. By contrast, the claustrophobic shots of Charlie and Allie inside their truck as they drive into Hatfield are indicative of Allie's
closed-mindedness and belligerence toward modern America.
Their journey from the same rural landscape into the town ends in
a similar way to the Lapps' ride: Eli's coach is seen marooned and
immobile near a crossroads, with traffic noise and road signs clustered around it, while Allie's pickup drives along a street fringed
with neon signs, refuse, and advertisements. Whereas in *Witness*
modernity shows genuine antipathy toward the difference of the
Amish, in *Mosquito* anger and aggression originate from Allie the
outsider and are vented on a lethargic community.

In Philadelphia, Samuel becomes a material witness to a homi-
cide, vital in terms of plot development and enlightening as a visual narrator, after the fashion of Billy Kwan in *Year*. The camera
gives us shots of his point of view as a defamiliarizing gaze on
1980s America, but the film does not sustain this limiting perspective indefinitely. John Book's presence, if not always his point of
view, takes over once he enters and observes the Amish community, in a commercially driven focus on the star and romantic content. However, Book's gradual ascendency over Samuel as the
film's narrative center emphasizes the very close association between the two characters, in dress, performance, action, and witnessing action. Varying styles of narration linked to Rachel,
Samuel, Book, and others, and later to Charlie and Allie in *Mos-*

quito Coast, rise and fall in importance throughout both films and imply the primacy of the concern with difficulties and differences in interpretation. This polyperspectival stance is reflected ironically in Eli's comment to Samuel on the Amish principle of pacifism over violence: "There is never only one way."

Initially, Samuel's perspective is the most important. His wonder at the railway locomotive, his view through the train window (looking at Daniel's cart running parallel to the track, waving to the hot-air balloon seen over the fields), and his walk through the station in Philadelphia are, in concert with Maurice Jarre's revelatory score, mystical reappraisals of everyday occurrences. These scenes, defamiliarized by Amish segregation and childhood, establish the boy as a naive viewer and narrator. The child's ingenuous narration and its association with the camera's (and therefore the viewer's) perspective is seen by the intrusion of just Samuel's hand into the frame of the train's window when he waves to the balloon and by the camera's assumption of his head height during his walk through the crowded station. As in the case of Billy Kwan, the stature as well as the perspicacity of the internal viewer/narrator influences the placing and movement of the camera itself.

Witness Lukas Haas (US 1985)
Picture from the Ronald Grant Archive

With the station murder, Samuel's immature perspective persists but is accompanied increasingly by that of John Book. Samuel's eye, constricted by the door and frame of the toilet cubicle, watches the death of the undercover cop, and shots of his entrapment in the cubicle (like those of the carriage ride) and close-ups of his hands fumbling to lock the door continue to stress his vulnerability engendered by age and upbringing. Similar frames—when Samuel is shown the face of a suspect squashed against the window of Book's car and when the camera again mirrors his point of view in the identity parade—emphasize his child's perspective. In the aftermath of the murder, when Book approaches Rachel and Samuel for the first time, his advance toward the camera (placed at their eye level) excludes his head and legs from the frame to leave a dehumanized torso.

Headless bodies walk around the mother and child and between them and the waist level camera as they await Book's arrival. A policeman's black-uniformed body, with hands behind his back and handcuffs on his belt, represents an authority visually similar to and as relentless as that of the Amish elders. Like Daniel at the family's departure, Book bends down to talk to Samuel and, significantly, Rachel, who sits at the same level as her son. The next day at the cafe, the camera reassumes the stature of Samuel as he receives the plate of hot dogs, and Book's headless chest occupies the rest of the frame. The strange foods are accepted as innocently as the opinions of Book's sister Elaine, which Rachel recounts over lunch. Rachel's naivety in this scene, which has been foreshadowed in her sharing of her son's wonder during the train journey as well as her similar stature during the interview with Book, is complimented here by Book's embarrassment when he begins eating while Rachel and Samuel say grace. By stooping to Samuel's level and by entering a world as foreign to him as Philadelphia is to the young boy, Book becomes a second, equally unformed and awkward narrator.

The crucial linking of the two narrators comes when Samuel identifies the murderer. Again, the camera copies his height and movements as he wanders around the police station. When Samuel recognizes Lieutenant McFee (Danny Glover), Book joins him wordlessly, bends down to his level, and tries to hide the revelation. Once in the Amish community, Book is more closely linked to Samuel by his view (shared by the camera) of the elders towering over his sick bed, by his ill-fitting Amish clothes reminiscent of the boy's costume, and by the sequence in which Samuel explains the workings of the farm to him. When Daniel courts Rachel, their wordless and adolescent afternoon on the porch swing seat is interrupted by Book, his awkwardness at the intrusion increased by his resemblance, in clothes and mannerisms, to her son.

Paul Schaeffer (Josef Sommer), Book's boss and former partner, remarks that the police are a cult or club like the Amish sect. The similarity is shown by comparable representations of police internal authority and narrow-mindedness when encountering a different culture. When Schaeffer and his colleagues have failed to extract news of Book's whereabouts from Elaine, Schaeffer is seen framed through the window of his car, cut off—like the Lapp family in their carriage—from the information he needs. When he contacts the rural police, the constriction of the city office (with blinds drawn and traffic noise intruding from outside) contrasts strongly with the wide expanses visible through the windows of the office of the more knowledgeable rural sheriff. When Book's partner Carter is brought before Schaeffer in another attempt to discover where Book has fled, the younger detective is seated and placed in a childlike position to the police chief, identical to Samuel's height before Book and Book's before the elders. The chief's headless body circles his subordinate officer in the chair while the camera remains at waist level. These visual representations of the Amish and police communities show that they function as hierarchies, demanding obedience from the lower orders (women and children, and men reduced to the status of children). "Shunning," a social non-existence in the case of the Amish, and actual death in Philadelphia, are the ultimate sanctions for transgression. Likewise, in *Mosquito Coast* Allie demands unquestioning loyalty from his family, telling his youngest son that if he resents his rule and wishes to leave the family, he can never return.

Having been reduced in status through his association with Samuel and his arrival in the Amish community, Book has his credibility as a hero of the western or thriller further eroded by the relinquishing of his gun. Giving up his firearm is, like acceptance of the codes of dress and non-violence, an illustration of his subordination to Amish authority. Book entrusts Rachel with the weapon after Samuel has found it in a drawer in his bedroom. Again the camera assumes the child's ingenuous point of view, peering at the gun over the top of the drawer while the small hands lift it clumsily. While Rachel expresses her anger, it is left to Eli, the household patriarch, to lecture the young boy on the principles of pacifism and abhorrence of killing. Don Shiach draws a comparison with the classic western *Shane* (George Stevens, 1953), in which the hero gunfighter instructs the son of the homesteaders he protects in marksmanship, noting the "Freudian implications of Samuel's fascination with Book's gun."[6] If these associations are traced further, we see Samuel's maturation in viewing (with the murder in Philadelphia as a kind of perverted primal scene) would coincide with interest in the phallic handgun, the "unclean thing" condemned by his grandfather.

The gun is encoded in the western and cop genres as the instrument of justice, wielded by the male hero in defence of family and society, but here the hero has been wounded, reduced to the status of an ingenue or child in an authoritarian society and emasculated by giving up the gun to the mother figure. In the film's linking of Samuel's perspective to Book's and the camera's, and Samuel's being witness to violent acts as yet unredressed, *Witness* provokes debate on the nature of retributive, morally justified violence in the western genre from which it draws its iconography, as well as on the viewer's observation of and participation in such acts through identification with on-screen characters. In answer to Eli's questioning, Samuel says that he would kill only "the bad men," whom he knows by their immoral acts of violence: "I can see what they do. I have seen it." Like a seasoned viewer of genre cinema, Samuel expects retaliatory violence from Book to provide cathartic resolution for the moral outrage built up by unpunished crime, but *Witness* seems unwilling to indulge this desire without qualification.

Feminist psychoanalytic criticism isolates the mechanism of the "look" as part of commercial cinema's reinforcement of patriarchal domination of media and society:

> The look is both a metaphor in films and an integral part of filmic structure. The cinematic apparatus is designed to produce the look and to create in the spectator the sensation that

it is she/he that is producing the look, dreaming those images which appear on the screen.[7]

In *Witness*, the "look" of the male characters on-screen at the action contained there gives the impression that external viewers share that look, and, because of the camera's association with the narrators and the moral drama they are observing, provides an analogy to and critique of the look of the spectators. As well as the linkage of Samuel to Book and of both to the camera, an additional connection of the gazes of characters, camera, and viewers comes from the process of identification, which causes the viewer to associate with the activity of the central (male) character in resolving narrative conflict:

> [I]dentification is a process which commands the subject to be displaced by an other; it is a procedure which refuses and recuperates the separation between self and other, and in this replicates the very structure of patriarchy. Identification demands sameness, necessitates similarity, disallows difference. Identification is a process with its own ideology.[8]

The difference enunciated by the look in *Witness* stretches across cultures and ideologies as well as genders, with self and other becoming the opposites of violence ("English") and pacifism (Amish). As Anne Friedberg implies, there are considerable repercussions for the female viewer in identification, which upholds the patriarchal status quo by making male characters attractive in their empowerment to resolve melodramatic narrative through moral or violent (or both) action and by the implied powerlessness of female characters to do likewise. Both the Amish and the police demand obedience to codes embodied in male authority figures. Book's individuality is encouraged in pursuit of law enforcement, but not when this leads toward the indictment of fellow officers. Similarly, in *Mosquito Coast* Allie is the archetypal American nonconformist, yet he demands loyalty from his family and will not tolerate the challenge of his sons.

Analysis of the desire for resolution and identification in *Witness* is made more complex by Book's semi-integration into Amish life, entailing a weakening or feminization of the hero through conformity to the rules of the male elders. Book and Samuel undergo mirror images of another psychological identification process that is central to mental, moral, and social maturation: the establishment of the ego in relation to the Super-ego and the Id:

> The Ego is at the centre of object relations, both as they are represented in our inner world and met in the outer world. The Ego is the mediator between the needs and demands of the inside world and the realities and opportunities of the outside world. In performing this refereeing task it has to heed the Super-ego, which is roughly equivalent to conscience, both in its conscious and unconscious aspects. The Super-ego is built from the internalized representations and standards of parental figures from infancy onwards, with contributions from later relationships with teachers and other admired or feared figures. We can distinguish further between the more primitive and punitive aspects of the Super-ego ("Thou shalt not . . .") and the more positive Ego-ideal or those precepts we may try to follow. The primitive Super-ego and the Ego-ideal are somewhat like the Gods of the Old and New Testaments, respectively. We may think out for ourselves, as adults, our attitudes to major issues of the day such as abortion or euthanasia, etc., but more frequently in many (often trivial) ways, such as queuing in shops, we operate according to the less conscious dictates of conscience. Indeed, society could hardly survive without them.[9]

Having lost his actual father, Samuel is presented with a choice between the patriarchal authority of his grandfather, a representative of the righteous Amish Super-ego, and an alternative in John Book, a father figure that in Amish terms incarnates the violence of the amoral Id. Book is faced with a similar choice between the unassailable moral position of the pacifist Amish Super-ego and Schaeffer, another father figure as Id, yet ironically one who represents a dark mirror to the Amish Super-ego as head of an exclusive and self-regulating cult. Both male heroes, finally perhaps the same persona divided into two, take heed of only part of the father's teachings. Samuel seems not to accept Eli's call to renounce all violent (and by extension, adult and individual) expression and yet helps to resolve the climax through peaceful means (ringing the farm bell to summon aid). Book responds to bullies in Strasbourg in "his way," in an explosion of physical violence, but leaves the final, retributive killing incomplete in favor of passive, communal resistance (silent witnessing of the enormity of aggression and transgression). This can be seen as a selection of individual rules from the law dictated by the elders of both sides, the creation of a personal ideology in the choices forming the Ego-ideal.

David Burton's personal negotiation of Aboriginal and non-Aboriginal custom and law in *Wave* represents a clear precedent for such a resolution. As such, the biblical nomenclature of the characters symbolizes the shift from the obduracy of the Old Testament Amish (Eli, Rachel, Daniel, and Samuel) to the mercy and compromise of the New (John). Book's and Samuel's resolution of the narrative, combining active and passive remedies, represents a personal compromise on their part and on the part of the filmmaker, defying the hallowed rules determining the conclusion of genre narrative. Where the hero figure is most often the embodiment of genre convention (in symbolic dress, ideology, and verbal and physical expression), the plural heroes of this film seek more than one way of resolving the conflict. Given that the narration has centered on them, it is fitting that their combined actions, whether they fulfil expectations or not, should conclude the drama.

The hero of the western is recognized by the significance of his dress, utterances, and actions. As the defender of order and protector of family and society against the savagery of the Indian, the outlaw, or in this case the corrupt police officer (with whom he does, however, share important features of knowledge, skills, and lifestyle outside civilized society), the good cowboy becomes a representation of the laws of the land (and the conventions of the films) that they all inhabit. According to Stephen Neale, the conventions of drama in the western

> find a particular focus in the body of the male hero. They articulate the space of the functioning of what is defined in the genre as the Law, and the space which is defined as outside it, as Other. The body of the hero is situated within a series of other bodies (those of Indians, outlaws, townspeople, farmers, and so on) across which this opposition is marked, hence the importance of dress, adornment, etc. It is marked also across a spatial economy whose polar instances are natural landscape on the one hand and the township/homestead on the other. Here, again, the body of the hero is located dynamically at the point of their intersection, oscillating between them.[10]

In identifying the duty of the hero as upholder and symbol of the law while noting his separation from the sites of civilized society, Neale gives an apt description of the role playing and performance expected from John Book. Where *Witness* complicates his duty, in diverging from the western or cop genres but accommodating a Weir trait, is in the culture clash, within which the heroes Book and Samuel act as the intersection of the worlds of Philadelphia and Lancaster County. In the new milieu, Book is inclined to conform to a new role rather than work on his old one of law enforcer, since Amish laws are at variance with those of Philadelphia. The result is the modification of both laws, new and old—the generic and violent law of the city wilderness and the old but renewed passive Amish law of the rural homestead. Inscription of the law on the hero's body implies the recognition of the law (in conventions of dress) and knowledge of the star incarnating him. The climax of *Witness* complicates these two pressures (identification of/with the star and expectation of the star's conventional duty to viewer and community) on the hero's body, but we can trace the origins of this struggle inside the film and the hero's persona in scenes preceding the compromise ending.

With the importance of witnessing and perception by Samuel established in the first half of the film, the increased significance of the character of John Book causes the analysis of looking, and the camera's point of view, to be taken over by him in the second half. The exchange of looks between Rachel and Book that begins after Daniel's visit and continues through the barn-raising scenes (where they appear almost immodest in their personal significance in the midst of collective endeavor) reaches its emotional peak when Book comes to watch Rachel bathing in the evening. At first he looks at her from the porch, seeing her move around the kitchen through the frame of a window. Like its predecessors in the carriage journey and in the cars, houses, and offices of Philadelphia, this composition suggests the distance involved in observation from outside a cult, culture, or ideology. While Rachel bathes, Book's face appears before her in a mirror as he watches from the doorway behind her. The framing of the face in the mirror recalls shots of Miranda in *Picnic*, encapsulating the notion of her as an icon, a center of desire, the creation of the admirers as much as an individual in her own right. The composition highlights the varied conceptions of Book, as the hero for the society, the star for the viewer, and the desired but forbidden lover for Rachel. When Rachel turns to face him, the camera gives their respective points of view, showing us Rachel's nudity and the conflicts of emotion and indecision in them both.

This sequence becomes a focus for the arguments of the sexual and social significance of the "look" and the place of the hero as a center for identification and expectation by the viewer. Shiach remarks on the pressures in modern cinema for nudity as spectacle and takes this scene as evidence of studio concerns overriding the director's reticence.[11] However, another interpretation is provided by the feminist critique of the "look" as an instrument of patriarchal dominance:

> In a world ordered by sexual imbalance, pleasure in looking has been split between active/male and passive/female. The determining male gaze projects its fantasy onto the female figure, which is styled accordingly. . . . Traditionally, the woman displayed has functioned on two levels: as erotic object for the characters within the screen story, and as an erotic object for the spectator within the auditorium.[12]

Amish society, as portrayed in the funeral gathering and the reproval of Rachel's behavior, is one of "sexual imbalance," and in this instance the male gaze of the camera (linked to the screen hero, our channel for the look and focus of identification) on Rachel's nakedness can be interpreted as a concession to commercial imperatives and a restatement of her social inferiority. However, the compromising of Book as a hero in giving up his weapons and his individual freedom of action is furthered in this exchange of looks. First, this meeting, although charged with desire, is not consummated in lovemaking, in contradiction of the commercial impetus for sexual spectacle. Second, the impotence of Book's and the viewer's look is challenged by Rachel's return of it on him, proving that the hero, also can become the erotic object of a gaze within the frame. We might go further and suggest that the meeting has been instigated by Rachel rather than Book, in her choice of the place and time for him to see her nakedness. Her gaze upon him stops the narrative in erotic contemplation, in the same way as the male objectifying gaze, and it complicates the hero's characterization. Third, the placing of Book's image within the confines of the mirror suggests his equivalence with Miranda as the idealized object of a gaze himself. Finally, the exchange of looks is broken first by Book rather than Rachel, as he looks away and retreats to his room, another example of dashed (audience, generic, and commercial) expectation. Rachel's return of the look is a subversive act, expressing her freedom of choice and acknowledging her sexuality in defiance of the patriarchal structures of her community and commercial cinema. Book sees more in the mirror than he bargained for and is forced to reconsider his role, conforming to expectation as a romantic hero, as a subordinate within the Amish community (as in the barn raising), or as a genre hero protecting society from without. The lack of resolution in this scene, depriving us of the voyeuristic thrill in consummation of Book's and the viewer's erotic gaze and depriving Rachel of the object of her erotic gaze, presages the genre disappointment of the violent climax. The sequence maps the inscription of patriarchal law on the bodies of hero and heroine. Her transgression in equaling his desire is betrayed by his indecisiveness, giving us another example of the hero's feminization. He becomes the object of an erotic gaze and is unable to resolve the problem that their mutual attraction poses to the status quo.

The next day, Book airs their dilemma when he states that if they had made love, he would have to remain in the Amish community, or she would have to leave it with him. His hesitation when watching her bathe recalls Samuel's impotence before the vision of the murder and recalls the childlike quality imposed on Book and Rachel within the Amish context. Confronted with several forms of transgression (his desire for the widow, covert viewing of her, and the discovery of her equal desire for him), Book assumes the passive role of woman and child, retreating before the spectacle, and although Rachel commands the look momentarily, she does not control the narrative. Rachel's marrying Daniel would satisfy the community, while her leaving with Book would complete a romantic narrative. Book's observation of Rachel bathing (and getting caught in the act) is decisive in resolving this issue, since it again places Book in the position of childlike viewer of things forbidden rather than mature witness to adult emotion. Despite Rachel's acquisition of the look, the hiatus in the narrative caused by the bathing scene is removed (and the action resolved) by the actions of the hero. By placing Book under her own gaze as well as the viewer's, Rachel unwittingly prompts him to resolve the narrative as demanded by his role as the hero and center for identification. Viewing the mother figure naked prompts Book to reject integration into the Amish community that the barn raising may have encouraged, to reattain maturity as an individualistic hero rather than remain and accept the patriarchal authority of the elders.

Book goes to Strasbourg with Eli and offends visiting tourists (we see them first through the windows of their coach as they disembark in foreign territory). He learns about the murder of Carter and calls Schaeffer at home. After threats of violence and exposure to his superior, Book has the opportunity to release his and our tension by beating up the youths insulting Daniel, and although this is an outburst of morally satisfying violence, it precipitates Schaeffer's discovery of Book's whereabouts. Back at the farm, Rachel finds that Book has given Samuel a toy, a series of chutes, wheels, and levers perhaps inspired by the mill itself. As a parting gift, the toy represents the order and harmony of Amish society, obeying certain rules and performing set functions. This present is juxtaposed with the reerection of the dovecote knocked down on Book's arrival. At a symbolic level, his departure will reestablish order in the commune, as Rachel will no longer have an alternative suitor. Rebuilding the dovecote symbolizes Book's resumption of heroic activity, defeating violence with violence in Strasbourg and later vanquishing the corrupt policemen with aggressive and passive means. Rachel watches Book and Eli reerect the birdhouse through the dividing and distancing frames of the kitchen windows, and when Eli comes in she hears that Book will leave in the morning. The maturer choice is reached, with Book returning to his world and expected role and Rachel accepting the inevitability of her submergence in the community. It is at this point that notions of naivity and maturity coalesce. Rachel takes off her starched headdress, symbol of her status and origin, her hands being seen in close-up as she does so, and joins Book in a wordless embrace outside. The close-ups recall shots of Samuel's hands at the moments of his new experiences: handling Book's gun, locking the door on the murderers. Rachel embraces a new experience for what she knows is the first and last time. In effect, the violent climax is a postscript to this resolution of the dilemma of identification, objectification, and genre expectation provoked by the meeting of the two communities, but is itself succeeded by a another lengthy exchange of looks that end the social, and genre, debate.

The mixture of methods used to resolve the violent action (gunfire, suffocation in the grain tower, and silent, passive witnessing) do not represent a formulaic and cynically commercial conclusion of the thriller plot. In sparing Schaeffer's life and overwhelming him with shame, Book defers to several higher authorities: the Amish wish for peace, his own sense of heroic fair play (giving up his gun to save Rachel, not shooting Schaeffer once he is disarmed), and the greater law-enforcement community (handing Schaeffer over to the police). He does not fully honor the creed of non-violence, but neither does he carry out his threats to Schaeffer. He has come out from among both schools of thought, returning to the model of the genre western hero without fully enacting the code of moral violence.

Echoes of specific westerns are discernible in the latter half of the film. Schaeffer, McFee, and Ferguson walk down toward the farm in a "deliberate evocation of *High Noon* [Fred Zinnemann, 1952],"[13] a western that also confronts the twin dilemmas of defense of society and pacifism. (There is also an echo of Weir's *The Cars That Ate Paris* [1974] in the menacing appearance of the policemen's car on the ridge overlooking the Lapp farm.) Having saved the community, Book should now ride into the sunset, but the difficult decision to resume the heroic role makes his departure painful. As Book stands on the porch with Rachel in the front doorway behind him, they exchange looks and then look away from each other twice before he summons the strength to leave. She is framed in the dark doorway, and in the background behind him is the road out of the farm to the open country. This ending combines *Shane* with *The Searchers* (John Ford, 1956), in which the hero Ethan Edwards's ambivalence toward the homestead is matched by the unconsummated desire for (and of) his sister-in-law. Book leaves, but hardly willingly, as he makes the decision to be shut out from the homestead and Rachel accepts being shut in. Like Ethan Edwards, Book returns to the environment to which he is best suited, and the seclusion of the family home prevents the rehabilitation of the hero. The male's discovery of his proper place and role, either choosing to remain forever outside society and the home (like Ethan Edwards and Shane) or taking the chance to join in and be softened by communal life (like Martin Pawley, once away from Ethan's influence), is made impossible by Book's recognition of his unsuitability to either environment. His resignation in returning to the city, which has been defamilarized through contact with Samuel and Rachel and the treachery of his colleagues, is not lessened by the realization that the city's marks upon him make him ineligible for Amish life. The triumph of the social order, implicit in Rachel's decision to stay and Book's to leave, is made emphatic by the sight of Daniel approaching the farm as Book departs. The final scenes are accompanied by the anthemic music of the barn-raising sequence, the epiphany of the cooperative society. In *Picnic*, the recapitulation of the "Emperor" symphony at the film's end heralds the defeat of the social system by the disappearances. In *Witness*, the Amish theme marks the victory of the community over the individual, the endurance of the farmers over the ephemerality of the fighters, echoing the muted ending of *Seven Samurai* (Akira Kurosawa, 1954).

Use of music and sound is one characteristic of Weir's style much in evidence *in Witness*, countering the notion that commercial considerations have laundered *Witness* of its maker's trademarks. The mystical strains of Maurice Jarre's score accompany the opening sequence (when the Amish rise out of the land) and Samuel's discoveries in the station and police offices (ingenuous kinship with a Hasidic Jew, awe at the angel statue, naive honesty in identifying the murderer).[14] The celebratory anthem also appears as the community runs toward the Lapp farm when summoned by the ringing bell, another affirmation of the society's strength in unity.

The music's power to mythologize the Amish community acts as a reinforcement to the significance of the art direction in the same scenes. Lighting, set design, and costuming on the farm recall works by Dutch painters of the seventeenth century in their dim pastel colors, the muted tones of the interiors, the lamp-lit rooms, and the representations of domesticity. This influence can be traced to a visit made by Weir and Ford to an exhibition of Flemish school paintings in Philadelphia.[15] Drawing on this style echoes the visual reference to Australian Impressionism in *Picnic*, and as in that film the recognition of their inclusion increases our awareness of the Romantic currents in the narrative. In *Witness*, the visual echo of art of the past authenticates the representation of the Amish way of life for a modern viewer and deepens understanding of its valuing of labor and family. Social structures, spirituality, and ideology are discernible in the idyllic depiction. In this context, the anthem accompanying the end credits is a vindication of the Amish prevailing over the intruders with cars and guns, shouts and music, and its mix of defeat and victory on personal and communal levels presages the downbeat ending of *Dead Poets Society* (1989).

The symbolic qualities of the western in representations of family, social communities, and the roles of the different generations and sexes of which they are composed are carried over from *Witness* to *Mosquito Coast*. The narrative of the source novel by Paul Theroux emphasizes the direct opposition and competition between Allie Fox and the missionaries in the Honduran jungle. The film adaptation goes further in this respect by making the Reverend Spellgood (Andre Gregory) Allie's sole adversary and by engendering internal opposition to Allie's despotism in his two sons. *Mosquito Coast* invites comparison with other depictions of Westerners, or more specifically Americans, journeying into the jungle wilderness. Parallels are evoked between this novel and its film adaptation and Joseph Conrad's *Heart of Darkness* and its extrapolation into *Apocalypse Now* (Francis Ford Coppola, 1979), as well as *Lord of the Flies* (Peter Brook, 1963) from the novel by William Golding, with its fragile establishment of civilized order on human and natural chaos.

The narrative of *Mosquito Coast* acknowledges and incorporates the resonances of these modern myths but also retreats further into the literary and spiritual past with its references to biblical and mythological texts (the Edenic garden, hell fire and flood, knowledge and its freedoms, and Promethean overreaching, as noted by George Robert Kimbal[16]). Allie is characterized as both a satanic opponent to God and godlike in his own powers, and demonstrations of his omnipotence and madness accord to cyclical patterns of moral fables and the particularities of biblical narrative. When the *Unicorn* is close to foundering in a storm, Allie does not join in prayer with Spellgood but saves the ship with his expertise.[17] Jeronimo and the garden paradise are destroyed and the family expelled when Allie takes a human life. Images of hell-fire and judgment recur in Allie's insane wish for immolation of the family by dousing them and himself in gasoline and then igniting it[18], and in Allie's torching of the Spellgood mission. The battle lines of belief in God or Allie and the division between the devout and the heathen are represented visually by parallel scenes, one showing natives paddling past the temple-like ice plant at Jeronimo, the other showing the ragged and exiled Foxes floating past the Spellgood mission to the sound of a recorded choir.

As in *Witness*, the changes in location and era do not disguise the concentration on western myths of establishing a garden in the wilderness and of an individual's coming out from among a group to build and defend a home and family, which will become the foundation of a new community. As in the earlier film, the discovery of or desire for a new frontier in *Mosquito Coast* reflects negatively on the previous one. As an "Eastern" western, *Witness* combines the fear of societal decay in the thriller territory of the east with a portrayal of older (but not unqualified) moral values in a geographical and mythical near-western setting. *Mosquito Coast* is a more convoluted revision of the same basic materials: The "higher civilization" of the Fox family imposes itself on a new and more primitive frontier, with the migration prompted by desire for a new homeland as well as by fear, loathing, and lamentation for the old. However, Allie takes too many of his society's artefacts and attitudes with him for the new Eden to be completely pure, and both the over-ambition of his scheme and its particular implementation doom the new frontiersman.

During the opening drive into Hatfield, Charlie's narration gives us his estimation of his father's authority: "I grew up with the belief that the world belonged to him, and that everything he said was true." The cynicism and eccentricity of Ford's performance and the camera's furnishing of views of urban decay encourage agreement with his opinions. The look of the camera and the son on the star and father serve to illustrate the viewer's identification and the son's admiration. Where exchange of the look undermines the cinematic structures of patriarchy in *Witness*, here the divergence of the star persona and the narrative itself from expectation perform the same subversive function.

Rejecting America does not prevent the recreation of its former zeal in Honduras. Captain Smalls of the *Unicorn* remarks that La Mosquitia is as primitive as "America before the pilgrims landed."[19] The first holiday in Jeronimo is celebrated by the Foxes as a traditional Thanksgiving Day, their first in "the new world." The nationalistic and religious nature of the celebration is made more significant by the incident occurring after the expulsion of Spellgood in Paul Schrader's screenplay. The pilgrims celebrate the cleansing of the land of their spiritual opposition, like the American settlers repelling the forces of darkness embodied in the Indians, before the new settlement is blessed.

The rapid transformation of Jeronimo from backward hamlet to self-sufficient village is accompanied by a headlong stream of Allie's vitriolic social commentary. The camera fixes on his head as he strides ceaselessly around the camp, expending as much nervous energy in expressing hatred of America's decline as he invests in Jeronimo's future prosperity. Schrader's script and Ford's performance reproduce the humor and rancor of his rantings, but these speeches are drawn from other parts of the novel and their insertion here emphasizes Allie's obsession with his country's decay. Even when removed from it he dwells on its failings and expounds his theories to the bemused locals. This is epitomized by the scene in which he asks a child, "Know what the biggest problem of the twentieth century is, son?" and then drowns out his own answer with a chainsaw, leaving only his axiomatic postscript of "double-digit inflation and a two-dollar loaf of bread!" The incongruity of this analysis to the Honduran jungle underlines the incongruity of the speaker's presence and the heedless imposition of both on a bewildered population. Forest must be slashed and burned for growing land and rivers dynamited straight for his superior civilization. In his massive effort of willpower and intelligence, building his own world and re-creating a better America, Allie has left nothing behind. He carries his country in his command of the natives and his speeches against it even in isolation, just as his children perpetuate what he sees as its failings (money, school, and church) in their play in their hideaway called "Acre."

The clash between Allie and Spellgood, the technological and theological evangelists, recapitulates the frontiersman's struggle and the western's conventions. Allie confronts the missionary on the "Jeronimo state line," recalling the standoff between Daniel and the bullies in *Witness* and Arthur's intimidation by the youths of Paris in *Cars*:

> Weir makes their meeting in the Honduran jungle echo back down every dusty main street in American film history: framed from behind, the tools of his trade slung at his hip, Allie advances to meet this trespasser in his paradise: "State your business, reverend."[20]

The film's Spellgood is robbed of the few victories the novel gives him in the battles of Biblical quotation in which he and Allie engage aboard the *Unicorn*, but conversely he is given extra lines here that make explicit Allie's atheistic authority over family and town: "And Pharaoh said, 'Who is the Lord that I should obey his voice and let you Israel go? I know not the Lord, neither will I let Israel go!' " Each father figure questions the other's right to the hearts and minds of the people, promising earthly or heavenly reward in return for obedience. Allie is addressed by name only by his wife (played by Helen Mirren), and she is known only as "Mother." Charlie and the people of Jeronimo know him only as "Father" or "Fadder." At the party in Hatfield commemorating the decision to emigrate, one of the migrant workers asserts this much to Charlie: "Your fadder is a great man. He my fadder too—we all his children." Allie is established as the jealous head of the flock, yet Spellgood insists that only "The Lord is your Father." Allie's belief in technological supremacy becomes indivisible from his disgust for missionaries who teach people "to put up with their earthly burdens."

Ascendancy to the position of absolute power may not have been Allie's aim, but it has been implicit in his riding roughshod over all opposition before and after arrival. His ambition, pride, and self-reliance are couched in terms of sacrilege and antagonism for his alter ego Spellgood, who mirrors his heedless determination. Theroux's Faust baits Spellgood and dares his creator in bolder terms than Schrader's and Weir's character: "Man is God.'[21] " 'Pray if you must,' Father said, 'but I'd rather you listened to me.' "[22] The creation of Jeronimo is accomplished with the swiftness of superior technology, but every stage of the construction is powered by Allie's dictating voice. Richard Combs mentions the

Amish barn raising as an equivalent to the building of the settlement in *Mosquito Coast*, but the tones of the two sequences vary
greatly. The barn is erected wordlessly, with celebratory music for
its assertions of unity of spirit and purpose in ennobling labor.
Jeronimo is hacked from the jungle in a cacophony of shouts, chain-
saws, and Allie's deranged dogma. Charlie's remembrance of the
back-breaking toil in his voice-over replaces the epiphany of pastoral life. The negative representation of technological and ideological imposition in mechanical labor presages the eruption of activity
brought to an inner-city district by the Green Guerrillas in *Green
Card* (1990). Allie is the power and word of creation, and to his son
and followers his will equals that of the Prime Mover: "He had
talked it into existence with the racket and magic of his voice."[23]

Once the new Jerusalem is completed, Allie embarks on his
greatest feat, with the construction of the much-enlarged version
of the Worm Tub, now named Fat Boy. This Frankensteinian project makes his word flesh, with his "baby boy" being a perfect technological gift to the world that its acknowledged Maker left
"incomplete." It is an improvement to life, but it is also the act of
one jealous for recognition, delivering ice as a "jewel" to those who
have never seen it before. Once his ice has been taken for granted
and Allie embarks on his abortive expedition, the consequences of
his actions begin to overtake him and his family. Spellgood might
have continued his quotation from Exodus: "Now shalt thou see
what I will do to Pharaoh."

In both novel and film, Fat Boy represents a secret covenant between Allie and Charlie. The eldest son is the only one to understand the motive behind the exodus from Hatfield to Honduras
and the building of Jeronimo. Fat Boy rises like a pyramid out of
the jungle, inspiring superstitious fear in the natives who help to
build it by hauling components up from the river like the slaves of
ancient Egypt. During a river trip, Allie finds his self-aggrandizing
beneficence undone by the discovery of a small, functionless image
of Fat Boy being worshipped as an idol.[24] His being asked to lead
prayers before it encapsulates his equation with the missionaries
by the locals and epitomizes the supernatural faith he places in the
science of Fat Boy as a gigantic false idol. Even after his death, Theroux's Allie is mistaken for a missionary,[25] an ironic testimony to
his likeness to Spellgood, who has also created a garden, enlisted

technology to his cause (recorded choirs, videotaped sermons), and killed the interloper (in Spellgood's case, Allie the Antichrist himself).

To Charlie, Fat Boy is more than his father's greatest work. When forced to climb through Fat Boy's innards, Charlie struggles to interpret what he sees there:

> [T]his was Father's head, the mechanical part of his brain and the complications of his mind, as strong and huge and mysterious. It was all revealed to me, but there was too much of it, like a book page, full of secrets, printed too small.[26]

Allie decries the Bible as "the God owner's handbook," but to Charlie, Fat Boy represents the companion volume to the workings and flaws of his father, sprung fully formed from his head. In his desire for freedom, Allie had enlarged the only truly private human space, that of the mind. However, the creation, in following the original model, is imperfect, and even Allie cannot live there comfortably. Attempting to enlarge the area further, in taking ice to the natives, leads to his undoing. When Fat Boy explodes, Allie's face, contorted in pain, is seen in close-up in the vivid orange light.

Charlie's understanding of his father is revealed to him, just as Allie considers true invention to be a revelation of existent facts that ease or explain life. Charlie's discovery within the workings of his father's child-project represents the beginning of his understanding of Allie's wish to create and his own comparable desire for self-expression. The children's frequent departure from Jeronimo to establish Acre, which maintains the reviled features of society to which they expect to return, is a maturer treatment of social tendencies than Allie's solution. Their answer is accommodation, in contrast to Allie's stated rejection and implicit preservation of technology and hierarchy.

The disintegration of the settlement and the family is caused by the challenge to patriarchal authority that Allie's sons represent. Allie is positioned as a third son by references to his wife only as "Mother" and his competitiveness toward Charlie and Jerry, giving challenges in which they can prove themselves to be men but scorning their failures as all that can be expected from children. The confusion of status is summarized by Jerry's anxiety before the announcement of the family's emigration. Mother remarks, that "when you're young, the world seems like a big and a strange place. If you think about it too much you start to worry." Jerry observes, "Dad's not young and he's worried," suggesting the naivety behind Allie's plans (and their failings) and the nascent mature perspective in the two boys that eventually undermines Allie's authority.

The breakdown of Allie's mental state and authority over his sons is signaled in several sites of conflict, where sides are drawn from the ranks of the family. During the building of Jeronimo, the Foxes are unified as a team and a family, and after Mr. Haddy delivers blue and yellow material to Mother, the whole settlement wears clothes cut from the same cloth. The family withstands the first conflict (the expulsion of Spellgood) relatively unscathed, but by the time Fat Boy is constructed, Acre already exists as an alternative to Allie's vision. The ice plant incarnates the conflict, being Allie's true offspring, a copy of the blueprint in his head rather than a competitive son/sibling. Concentration on Allie's (god)head as a visual representation of Theroux's text marks the inventor's body as the principal battleground where his sons fight for emancipation.

Allie becomes alienated emotionally and physically from his sons during the ice march into the hills. Charlie sides with Jerry in the face of their father's vitriolic outpouring when they camp for the night. Allie sits with his back toward the boys, who sit by the fire they have made. Testily, Allie tells them to put the fire out as it is melting his ice, an epigrammatic representation of their opposition to his authoritarianism and their eventual prevalence over him. His ice will melt, the plant that made it will be destroyed, and he will die as his sons outlive him. An identical scene succeeds the expulsion from Jeronimo. On reaching the sea, Mother and the children play in the surf and think of returning home while Allie collects objects washed up on the shore to support his new plan for a beachcombing life. In an echo of the confrontation with Spellgood, Allie is seen from close behind at waist level, clutching the detritus of the previously rejected world while the rest of the family cavorts in the background. They have become Allie's enemies because they dare to contradict his word. As a desperate measure to retain their support, Allie lies about the destruction of America, making their return impossible. The twins and Jerry half-believe him, Mother treats his words as a cruel joke, and Allie seeks Charlie's support with a conspiratorial wink, a second secret bond between them that Charlie feels unable to respect. That night, Allie sits apart from the main group again. The children sit by a fire while Mother gives her qualified support to her husband's subjugating falsehood.

Father asks for faith without proof in this new chosen home, built literally on sand. Mother and Charlie comply for the time being while knowing that their compliance has been gained unfairly. When the boys' loyalty is exhausted and they attempt to abandon Allie on the houseboat, Father turns his back on them for the last time. Their "treachery" appears as a wish to save themselves and Mother from Allie's harm in an archetypal Oedipal situation. In addition to the location of the conflict in Allie's physical separation from the family, this incident again emphasizes the dominance of Allie's head as the seat of the word of authority: "There was Father's wet streaming head, the beard brushing the rail, the clunk of the brass propellers hitting the boards, and his howl, 'Traitors!' "[27] The brothers' act separates them permanently from the family. Allie retains control over only Mother and the female twins. By presenting his back to the boys again while they are towed behind the houseboat, Allie incites them to contemplate killing him. They imagine attacking the two areas of the patriarch's body that have characterized the struggle: Charlie thinks of sticking a knife into his back, and Jerry says aloud how easy it would be to kill him with a hammer blow to the head. Charlie's reproval of Jerry's outburst shows his guilt for his own thoughts, and Jerry's assertion that he was thinking the same (validated by the voice-over) illustrates how the two boys now seek to challenge their father.

Throughout the journeys from Hatfield to Jeronimo, Jeronimo to Brewer's Lagoon, and back to the sea, Allie's mastery of the action has been complemented and eventually eroded by Charlie's narration. His voice is even greater than his father's because its retrospection has benefited from the experience of this journey and has transcended it in comprehension. Allie's wish for a new world becomes a disconcerting reality for him and his family, and when the brothers' wish for Allie's death comes true, Charlie realizes that loss of the father will sweep away the security of childhood and present them with the wealth of potential offered by adulthood. This is encapsulated in the long shot of the ocean at the opposite end of the river that closes the film. Where Charlie is left as an unfettered voice in this space, our last view of Allie is just of his head, the only part of him still "alive"[28] after being shot and paralyzed by Spellgood. The son outgrows the father, seeks his own independence and beliefs in opposition to and emulation of the father's creed, and gains his own voice as narrator and creator of his own history.

Mosquito Coast becomes, like *Witness*, an analysis of the roles of the father, mother, and offspring within family and patriarchal society and of the influential position of the male star as hero in the narrative when the narrator function is as divided as the family represented in it. The casting of a well-known star who is then displaced from the center of the narrative (and divorced from audience sympathy and identification) by a younger, lesser character provokes a reassessment of this defamiliarizing use of the star persona and a closer examination of the narrative methods that herald this displacement—and of the disappointment of audience expectation.

Visual and verbal channels of information in *Mosquito Coast* are shared between the characters of Allie and Charlie. While this may appear similar to the narration of *Witness*, several important differences heighten the parabolic nature of *Mosquito Coast* in contrast to the genre and melodramatic strengths of *Witness*: Allie is Charlie's natural rather than adoptive father; Charlie's voice-over uses a reflective past tense as he reviews the events that have formed his present self; Charlie and the other children, both natural and spiritual, face a bitter conflict with the father's authority before they can achieve independence; and the symbolic opposition of one father to another (Allie against God, or against Spellgood) forces a moral choice upon viewer and child alike. Charlie's voice-over narration places him outside the narrative with the viewer and within it on the screen. From without, we observe (and judge) Allie dispassionately, the viewer with the benefit of distance and Charlie with that of hindsight.

Recounting his rite of passage, Charlie leads us to expect the revelation of details and incidents that have not only made the story worth (re)telling but also (in)formed him sufficiently to make him a mature and engrossing narrator. Charlie's distance in time from the events he relates, though indeterminate, gives him the prescience of the external viewer. By the time he comes to narrate the story to us, he knows as well as the viewer that Allie lied about America's destruction, but the earlier self that he and the viewer observe in the diegesis remains in a younger, impercipient form. This distinguishes Charlie from the child narrator of *Days of Heaven* (Terrence Malick, 1978), who, although distanced in time and recounting events as full of biblical imagery (hellfire, plagues, and covetousness), gives little or no insight to the possible parabolic interpretation of the narrative. The delicate balance between former and latter states of knowledge, with the narrative as the spanning journey/time, is found in other filmic rites of passage, and particularly in the contemporary Australian cinema in the films of John Duigan (*The Year My Voice Broke* [1987]; *Flirting* [1989]).

Apocalypse Now is also framed by the voice-over of Captain Willard. The film begins with an hypnotic dream-like sequence, in which images of the Vietnam War merge and cross-fade with close-ups of Willard's face. The visions of the face, the mind it shields, and images of the war the mind contains suggest the narrational and psychological complexity of treating such subject matter. Whether these images reflect Willard's experience of the war prior to the mission that forms the narrative or they are the condensation of images of the mission he and the viewer will see remains unclear, but the first line of his voice-over declares, "I'm still only in Saigon." The immediacy of this present tense clashes with his later admission that the story of his mission to find Colonel Kurtz is really a "confession." He becomes, like Conrad's narrator Marlow, the caretaker of a memory that encompasses himself and another. The voice-over is both the narration of an omnipotent storyteller and the personal, limited consciousness of a character locked within a present narrative. In *Apocalypse Now* and *Mosquito Coast*, dramatic irony consists of a difference in the information open to the narrator and viewer and in the character of the narrator within and without the diegesis. This is a very different situation to Billy Kwan's, who aspires to omnipotence over *Year*'s narrative but whose voice-over only accompanies or succeeds events already viewed by himself and the viewer. As a character still in the diegesis he is prey to unenvisaged turns in constantly current events. His release from the narrative and full knowledge of it come only with death.

The river journey of *Apocalypse Now* is replicated in *Mosquito*, but whereas the flow in Coppola's film and the accretion of knowledge stop when the "end of the river" is reached, in *Mosquito Coast* the journey is traced into and back out from the heart of darkness centered on the mind of the father figure. Willard is closely associated with the man he seeks; they have witnessed the same "horrors" and do not have the right to judge each other's actions. During the river trip, Willard reads a letter sent by Kurtz to his son, explaining his actions. The recital of the letter by Willard links him to its writer, while his reading also makes him seem like its intended recipient. Father and son, teller and listener, converge with this episode. These resemblances, in addition to the shared confession and expiation of the narrative, make them appear as two sides or versions of the same character. The journey is the only available exposition or explanation of events, as the trip through the war is also a voyage through the minds of the warriors themselves. The film's images offer an experience equivalent to seeing the same horrors as Kurtz and Willard and bring us to Willard's level of comprehension of "causes," so that finally meeting and witnessing the "effect" in Kurtz represents no added enlightenment.

The duration of the trip and Willard's voice-over are the sole sources of information about what has become of Kurtz; there are no answers forthcoming from Kurtz himself. The river journey and the sights it encompasses have to explain the situation and psyche of both men, Willard and Kurtz, who can be seen as essentially the same man traveling from youthful inquiry to maturer knowledge of the world and himself. The mental development (or degradation) of the journey is evident in the concentration on the heads and faces of the characters. Kurtz talks in the shadows of his temple, with only his crescent face lit in the darkness, and once Willard decides to complete his mission and kill the colonel, he assumes a similar disembodied power:

> Willard, on his way to murder Kurtz, rises from beneath the surface of the river, his head smooth, glazed with the mud of the unconscious. He has brought the darkness of his deepest self to the surface and, as a result, has taken on his closest resemblance to Kurtz.[29]

The film ends as it began, with shadowy superimpositions of Willard's face over the surface of the jungle and the stone idols of the temple, as the heralded air strike levels Kurtz's compound.

Willard slays his older self so that the journey, and his progress from a state of ignorant grace to knowing damnation, survive only in his transformed, storytelling self. As well as being a quest for the meaning and causes behind events, the trip is a search for the authority that has sanctioned them (Willard's struggle for command of the boat on which he travels, the search for the commanding officer at the Do Lung bridge, and the radio messages to the higher command that has sent him to kill Kurtz). Willard kills the older man, the god and father figure he has sought out for answers and motives, both for Kurtz's actions and his own (Kurtz's murder of Vietnamese double agents, Willard's alleged assassination assignments), although officially he acts under the authority of the generals at Nha Trang. As cruel gods of the Super-ego, the generals' instructions and punishments both end in death, and as in *Witness*, violence posited as the id (Kurtz, who wishes to wage war "without judgment," Schaeffer and the corrupt cops, who have "lost the meaning") becomes transformed into controlled and purposeful aggression that preserves a memory of its own (Book's defense of the Amish mixing violence and pacifism, Willard's slaying of Kurtz to keep alive the truth behind official policy). Ironically, these individual compromises of the Ego-ideal receive the benediction of the authorities they defy. Book's violence scandalizes the Amish but rehabilitates him into the law-enforcement community. Willard's successful completion of the mission ensures his promotion to major, even though he considers himself no longer "in their army." Both actions represent an accommodation of the lies of higher authorities—in obeying orders for different reasons or combining violent and passive measures for concluding action—which is also present in Charlie's final unwillingness to judge Allie, despite complicity in his father's plans and lies.

The final lines of Charlie's narration undergo a subtle change in adaptation from novel to film:

> Once I had believed in Father, and the world had seemed very small and old. He was gone, and now I hardly believed in myself and the world was limitless.[30]
>
> Now he was gone, and I wasn't afraid to love him any more, and the world seemed limitless. [film dialogue]

Charlie's ability to love his father has had to prevail over his propensity to fear and believe in him. Having been brought up with the belief that all his father said was true and that the world belonged to him, Charlie's realization that his father is fallible and can lie opens up possibilities for a threatening but new world beyond the confines of family. Faith in his father's better intentions, charity for his failings, and love for him as an individual outside of familial obligation create Charlie's love for and faith in his father on terms that Allie himself has laid down: "Faith is believing something you know ain't true."[31] Charlie starts to travel downstream when the journey has been completed. He has challenged the patriarch's authority and divine rule, and the experience has adapted him to the world he will face as an adult. Allie is a "dead thing traveling downstream" since he cannot adapt to the realities of the world and the world cannot endure the imposition of his plans. The landscape of Jeronimo and Brewer's Lagoon that Charlie and the family have inhabited has been, like that of *Apocalypse Now*, a projection of the inside of the father's mind and a realization of his plan (true, asexual creation and total, amoral war). In return, Acre has been as much a recognition of eventual adult responsibility as a symbol of Charlie and the children evading patriarchal authority.

Ironically, Jeronimo and Acre represent the two extremes of the boys' societal organization in *Lord of the Flies*: idyllic pastoral existence and tribal warfare. Jeronimo, despite its sophistication, harbors Allie's violence and immaturity, and Acre, despite its primitiveness, is a more stable preservation of the principles of society. His sons' maturation and his own mortality are beyond Allie's control, yet his death propels the boys into a new world that claims not to embody heaven or hell but simply the potential for both. Allie the child dies on the way downstream, allowing Charlie (whose name seems to be an enlargement of that of the patriarch) to live on in maturity, ready to narrate. Recounting and narrating events from the "foreign country" of the childhood past is proof that Charlie has reached the new world of adulthood.

Witness and *Mosquito Coast* are reappraisals of thematic and genre patterns in American cinema. They provoke a reassessment of the hero's ideological function, his individual failings, and his very nature since he is a reflection upon if not of the society he protects. *Witness* is as valid a reassessment of the Fordian frontier family and alienated hero as *The Searchers*, but through its modern setting as a parallel to the West it shows a contemporary society shaped by the experience of the past and the mythologizing of that same past enacted in genre cinema. The latter-day settings reinforce the assumption of generic acquaintance in the viewer. The films we watch now bear witness, as do we, to films we have seen before, and the past can be relived continually in recitation and reinterpretation, as it is by Charlie and Willard.

The hero's violent action is expected to follow the dictates of commercial cinema, western convention, and the moral outrage of the modern audience besieged by crime. *Witness*'s frustration of these expectations forces us to admit the unsuitability of conventional solutions to the moral difficulties encountered in modern multicultural society. *Witness* enunciates the hero's vulnerability to the societies or families he protects. The very action that marks him as an individual distinct from the homesteaders is defined by conformity to a code by which he is expected to live and die. Ironically, individualism is attained through obedience to higher authority, emasculating the hero in the same way as Book's gradual integration into the Amish household. In Weir's film, the hero redefines his own action but cannot change his role. He bends the rules in the course of completing the tasks expected of him by viewer and society but still leaves, unhappily, as conventions dictate. In the confusion of several social codes and the conventions of several genres with which he must comply, Book (like Guy Hamilton in *Year*) displays the impossibility of heroic action according to the old codes within the (post)modern multicultural and multigeneric environment.

Witness represents a reconstruction of the western drama of society defended by a lone, alienated hero, with the expectations of genre mixed with aspects of the thriller and the identifiable characteristics of Weir's style. By not disappointing prospective audiences for a genre-based entertainment picture with a well-known star and a stylistically based film by an art-house director, the filmmaker arrives at the result pinpointed by the producer: a "hybrid" form with wide commercial appeal, more successful than *Year*'s parallel attempt. The scripted elements of culture clash, the title's emphasis on the act of viewing, and the visual composition and musical reinforcement that illustrate the familial and sexual pressures on the protagonists reflect this convergence of form and content. The marriage of the formulas of entertainment cinema and personal artistic contribution underline Weir's wish to emulate classical Hollywood directors.

Mosquito Coast draws on the same expectations of entertainment cinema but disappoints them in terms of its characterization and narrative. Weir outlined his motives behind the deliberate frustration of commercial and genre expectation in an interview:

> I enjoyed it in terms of looking at it as a Shakespearean character . . . one of his flawed heroes, the Macbeth, the Othello, where the quality that has made them great is accompanied by a hair-line crack that will widen with their having gained power . . . and I thought how exciting on many levels, here particularly with Harrison, here was a classic movie hero who did solve problems who starts off with the hair crack, which might widen but then is closed over and healed and they ride off into the sunset, the John Wayne in many films, and I thought "People will love seeing it go in the other direction," and of course that was not the case.[32]

This misuse of the star persona caused confusion and disappointment in an audience expecting a narrative of heroism and adventure simply from the casting of Ford as Allie Fox. The compromise of Book's heroic action in defense of family and society springs from the ideological conflict caused by his contact with another culture. Allie's refusal to acknowledge any other culture but his own in the country he colonizes, and his provocation of conflict within the American family rather than his defense of it as a social and moral institution, leave the concepts of the hero and the family as ideals reproduced from the western model so demoralized as to offer no uplifting message.

In an interview, Weir admitted his intention of turning away from his recognizable style in the filming of *Mosquito*, even to the extent of filming and subsequently discarding a "Peter Weir-style opening" since this "might be too close to *Witness*."[33] Ironically, in eliminating trademarks of composition (in favor of faithful adaptation of images from the novel, such as concentration on Allie's head) and frustrating expectations of the hero and narrative, *Mosquito Coast* emerges as a more idiosyncratic and art-cinema film than *Witness*, which deals with the hero, the narrative, and the genre equally subversively. The submergence of the director's style in a classical, unembellished Hollywood narrative did not succeed on the basis of misrecognition. Since *Mosquito Coast* resembled staple entertainment in its seamless storytelling, the tragic qualities of the hero appeared mismatched and the downbeat ending, though characteristic of Weir's films, bleak and unforgiving. The parabolic tone in which Allie's fall is depicted and the near-eradication of Weir's characteristic style from the film leave little comfort for the viewer seeking either genre entertainment or art-house stylization.

The reappearance of the frontier hero and father in *Mosquito Coast*, played by the same actor, makes us reexamine the heroic construct, this time in the late twentieth-century context of American overseas influence. The relocation of the frontier necessitates a fresh perspective on the power and rights of patriarchy that dominates families on one scale and colonizes continents on another. Reassessment of present sociopolitical conditions through recourse to past cinematic models allows us to see the lies hidden behind the myths, like the secrets in the garden's undergrowth or in the corners of a diseased mind as revealed in *Blue Velvet* (David Lynch, 1986). Reintroducing the iconography and expectations of previous films and earlier genres in contemporary settings makes the conflict between youth and age, or violence and tolerance more disconcerting, since the older cinematic models, like the older patriarchal figures, are no longer representative of security. Charlie's father is heroic in his achievement but diabolic in his despotism. In *Blue Velvet*, Geoffrey's father suffers from a debilitating physical illness, while Frank Booth's mental illness endows him with a maniacal criminal and sexual energy that is both subversive and seductive. The head of an all-American family can be sick; the nostalgic small-town environment can secrete modern perversities of sexual and narcotic degradation. By externalizing the mental processes of the preeminent male characters as the landscape other characters have to inhabit and by referring constantly to America's mythic self-perceptions of the social and cinematic past, these films heighten their parabolic resonances. The use of the defamiliarizing gaze of a younger narrator on the structures of social and cinematic convention and on the patriarchal figures that embody them marks these films as rites of passage for their protagonists and their viewers. We have been assured of stability and continuity until now, genre recognition being an indication of the viewer's immaturity. Transformation of convention, displacement of star and narrator, and the (re)telling of stories accompanying the updating of genre, illustrate the uncertain social and cinematic futures finding expression in the maturation of postmodern film and of its viewers.

The varying thematic and stylistic balance struck between Australian and American elements of *Witness* and *Mosquito* accounts for the difference in their fortunes as examples of popular film. However, the differences between them are also indicative of the continuing development of the director's techniques and influences during this second period of his career. The open-endedness of the narratives, in recognizing the possibilities for growth and change within even the most restrictive circumstances, is a representation within the films of Weir's openness to new material, experience, and change, while pursuing a goal of uniting disparate forces from popular American films of the past and the earlier, personal Australian films. Like his youthful narrators' desire for new experiences and his star's breaching the boundaries of his persona, Weir's relationship with film narrative and genre models of the past is a work in progress, with the continuities of style and subject finding new surroundings in the transformed landscapes of post-studio American cinema.

Notes

1. Minty Clinch, *Harrison Ford: A Biography* (London: Hodder & Stoughton, 1988), p. 219.

2. Michael Bliss, "Keeping a Sense of Wonder," *Film Quarterly*, 53 (1999), pp. 2–11 (p. 4).

3. Clinch, *Harrison Ford*, p.220.

4. Robert L. Berner, "Old Gunfighters, New Cops," *Western American Literature*, 21 (1986), pp. 131–134 (p. 131).

5. Brian McFarlane and Geoff Mayer, *New Australian Cinema: Sources and Parallels in American and British Film* (Cambridge: Cambridge University Press, 1992), p. 29.

6. Don Shiach, *The Films of Peter Weir* (London: Letts, 1993), p. 131.

7. Sandy Flitterman, "Woman, desire and the Look: Feminism and the Enunciative Apparatus in the Cinema," in *Theories of Authorship* ed. John Caughie (London: Routledge & Kegan Paul, 1981), p. 243.

8. Anne Friedberg, "A Denial of Difference: Theories of Cinematic Identification," in *Psychoanalysis and Cinema*, ed. E. Ann Kaplan (London: Routledge, 1990), p. 36.

9. Dennis Brown and Jonathan Pedder, *Introduction to Psychotherapy: An*

Outline of Psychodynamic Principles and Practice, 2nd ed. (London: Routledge, 1991), pp. 47–48.

10. Stephen Neale, *Genre* (London: B.F.I., 1980), p. 38.

11. Shiach, *Films of Peter Weir*, p. 134.

12. Laura Mulvey, "Visual Pleasure and Narrative Cinema," *Screen, 16* (1975), pp. 6–18 (pp. 11–12).

13. Richard Combs, "Witness," *Monthly Film Bulletin, 52* (1985), pp. 166–167.

14. Bruce Johnson and Gaye Poole, "Sound and Author/Auteurship: Music in the Films of Peter Weir," in *Screen Scores: Studies in Contemporary Australian Film Music*, ed. Rebecca Coyle (Sydney: AFTRS, 1998), p. 136.

15. Clinch *Harrison Ford*, p. 221.

16. George R. Kimbal, "*The Mosquito Coast*," *Films and Filming, 389* (1987), pp. 40–41.

17. Paul Theroux, *The Mosquito Coast* (London: Penguin, 1981), pp. 98–104.

18. *Ibid.*, p. 323.

19. *Ibid.*, p. 82.

20. Richard Combs, "Beating God to the Draw," *Sight and Sound, 56* (1987), pp. 136–138.

21. Theroux, *Mosquito*, p. 93.

22. *Ibid.*, p. 203.

23. *Ibid.*, p. 279.

24. *Ibid.*, p. 201.

25. *Ibid.*, p. 383.

26. *Ibid.*, p. 168.

27. *Ibid.*, p. 340.

28. *Ibid.*, p. 372.

29. William J. Palmer, *The Films of the Seventies* (London: Scarecrow Press, 1987), p. 215.

30. Theroux, *Mosquito*, p. 383.

31. *Ibid.*, p.16.

32. Interview with the author, June 1993.

33. Pat McGilligan, "Under Weir . . . and Theroux," *Film Comment, 22* (1987), pp. 23–32 (p. 30).

Chapter Six

Dead Poets Society (1989) and *Green Card* (1990)

Like Peter Weir's first two American and his last Australian films (*Gallipoli* [1981] and *The Year of Living Dangerously* [1982]), *Dead Poets Society* and *Green Card* reflect the commercial and personal sides to the director's choice of work. Like *Witness* (1985), *Dead Poets* was a studio production to which Weir was recruited, his input becoming crucial to the film's visual expression and handling of familiar themes of freedom and oppression. For *Green Card*, Weir not only served as director but also as writer and co-producer. In another parallel to the preceding films, the writing of *Green Card*, begun after *The Mosquito Coast* (1986), predated Weir's involvement in *Dead Poets*. Where funding difficulties had postponed *Mosquito Coast*, *Green Card* was delayed by the non-availability of lead actor Gérard Depardieu.

Dead Poets united the director with a production unit team mixing old and new: John Seale was again on camera and Maurice Jarre once more provided the score, but the original script by Tom Schulman and the central starring role for Robin Williams (as John Keating) illustrate Weir's deeper integration into the Hollywood mainstream. French reviewers such as Jean Douchet, among Weir's staunchest supporters or most concerted critics, perceived problems with *Dead Poets'* contemporaneity, despite its setting in the past:

> Sociologically, this film meets an expectation. After fifteen or twenty years of economic privations, psychological frustrations, and others of life's troubles, the offer of epicurean pleasure seems like the light at the end of the tunnel. "Carpe

Diem" becomes the password, the recognition of a sect; but without the renunciation of any of Reagan's or Thatcher's moral prescriptions that reemerged after the Dionysian freedoms of '68.[1]

Douchet also compared Weir's film with *Zero de Conduite* (Jean Vigo, 1933), another treatment of the education system as a microcosm of society, made in a period of similar political and economic difficulty. Again, reviewers stressed the applicability of Weir's chosen material to wider cultural and filmic concerns. The juxtaposition of *Dead Poets'* setting (1950s conformity) with the commercialism and philistinism of its own era (the Reagan and Thatcher 1980s) draws attention to the intervening years of youth rebellion and social unrest in Europe, which the director himself had experienced and portrayed with varying degrees of explicitness in his films of the 1970s. The historical and ideological location of "1959" resembles the "1900" setting of *Picnic at Hanging Rock* (1975), with a similar depiction of a hidebound establishment, apparently secure but soon to be challenged. Further similarities to *Picnic* are visible in *Dead Poets* (and *Green Card*), with the director's style and themes emerging within studio-produced material. The presence of an art-film mentality (meticulous art direction, arresting visual composition, and references beyond the stated narrative) in what appear to be Weir's most outrightly commercial pictures illustrate the persistence of his stylistic hallmarks and his assimilation of personal style and studio project.

Another filmic inheritance, beyond that from Vigo's film, was apparent to other critics, in this case from Weir's own past.[2] In explicit thematic terms and in subtler stylistic ones, the spirit of *Picnic* is reinvoked in an American context. The needs of American commercial entertainment and the approach of earlier Australian art-house cinema coexist for comparison, with Weir addressing an ostensibly American theme in a style reminiscent of his own previous work and Hollywood's classical period. The film's time setting (1959, at the end of the first decade of the Cold War and the beginning of the new decade of liberation) can be compared to those of *Picnic*, *Gallipoli*, and *Year*. Here, the defamiliarizing gaze on the past parallels the Australian director's perspective on American film, history, and society. The structures of school (from *Picnic*) and family (from *Witness* and *Mosquito Coast*) are again reviewed critically under unusual circumstances (an inexplicable disappearance, immersion in alien cultures, the arrival of an eccentric teacher). A pivotal moment in history is used to locate a reflexive and parabolic drama about the loss of innocence, youth, and freedom again being opposed by age and conformity. Structures of control and attempts to retain authority within the narrative highlight the conventions of the medium and the tropes of genre laid bare by stylistic and thematic traits of Weir's work (*Witness*'s autumnal colors and patriarchal discipline, the stress on the passing and preciousness of time from *Picnic*, the lure of the spiritual above the mundane from *The Last Wave* [1977], and the individual's resistance from all Weir films). However, *Dead Poets* is not just a version of *Picnic* defused and simplified for a popular American audience. The definitively American qualities of *Witness*'s justice and *Mosquito Coast*'s frontiersmanship are replaced by a parable of democracy set in the context of conflict between younger and older orders, individuals against authority, familiar to viewers of *Picnic*.

While maintaining Weir's characteristic forms of visual expression, *Green Card* also shows a debt to past genre cinema, drawing some of its inspiration from the screwball comedies and odd-couple movies of the 1930s and 1940s. In an interview, Weir admitted these influences and the desire to reinterpret their formulas, expressing admiration for *It Happened One Night* (Frank Capra, 1934) and *The 39 Steps* (Alfred Hitchcock, 1935).[3] Weir relished the "technical exercise" of updating screwball comedy to modern New York and the handcuffing of the central characters in the latter film formed the basis of the comedic situation of the "green card" marriage. The circumstances of the enforced relationship between reserved upper-middle-class female and passionate lower-class male within the confines of an apartment recall those of *The Plumber* (1979). The similarities extend as far as the musical aspirations of both male characters: Both engage in spontaneous "composition"—Georges (Gérard Depardieu) at the dinner party on the piano, Max in the bathroom—and the music they make has a considerable effect on the films' soundtracks. Georges' compositions revolve around his growing affection for Brontë (Andie MacDowell), and the fabrication of their courtship is centred on "Africa," as the café where they meet, the country he pretends to visit, and the state of mind they need to attain to live together. Georges' music and that of the soundtrack mix tribal rhythms and drumming (the first sound of the film) with classical pieces heard in Brontë's apartment. The classical melodies are gradually displaced by the vibrant immigrant sounds, associated with Georges and other foreign communities, creating an aural representation of Brontë's change of heart.

The juxtaposition of classical pieces with contemporary sounds and natural rhythms is one of *Green Card's* many resemblances to *Picnic*. Brontë's botanical work and the desire to own the apartment with its extensive greenhouse motivate the superabundance of flowers. The symbolic nature of the flowers in *Picnic* adds new layers of meaning to *Green Card*, illustrating Brontë's similarity to the girls of Appleyard College, and it reflects the separation between garden and park and greenhouse and (rural or urban) wilderness apparent in the differences between Brontë and Georges. Like *Dead Poets*, *Green Card* draws on the visual and musical idiom of *Picnic* to tell similar American stories of freedom and repression, nature versus artifice, using recognizable tropes that helped to establish the director's style. In *Green Card*, the ubiquity of music and flowers indicates their importance, with their integration being reinforced by their association with the main characters.

The production and narrative of *Green Card* reflect the experience and concerns of the director and star in subtle ways. Depardieu was well known to art-house and film-festival audiences in America but not to mainstream Hollywood filmgoers, and both he and Weir viewed the American film industry from the position of outsiders. The modification of the comedy genre in *Green Card* follows the established pattern of genre transformation found in all Weir features. In Weir's American films, the significances of the genre to past and present societies and the cinema's representation of them form the basis of this genre quotation. The western hero and the society he protects are scrutinized in *Witness* and *Mosquito Coast*; family, friends, and education as a preparation for life within the establishment are criticized in the bildungsroman of *Dead Poets*, and issues of gender and race in contemporary society are raised in the romantic comedy of *Green Card*. The principal theme of Weir's American films, in recapitulating but transforming traditional formula cinema and examining the society it reflects, and the persona of Gérard/Georges, the immigrant arriving in the "land of opportunity," endow *Green Card* with more contemporary relevance than a simple remake of Hawksian sexual conflict might otherwise suggest. For both *Dead Poets* and *Green Card*, an acquaintance with genre models is as important as a knowledge of Weir's previous work to appreciate their breadth of reference, both as films representative of the director's canon and as revisions of a wider genre inheritance.

Where *Picnic* embraced a variety of other art forms, *Dead Poets* adopts the language of American Romantic poetry. Keating's enthusiasm is transmitted through this medium, not as an end in itself ("we're not talking artists, we're talking free thinkers") but as the beginning of a new, or the reawakening of an old, mentality in his students. The sources quoted in the film, from Whitman and Thoreau to Tennyson and Shakespeare, require as close an analysis as the references to the visual arts in *Picnic*, and the poems included elucidate the undertones of *Dead Poets* just as allusions in *Picnic* extend the film's debate on individual and national determination.

Keating's insistence on "seizing the day" seems at first to be an assertion in tune with the recognition of the preciousness of time found in *Picnic*. In fact his urgings of "Carpe Diem" arise from a preview of death, as he and his class are "food for worms." This is furthered by the reading from Herrick ("Tomorrow will be dying") and later by Neil's choice of verse from Tennyson's "Ulysses" at the first Society meeting ("my purpose holds / To sail beyond the sunset"). Poignantly, Neil (Robert Sean Leonard) is shown singled out in a cut when Keating describes death. Thoreau's poem "Carpe Diem" seems to advocate a more selfless attitude when read in full:

> The task of the present
> Be sure to fulfill;
> If sad, or if pleasant,
> Be true to it still.
>
> God sendeth us sorrow
> And cloudeth our day
> His sun on the morrow
> Shines bright on our way. (ll.13–20)[4]

Faithful abstention in place of Romantic expression seems to be the order of the day. The poem might score high on the scale of Pritchard's axis of "importance," at least in character formation.

The Society's invocation, from *Walden—or Life in the Woods*, appears a truer representation of the Romantic sensibilities Keating seeks to pass on to a new generation. Thoreau's character determines to "live deliberately" and enjoy a plain but untainted existence separated from ordinary mankind:

> I did not wish to live what was not life, living is so dear; nor did I wish to practice resignation, unless it were quite necessary . . . to drive life into a corner, and reduce it to its lowest terms, and, if it proved to be mean, why then to get the whole and genuine meanness of it, and publish its meanness to the world.[5]

The teacher's exhortations to his class have this uncompromising tone, combining ideals of adolescence with rustic idylls of a more distant (but equally unattainable) utopian age. Perhaps his words are ill-chosen or his enthusiasm more infectious than he realizes. Arguably he is appealing to a receptive audience in the most attractive but misleading language available.

Walt Whitman is uppermost in the quoted writers, and his "Song of Myself," although not included, lies behind Keating's calls for self-expression:

> I celebrate myself, and sing myself (1.1)
>
> I think I could turn and live with animals, they are so
>   placid and self-contain'd, . . .
>
> They do not lie awake in the dark and weep for their sins,
> They do not make me sick discussing their duty to God,
> Not one is dissatisfied, not one is demented with the
>   mania
>   of owning things,
> Not one kneels to another, nor to his kind that lived
>   thousands of years ago, . . . (ll.684–690)[6]

Such lines might stir rebellious dissatisfaction in the minds of impressionable schoolboys, but in fact their revolt is quite muted. Neil's acting ambitions are advanced outside Welton, Charlie's pranks do "not speak for the group" as a whole, and perhaps only

Overstreet's courage with Chris is fueled by Keating's philosophy: "'Carpe Diem' if it kills me!" By contrast, Todd (Ethan Hawke) is raised the highest (by the emotional and expressive maturation that Keating and love of poetry engender) to fall the furthest with the realization that words and ideas cannot change the world. In another parallel to the fates of Sara and the seniors in *Picnic*, Neil's mythologized death or "disappearance" (suggested by the film's French title, *Le cercle des poetes disparus*) is, finally, a preferable fate to that of those who remain:

> All goes onward and outward . . . and nothing collapses,
> And to die is different from what any one supposed, and
> luckier. (ll.120–121)

Comparisons between *Dead Poets* and *Picnic* produce a range of significant similarities and divergences. Again, escape from a restrictive and self-serving educational system is embodied in a retreat to the wild, but the journey is short and furtive, repeated but impermanent, like the Fox children's excursions to Acre in *Mosquito Coast*. Charlie (Gale Hansen) uses the Indian cave as a safe area for performance of his favorite roles (of musician, sexual explorer, and peer group leader). Overstreet (Josh Charles) examines his feelings for Chris during the nights in the open, and this helps him reach a decision for action. Todd cannot overcome his embarrassment either in the cave or in the classroom, and it takes individual attention from the teacher (they spin around wildly before the rest of the class, in an echo of the rapid disorientation of Irma's last visit to Appleyard's gym hall) to drag his "verse" out of him. The quickly circling camera, which records the rapture of Todd's oracular outpourings, is seen again in *Green Card*, when Georges and Brontë dance with abandon in the flat to create images of their fictional wedding day (at a point where their emotion is only half-felt), and later as they embrace outside the Afrika Cafe before Georges is deported (when the love is genuine and reciprocated). The camera technique that originates in *Picnic*, as a signifier of emotional disturbance and confusion reappears as a recognition of spiritual growth, an upheaval with a positive outcome.

Neil's re-creation of the Society is part of a wider campaign of disobedience, rather than a particular wish to conjure poetry into his life. Being closest to Keating sets him apart from the other boys, and the Society seems to be bonded together most strongly (until Cameron's betrayal) when under threat after Neil's death. Freedom through the indulgence of the forbidden drama demands a greater journey than the nightly trip to the cave; it demands the crossing of a mental distance in imagination and individual fulfillment and requires a similar leap in parental leniency. The drama (inevitably, perhaps, *A Midsummer Night's Dream*, with escape to the freedom, confusion, pain, and truth of the forest followed by a return to the censure of civilization) provides Neil with the necessary milieu and means of expression.

The territory of Shakespeare, with Neil as Puck, the sylvan spirit who begs forgiveness for his mischief and exuberance, is further afield in terms of familial, educational, and adolescent exploration than any of the other boys dare go. Once there, Neil is as lost to society and his peers as the girls on the Rock. *Picnic*'s dream of individual freedom, within a dream of art film free from narrative constraint, is transformed in *Dead Poets* into a performance played out before an unsympathetic establishment audience, with the illusion of liberty erased by narrative closure.

The many parallels to *Picnic* vary between the similarities of subject (an all-male rather than all-female college, a comparable short narrative span of one or two terms, a calling to freedom of expression prohibited by the existent educational regime) and near-identical compositions, editing, and mise-en-scène (again appropriating art, statuary and natural and man-made signifiers of passing time in symbolic support of the narrative). As in the earlier film, other art forms facilitate interpretation of a wider, hidden intention that is related through their connotative meanings, although in *Dead Poets* the narrative is not left unclosed, and previous ambiguities are replaced by a linear drama. It is as if concentration on the mechanics of the educational system (seen in a succession of Latin and science classes that precede Keating's first literature lesson), compared with the inanities of Victorian female schooling (rote learning of poetry, drawing, and dance) seen in *Picnic*, reveals the permanence and authority of the system. School leads inevitably toward orderly, respectable adult life rather than the attractive but illusory alternative spiritual existence, which the groups of adolescents in both films nonetheless crave. Absolute escape and revocation of authority in *Picnic* become a temporary vacation from control in *Dead Poets*. In the later film, the return to Welton (for Keating as a former pupil as well as for the current students) also brings a reckoning for their transgression. The exercise of control in the narrative extends to the form of the film itself, with *Picnic*'s open-endedness being replaced with a linear and melodramatically motivated narrative.

The inclusion of American literature connects the film's visual references to *Picnic*. One of the most obvious allusions occurs when the older boys meet up again after the vacation and Todd is invited to their evening study group. Todd is seen at his desk, winding his alarm clock as the school clock chimes outside. There is a cut to the clock tower, with the view up at its face from below zooming in as it strikes. Next we see the nearby river bank, where the sound drives birds into the air. Successive shots show birds flying right to left over flat, golden fields, with the camera panning to follow them as they disappear among autumnal trees, and black geese flying upward from left to right into the pale sky. The sequence ends with the camera looking upward, positioned at the center of the winding staircase and rotating as the boys descend to their classes, recalling the girls' noisy appearance on the morning of the picnic.

In seven shots, we have been alerted to the reappearance of some of *Picnic*'s themes: the passage and dictates of time, the antipathy of the human establishment toward nature and natural impulses, and the potential for youth to challenge authority. The coloring of these shots recalls the pastoral landscape of *Witness*; the rural setting provides an indication of the changing seasons and cycles of action in human and natural affairs (fruitful autumn at the start of the term, winter at its tragic conclusion). The panning shots of birds resemble those seen on the arrival at the picnic grounds, but in this case the sharpness of the cuts (compared with the eerie superimposition of images of Miranda, the birds, and startled horses in *Picnic*) shows nature frightened by human action rather than humanity disconcerted by the presence of the wild. The example and atmosphere of *Picnic* are reinvoked but are already being altered subtly by the greater control and resilience of the establishment symbolized by Welton Academy.

Todd's association with the clock is an indication of the shift in Weir's treatment of these themes. Todd writes "Seize the day!" in an exercise book after Keating's first lesson, but immediately afterward he screws the page up and turns to his pile of textbooks. This is followed by a shot of the ticking clock in the school foyer, where Overstreet waits for one of the masters to take him to meet Chris for the first time. A similar shot of the clock and the staircase to the headmaster's office precedes our (only) view of the coercion the boys suffer to sign the affidavit against Keating, when Todd is summoned before the head and his parents. Unlike *Picnic*, the clock does not stop and the establishment retains control, answering poetic mysteries with crushing conformity. In effect, Todd becomes the Sara to Neil's Miranda; Neil and Keating are unsparing in bringing out his poetic potential, but he is the most sensitive of those left behind. Todd's run through the snow, on hearing of Neil's death, parallels Irma's flight from Michael by the lakeside, when the loss of childhood and childhood friends can no longer be denied. Both scenes are followed by an epigrammatic hymn. However, the fear of the unknown and doubt in the establishment provoked by "Rock of Ages" in *Picnic* is replaced by fear of the establishment and its retributive powers when Psalm Twenty-three, demanding humble subservience, is sung in the school chapel. Escape to the cave, linked to the mystical score, is periodic but impermanent, and although Neil's suicide (accompanied by the same music) is treated in the same manner as the *Picnic* disappearances (slow motion for Neil's preparation and his father's horrified discovery, and the absence of diegetic sound, including the gunshot), it is a definite, if unseen, death rather than an inexplicable and liberating departure.

If the literary quotations in *Dead Poets* have appeared ambiguous or as useful to the establishment as to Keating's Romanticism, Weir's visual signposting does, in comparison with *Picnic*, use similar iconography for different ends. One pertinent sequence covers the range of classes the boys attend. The chemistry teacher requires homework for the next day, the Latin master gives endless repetitions of verb conjugations, and the trigonometry teacher demands absolute precision in their work. When the pupils reach the English class, the teacher is hiding in his closet, and when he emerges it is to remove the class to another part of the school. In the trophy room—a combination of baronial hall (animal heads), private chapel (the banners representing the Four Pillars), and school museum (sepia photographs and memorabilia)—Keating outlines his philosophy to the boys and encourages them to make their lives "extraordinary."

However, Keating's use of human examples from the school's past (the generations seen in the faded photos) hardly differs from the implicit promptings of admirable history and honored tradition found in the sculpted bust and carved Roman head flanking the Latin master's blackboard or the Victorian symbols seen in Mrs. Appleyard's study. As witnessed by Neil's death and the Society's last pledge of allegiance to its mentor, it is the Romantic, libertarian values that are in retreat, not those of the authoritarian establishment. The photos, as of those missing on Hanging Rock, depict those now beyond the reach of establishment control and are a painful reminder rather than an inspiration to those left behind. Death and its concomitant impression of failure and missed opportunity are emphasized before and after Neil's suicide, whereas *Picnic* registers only a bizarre sense of loss (of understanding and control) when the girls disappear. The two films' titles underline this difference. *Picnic at Hanging Rock* relates the circumstances of an ephemeral event transformed into an unending mystery, which is reviewed in a constant present and is never "closed" or explained. Like the lost girls preserved in the photographs, portraits, and the film's own images, the narrative is unable to move forward, barred from change or conclusion. *Dead Poets Society* shows a young secretive group recalling the exploits of illustrious predecessors—dead poets and former pupils—in an imitation and attempted recovery of vanished glory. The exercise perhaps equips them for their own "extraordinary" deeds, such as Neil's desperate decision to end his life and Todd's career-threatening disobedience, but at the same time the narrative signals the futility of such actions.

A telling reinvocation of *Picnic*'s aura of grief comes when Neil visits Keating in his rooms. There is a framed portrait of a young woman on the writing desk, and the "Emperor" symphony plays on the record player in the background. The events of *Picnic* could almost be a memory for Keating, with the framed picture like Miranda's and the melancholy music from the earlier film's soundtrack there to remind him and us. The teacher has not completely rebelled or fully complied with the establishment's standards, even from his own school days at Welton. He describes

J. Evans Pritchard's preface as "excrement," one of the boys' alternative Four Pillars. In the idiom of *Picnic*, he has neither vanished on the Rock nor returned unchanged, and the frequent but reversible forays into the wilderness have left him subtly altered and unsuited for his vocation.

Keating's return to Welton to replay his adolescent revolt only reinforces the gap between youth and age, and the compromises the former villifies only to accept them at the later stage. The "Emperor," heard during *Picnic* with scenes of the Victorian values in retreat, suggests here, with the portrait of Keating's distanced love, that it is the Romantic mentality that must change or die. From this duality in Keating come the ambiguities that puzzle his students. He challenges the school system, urges them on to extraordinary feats, and eulogizes the past Dead Poets Society, but he subsequently upbraids Charlie's pranks (being expelled will deprive him of education's "golden opportunities"), says the present administration would frown on a re-formed Dead Poets Society, and stops Charlie from intervening between Neil and his father ("Don't make it any worse than it is"). The very existence of a compromise between static conformity and fleeing rebellion, which defines Keating's character and was an unattainable quality in *Picnic*, shows the narrative of *Dead Poets* being filtered through a sadder, wiser, and more worldly vision.

Don Shiach notes Robin Williams's star status, acquired through his performances in films such as *Good Morning, Vietnam* (Barry Levinson, 1987), and the influence of his "screen persona of caring non-conformity"[7] on the reception of *Dead Poets*. As in Weir's previous Hollywood pictures with Harrison Ford, popular perception of the male star assumes considerable importance in the audience's reading of the film. In highlighting the comic elements of Williams's performance, viewers and pupils are left in no doubt as to Keating's sincerity and motivation in more serious moments. The most obvious quality of Williams's characterization in both *Good Morning, Vietnam* and *Dead Poets* is that his performance underpins the urges of the characters of Adrian Cronauer and John Keating to "perform" to their respective audiences. The characters teach others about the harsh realities of life in authoritarian organizations through their unconventional conduct, but they also appear naive in not foreseeing the consequences of their actions and the vengeful power of the establishment.

Neil, as Keating's most ardent admirer, also chooses performance as his means of expression and escape. The "dream" of the play, in its poignant narrative and performance by the students, allows temporary release from parental constraint. *Picnic* alludes to *The Tempest*, suggestive of a dreamlike journey away from conventional society into a magical and liberating setting. *Dead Poets* quotes from another magical play that demands a return to everyday reality after experiences in the removed realm, and acknowledges its artifice with an epilogue asking for the audience's tolerance. Like the forays to the cave, the play's freedom is short-lived, and Keating's career and Neil's life are tragically curtailed. The upholders of authority have not "slumbered," and do take offense at the dream of liberty.

The naivety of Williams's persona in Levinson's film becomes a willful near-sightedness in Weir's, which gives rise to his contradictory stance, urging the pupils to liberate their minds while suggesting caution in their conduct in the academy. The idealistic belief that "words and ideas can change the world" (supported unequivocally by Cronauer, who broadcasts unedited news to troops in Vietnam to reveal the true nature of the war, but only stated by Keating, whose conduct and ultimate fate deny the principle) can again be traced to the film's literary sources. The Romantic idealism of Thoreau and Whitman reflected the humanitarianism of Abraham Lincoln but foundered upon the disillusionment of the Civil War. In *Dead Poets*, the portrayal of the United States in the 1950s, with conservatism and authoritarianism permeating social and political life, makes the poetry's message another unattainable dream. Weir's films in Australia and America often feature downbeat or qualified endings, but in *Dead Poets* there is the feeling of a necessary, if hard, formative lesson in hierarchical responsibility having been learned. Having peeped like Puck over the boys' shoulders as they gaze at the pictures of their predecessors and offered them magical, meddling suggestions, Robin (Goodfellow) Williams's character later asks for leniency and understanding. However, as in Shakespeare's play, the repercussions of drama and mischief can be genuine and dangerous. He has not "mended" and therefore will be "reprehended."

Individual freedom is difficult to attain under the Victorian constraint of Appleyard College and the Cold War sobriety of Welton Academy. The examples set by American male cinema heroes in Weir's generically adaptive material (the problematic personas of Harrison Ford and Robin Williams) always have far-reaching effects on actual or adoptive male offspring (Samuel Lapp, Charlie Fox, the Welton class of '59). Weir's concentration on the American establishment (in terms of conventional film and conservative society) reflects subjects addressed in both his Australian and American work. These can be seen in the deluded idealists and disempowered heroes of *Gallipoli* and *Year* and in the questioning of family and society in *The Cars That Ate Paris* (1974), *Wave*, and *The Plumber*. Stylistically, *Dead Poets* recalls *Picnic* most closely, but its themes and characterization portray a steady development of societal questioning and analysis of human action under communal constraint from *Michael* (1971) and *Homesdale* (1971) onward.

The history of American film and society in the McCarthy era provides *Dead Poets* with its most obvious subtext. There is more than a hint of the proceedings of the House Un-American Activities Committee (HUAC) in the headmaster's search for a scapegoat:

> One finds in *Dead Poets Society* the search for origins, the examination of the foundations of civilization, the discovery of a magic world beneath the rationality of the everyday, the rites of initiation, this time within the form of a parable of education. . . . [T]he first parable hides a second, that of totalitarianism, and more specifically, of McCarthyism, with its rituals of denunciation.[8]

Michel Sineux's two parables suggest, with Douchet's view of contemporary social and economic concerns, three rituals of initiation in *Dead Poets*, awakening the viewers and protagonists to Romantic ideals, realistic disillusionment, and artistic and historical precedents (*Picnic* in the director's past and HUAC in the industry's). Victorian schoolgirls, the pressed flowers of their age suited only for service or marriage, and 1950s schoolboys, the forced flowers needed for the financial, legal, and political edifices of Cold War America, are both able to comment on the capitalist advancement and moral retrenchment of Thatcher's and Reagan's policies of the 1980s.

In place of the "Emperor," the classical music (again by Beethoven) included in *Dead Poets* accompanies scenes of Keating inspiring the boys during sports matches. While the music and images suggest the ideal of beauty and enlightenment in all scholastic activity, the musical selection implies the outdatedness of such endeavors. The establishment wants doers rather than thinkers. *Dead Poets* ends with the stirring strains of martial music, previewed by sights of the school piper playing at the opening ceremony and later by the river at dusk. The image and the music recall earlier times, associated with the 1930s mural in the hall showing schoolboys clustered around the flag of the Union, with the same restrained hues and calm certainty of images of the Amish in *Witness*. This ending can be seen to continue the portrayal of painful but transcendent experience that concludes Weir's earlier American films. In each case, the ending does not equate with definite closure (what becomes of John Book in Philadelphia, Rachel in Lancaster County, and the Foxes in Honduras?) and this open-endedness is inherited from the Australian films. The uplifting sight of Todd's resistance is tempered by the recognition of the establishment's unassailable authority, as Keating, like Book, is forced out of a mistaken idyll.

In addition to visual patterns from Weir's earlier films, camera angles in *Dead Poets* provide an indication of the characters' physical and authoritative stature, an inheritance from *Year* and *Witness*. Camera angles in the classroom indicate the drama's progression. During the lesson on the Pritchard text, we see Neil from Keating's lectern as he reads the Preface aloud. Later the teacher assures all of them of their ability to "contribute a verse" to the world's "powerful play." Keating looks up from where he crouches between the desks, and the camera follows his gaze into Todd's face as he asks, "What will your verse be?" When he asks the boys to express their own feelings for what they read, he exemplifies the fresh perspective by climbing on his desk to "get a new angle on things" and encourages them to do likewise. Rising physically and mentally from their places, they tower over the camera.

The decline is signaled in the same form, when McAllister looks down from a window on the courtyard where Keating's class discusses the danger of conformity. This is mirrored later by Keating, now suspended, looking down from his room on McAllister escorting the parents of prospective pupils around the grounds. The symbolic, confining framing of characters within doors and windows can also be seen here, indicating McAllister's powerlessness to help or imitate Keating if he is sympathetic to his ideas, or his duty to inform the headmaster of what he sees. The first suggestion of parental control in the form of Neil Perry's father also is shown in this way. Mr. Perry appears in the doorway to Neil's room, where the group is relaxing after the opening ceremony. The dispute over Neil's extracurricular activities is enacted with Mr. Perry still framed in the doorway and Neil seen against the barred window. The inflexibility of one and the entrapment of the other are signaled in a composition reminiscent of *Michael* and *Wave*. When first Todd and then others climb on their desks in a final salute to Keating, the camera shares the looks they exchange: Todd frightened but determined and Keating shrunken and dejected as he heads for the door.

The triumph of the final music mixes Todd's rise in confidence and Keating's admirable qualities in defeat, with the attendant victory of the dominant power and the uncertainty of the younger and older men's future. The film's literary ambiguities are present at the conclusion, with Whitman's "O Captain! My Captain!" as the class's rallying call:

> O Captain! my Captain! our fearful trip is done,
> The ship has weather'd every rack, the prize we sought is
>   won, . . . (ll.1–2)[9]

The eulogy to Lincoln applauds his and the nation's spiritual victories but was written after his death, and in this case we might question whose is the prize and what victory has been gained. Where *Picnic* begins and ends with a dream of individual and cinematic freedom, *Dead Poets* is a waking dream of imprisonment, an allegory of American confinement made by a free thinker inside the filmmaking establishment. One of the director's most commercially successful productions emerges as one of his clearest examples of artistic control and authorship.

The narrative and visual expression of *Green Card* illustrates a further integration of directorial stylization within commercial cinema. Weir embarked on writing the screenplay during a period in which none of the studio projects he was offered were interesting enough to attract him. The desire to make a straightforward commercial picture, allied with viewing of comedy films from the 1930s, only reached fruition through the contribution of Gérard Depardieu, "the Cary Grant I couldn't find."[10] The notion of an established Hollywood comedic model to follow (or diverge from), together with the inheritance of Weir's previous work, creates (as in the cases of *Year, Witness,* and *Mosquito Coast*) a transformation of genre principles through the medium of the director's thematic and stylistic concerns.

The allusiveness of Weir's films and the breadth of their references to and quotations from other films require a knowledge of the genre or medium under examination to appreciate its extrapolation into parody or pastiche. For *Green Card,* screwball comedy provides a well-known basis for modern innovation. The label of "screwball" was applied to a trend in film comedy, which combined some of the excesses of slapstick with clashes of personality, sex, and lifestyle. The conflict caused by the characters' meeting went beyond differences of sex, class, or wealth to suggest a reversal of courtship rituals, with an unconventional or eccentric female hunting a staid and introverted male (e.g., *Bringing Up Baby* [Howard Hawks, 1938]. The genre also was capable of quite acerbic social commentary, addressing contemporary economic or political issues (*Holiday* [George Cukor, 1938], *His Girl Friday* [Howard Hawks, 1940]) and sexual behavior inside and outside marriage (*The Philadelphia Story* [George Cukor, 1940]). All these narratives have the central theme of attraction/repulsion of opposites (rich and poor, introvert and extrovert, conservative and liberal, male and female). However, there is an inherent paradox in the apparent iconoclasm of the genre's reversal of sex roles:

> Despite the general superiority in the genre of the female over the male, with her apparently antisocial approach to the traditionally male-dominated courtship ritual, the game still has the most conservative of goals: the heroine's madcap maneuvers are often used to capture a male and break him—or save him—from any real antisocial rigidity. This is best summed up by the term *marriage,* or the promise of marriage, which ends the screwball comedy, reaffirming one of the most traditional institutions in Western society.[11]

Weir's film asserts its difference from the very beginning, starting with the marriage of strangers and redefining marriage for consumerist America as a prerequisite for another kind of possession (Brontë Parish gaining her greenhouse). It also re-reverses the sex roles, in casting Brontë as the reserved and reclusive female and Georges as the relaxed, lower-class but romantic male (returning, ironically, to the characterizations of an archetype of the genre, Capra's *It Happened One Night*). *Green Card* adds the issues of race and immigration to the barriers of difference between the odd couple, creating a tension redolent of bigotry and isolationism in the midst of the comedy. The racial, sexual, and class-based prejudice lying behind the fantasy narrative of *Wave* and the thriller material of *The Plumber* finds a new mode of expression in contemporary romantic comedy in multicultural New York.

The eccentric character's behavior needs a foil within the narrative as well as a pleasantly scandalized audience without. In addition to the conventional future spouse, there must be a conservative (older) societal group and a stable (more wealthy) setting with which the eccentric's antics can contrast. *Green Card* includes the guests at Mrs. Adler's elegant soiree who, although embarrassed by Georges' composition on the piano, are won over by his poetry. Georges' efforts on Brontë's behalf secure the Adlers' gardens for her group of environmentalists; again, Georges is an aid to Brontë's acquisitiveness. Instead, Georges encounters genuine animosity from a younger generation, in the form of the supposedly radical Green Guerrillas, who appear, within their own clique, to be more conventional than the establishment. Their intolerance and superiority recall the unsympathetic alternative society in *Michael*.

The Adlers and the Green Guerrillas supply another staple of the genre, the possibility of other partners for the protagonists. Brontë's partner Phil appears too infrequently (and unsympathetically) to represent much opposition to Georges, but Lauren Adler (Bebe Neuwirth) is potentially a better partner for Georges, being closer to conventional screwball heroines in her unconventional behavior. Ironically, it is Lauren who predicts that Brontë will "wind up like some grand old Kate Hepburn." Comparing the solitary Brontë to the archetypal 1930s comedy actress (who could embody both aloof reserve and eccentric extroversion in her films

with Hawks and Cukor) not only indicates the intentional referencing incorporated into Weir's film but also emphasizes its divergence from the genre model. Academia and personal reserve,
associated with the male in *Bringing Up Baby*, are attributed to the
female in *Green Card*, while the "female" characteristics of spontaneity and passion, present in Lauren, are connected chiefly with
Georges. This polarization of male and female characteristics accords with that seen in *The Plumber* (Max the singer versus Jill the
academic), and perhaps also lies behind the chaotic relationship
between the libertarian, venial French male and distressed and self-
deluding American female in *French Kiss* (Lawrence Kasdan,
1995).

In its mixture of fidelity to and divergence from genre conventions, *Green Card* prompts a reassessment of screwball comedy
and its applicability to contemporary society. Weir called *Green
Card* his "second flat-out genre picture"[12] without indicating
which preceding film he rated as his first, but since the majority of
his films acknowledge conventions of narrative, characterization,
and ideology and engage in the realignment of such codes and audience responses to them, the distinction between art cinema and
genre film appears increasingly irrelevant:

> Genre films deal just as surely and deeply with social issues,
> considerations of life and death, and the unknown as do art
> films. The very persistence of genre films argues that they
> must be dealing with basic aspects of existence and
> social/psychological interaction, or they could not continue
> to be made.[13]

In the role of writer-director for a studio project, Weir's
achievement in *Green Card* shows a combination of art-cinema individualism and Hollywood entertainment, a meeting of popular
entertainment and personal style that echoes the works of the first
American auteurs.

As in *Dead Poets*, another register of reference beyond that of
allusion within the genre or medium is apparent in *Green Card*,
when structural similarities and recurrent motifs carried over from
the director's other films are recognized. In the opening sequence,
the relentless rhythm of the boy drumming outside the subway is
heard before he is seen. This introduces the importance of music

and the motif of drums, associated in Georges' mind with Africa and the fiction concocted for the Immigration and Naturalization Service (INS), and in the mind of Mrs. Bird with the "jungle" and unwelcome, disruptive immigrants. Brontë is seen buying a flower at a stall nearby; the drumming makes her forget her change, which she puts into the bucket next to the boy. The hand that drops the money holds a white rose, a link to the pressed flower seen at the beginning of *Picnic*.

Brontë's obsession with plants and the images of them in the decoration and furniture of her apartment recall the ubiquitous flowers of *Picnic* and connect Brontë with the reserved or preserved girls of Appleyard and their headmistress. Mrs. Appleyard's study also displayed floral decorations, although of a more limited and regimented kind, and she only leaves the college's confines once, like the pupils, for her fateful encounter with the Rock. Brontë's regulation and private enjoyment of the specimens (with)held in the greenhouse suggest a similar narrow-minded attitude that, when embodied in Mrs. Adler's refusal to donate her trees (contained in a classically appointed garden) to the environmentalists, becomes an obstacle to her ideals.

Brontë's return to the apartment after forays outside recalls John Keating's attempt to balance the liberty of poetry in the cave with the demands of the Welton establishment. Neither of them escapes the literal or metaphorical confinement of the establishment, although both transgress. Brontë's retreat, an exclusive apartment building, is as angular and ancient as Appleyard College. She divides her time unequally between the outside world and her apartment (Phil asks if it is a "girls' dorm"), and the apartment itself is subdivided between living rooms and the greenhouse, her "special place." The old building has no polar opposite, such as the Rock confronting the college; what opposes Brontë's life, defined in her living space, is Georges, a monolith from a foreign land.

The first barrier interposed between Georges and Brontë is the large window of the "Afrika Cafe. We see Brontë look out while she waits with Anton, and Georges crosses in front of the camera—the screen of the window being the frame of the action—before he walks back to gaze at her. His positioning on the other side of the divide and upon a rectangular replica of the cinema screen provokes comparison with the opening of *Year*. In both films, this framing device causes viewers to reconsider their position before the dramatic construct (evidenced by Brontë's comment to Anton, asking if she looks the part for the artificial wedding), either recognizing a famous face or accepting genre convention. It also recalls the limiting compositions of *Wave*, *The Plumber* and *Michael*, which highlight the ideological constraint on middle-class characters unable to comprehend or tolerate differences of race, class, or generation.

Such compositions recur in *Green Card* with similar relevance. In the wake of her cross-examination by the selection board of the apartment block, Brontë enters the rooms and greenhouse for the first time. As she begins to explain the needs of the collection's neglected plants to the trustees, classical music blooms on the soundtrack, replacing her voice just as the room and her interrogators are succeeded by a shot of her standing in the doorway to the apartment. She appears in a narrow strip of light in the frame of the door, with darkness dominating both sides, in a composition reminiscent of scenes in the Burton household. The music continues as she walks through the rooms with their old-fashioned furnishings and then rises triumphantly as she enters the greenhouse and gazes at the domed ceiling. The cultural refinement signaled by the image and sound reinvokes the tone of Victorian aspiration from *Picnic*, but the seclusion of Brontë's new home, her subterfuge in acquiring the apartment, and the later defense of her property recall the remoteness and manipulation of *Picnic*'s social establishment. The selection of classical music for certain scenes and characters in Weir's films (Billy Kwan, Jill in *The Plumber*) implies a criticism rather than approval of their learning or taste.

In narrative terms, these scenes establish Brontë's desire for possession of the greenhouse. Her activities with the Green Guerrillas and her falsification of marriage suggest her credentials as an unconventional and anti-establishment character. However, the accumulation of allusion to Weir's other works in this sequence (*Picnic*'s imagery, *Wave*'s framing) provides clues to Brontë's character. The straitened composition introducing her to the apartment echoes the insularity of the middle-class Burtons. We see her in the same narrow band of the frame when she admits Georges grudgingly through the front door (and Mrs. Bird observes them, too, through her slightly open door), and again when she is glimpsed through the kitchen door, having retreated there while Georges surveys the room. These shots resemble the confining compositions of *The Plumber*, when Jill observes Max around the dividing doors. Leading up to their first argument, the couple walks in parallel through the rooms and greenhouse, Brontë dominating the foreground and Georges framed in the background by the succession of doors and windows. The frames symbolize the social, psychological, and sexual distance between them, which Brontë seeks to maintain.

The restriction of the frame around Brontë (or its imposition on Georges) indicates her wish to exclude others and control her environment, but it also echoes the reserve and remoteness of the traditional screwball hero, which the disruptive heroine seeks to overcome. Extrapolating the characterization of females from *Picnic*'s Mrs. Appleyard and Annie Burton in *Wave* to Jill in *The Plumber* and Brontë in *Green Card*, we can see that the varying combination of framing, compositions, imagery, and music posits women as being the preservers of, and being preserved by, established society. This tendency in Weir's films explains Brontë's characterization, merging male academic (f)rigidity from *Bringing Up Baby* with the aloofness and class distinction of Katharine Hepburn's Tracy Lord from *The Philadelphia Story*. The latter film represents a possible structural basis for *Green Card*. At its end, Tracy abandons her upwardly mobile fiancé, to remarry her first, upperclass husband. Despite personality clashes, like (re)marries social like; in Weir's film, the mistaken marriage is reinstated but the couple remain decided opposites in habits, backgrounds, and beliefs. The conservative characterization of women in Weir's films produces an ending in which barriers of class, race, language, and ideology are crossed successfully by the characters, if not by the establishment.

That a satisfactory genre ending may be reached despite the evident subversion of codes is suggested by further development of the same stylistic features. When Georges makes "real" coffee in the kitchen, Brontë joins him there, and the division of the frame and the characters is absent (although they still sit at opposite ends of the flower-decorated table). Georges is welcomed (in French) to the Adler soiree after Lauren has shared the doorstep and doorframe with him. After having continued her conversation with

Georges unwillingly, peeping around the lounge door as he makes his bed on the sofa, Brontë reenters the room to work on their fictitious marriage, sharing her space, photo albums, and past with him.

The music of *Green Card* also plays a considerable part in the signposting of national and narrational emphases. The first sight of the greenhouse, as well as every subsequent sequence set in it or showing Brontë's work, is accompanied by Mozart's music. This apparent refinement, like *Picnic*'s use of Beethoven, highlights the reservation of public (the school) or private (Mrs. Appleyard's study and Brontë's greenhouse) locations and institutions to cope with the intrusive and unconventional. *Green Card*'s Mozart, driven from Brontë's apartment by the upsurge of Enya's rhythmic drums, presages a comparable revolution in her state, set in motion by the foreign male who is connected with the appearance of music in her life. His alien habits and opinions and the reappraisal of Brontë's existence that they provoke are heralded by the proliferation of unfamiliar and extraneous musical forms on the soundtrack.

The interpenetration of cultures in America, and the consequent debate on immigration and mixed urban communities are represented by the soundtrack's variety of music, voices, and languages. From the opening sequence, juxtaposing Brontë's buying of the flower and the young black child's drumming for change, Brontë's closed life and tranquil airtight greenhouse are contrasted to the city's myriad inhabitants and sounds. These external forces are personified in Georges, whose bulk looms over Brontë like the skyscrapers in the background while they argue on the roof about her "good works" in the ghettos. Traffic noise and sirens fill the background and accompany Georges' murmuring "chaos" and "despair" after she has left the roof. His physical presence and ardor recall the character of McTeague in another treatment of immigrant marriage, *Greed* (Erich von Stroheim, 1923). The couple's black-and-white costuming and the pair of caged birds in the greenhouse are perhaps other debts to this film. Georges' accented English or the French spoken with Anton and the waiters in the restaurant (offering meals "from all nations" for cosmopolitan New Yorkers), his attack on the Adlers' piano, and his composition "for Brontë" are the static on Brontë's wavelength, the interference to her view and plan of life, and definitely "not Mozart."

The nature of the foreign is often unspecific, given the range of cultures finding expression in the city. Perhaps its only definition is Brontë's antipathy to it. She does not speak Georges' language, unlike Lauren and the Adlers' guests, who prize the elitism associated with esteemed European culture (Lauren's French movies, her mother's "soiree," seeking a relation between Georges and "Gabriel Fauré," and the female guest's anecdote concerning her ancestor and Lafayette). When the trustees of the apartment block inquire, hearing that Mr. Fauré is in Africa, whether he himself is African, their relief at Brontë's assurance that he is French is set against her own enigmatic expression, perhaps reflecting righteous disdain for their need to ask or a similar relief that she can give an acceptable answer. Such awkwardness is paralleled in *The Plumber*, when Brian brings African, Indian, and American representatives of the World Health Organization home for a meal. When Dr. Japari expresses interest in Jill's famous curry, she remarks, "But I've never cooked for a . . . "

The sequence showing the Green Guerrillas garden project in the inner city provides another illustration of this attitude to the city's non-American elements. The group's van arrives at the site, where stereotypes of urban deterioration abound: youths on street corners, crumbling red brick, leaking hydrants, rap music. Brontë works on a flower bed ringed with brick rubble, and such incongruity features in the succeeding scenes. The liberal concerns lambasted in the processes of legal aid in *Wave* give rise here to a heedless intrusion into a neighborhood far from Brontë's home. Despite the laudable intention behind this invasion, its representation suggests that the group's motives are at variance with the environment and wishes of the community. In a rapid montage reminiscent of the construction of Jeronimo in *Mosquito Coast*, the environmentalists remove the refuse and create a multicolored garden with flowers and bright paints. The local Latinos and blacks watch or help in a bemused fashion. The city fathers have blessed the project, but it is unclear whether the opinions of the inhabitants themselves, like those of Allie Fox's flock, were even sought. The devotion and community spirit of the Amish barn raising is succeeded by self-gratifying labor that ignores, recruits, or patronizes the local inhabitants.

When Phil, Brontë, and the others leave for dinner, their philanthropy is replaced by impatience at the restaurant and by Brontë's fearful glimpse of the equally foreign and intransigent Georges. Working as a waiter in the neighborhood, Georges is reduced to an inferior other and is classified as such by the incongruous background music from *Zorba the Greek* (Michael Cacoyannis, 1964), another filmic clash of reserved and expansive (foreign) behavior.

Brontë's middle ground between the apartment and the city is the park, a larger and less structured version of the greenhouse. The strength of the contrast is made plain when, after moving into the apartment, Brontë walks through the park to the ghetto project. As Mozart fades from the soundtrack, views of the greenhouse are replaced with a shot of a black, bare tree against the sky, accompanied by traffic sounds. Moving down the tree and panning across the street, the camera's gaze takes in the old apartment building and Brontë leaving by the front door. Next, we see the landscape of tall buildings in the background, with the verdant boughs of trees surrounding them from the foreground as she enters the park. The shot recalls similar compositions in the earlier films: Appleyard College hemmed in by vegetation; the church in *Wave* surrounded by hedges and shrubs; Welton Academy encircled by autumnal woods. The significance of the shots in the other films—symbols of human order under threat from natural forces—is applicable in this case, although limited to one taciturn individual.

The park's significance is seen when Brontë meets her lawyer there to discuss her alternatives before the full inquiry. She asks why Georges could not meet her in the park to agree on details of their fictional life together, rather than stay in her apartment. Her preference is to complete the proceedings "without anyone knowing" and for her life "to continue as before." The park is the midpoint between the ghetto environment where Georges admits he grew up and the apartment Brontë wishes to keep sacred. As in the restaurant and later in their final argument, when she brands him as being from the gutter and bound to return there, her facade of middle-class liberalism slips to reveal prejudice. Brontë's masculine clothing in this scene, as an outward representation of the assumption of male roles Wes Gehring attributes to screwball heroines,[14] contradicts convention. Where the female's unconventional behavior and dress illustrated her assumption of the male courtship role, here Brontë's vehemence is not only anti-courtship but also anti-contact. Ironically, it is left to her lawyer to restate the traditional line, that marriage should be based on love.

Brontë's seclusion must be overcome if any, let alone all, of the conventions of romantic comedy are to be satisfied. As in *Year*, the strength of the character's desire to dictate as well as narrate must be quashed by the inexorability of film narrative and genre convention. In *Year* and *Witness*, the actions and reactions of the male characters are modified as they encounter different cultures and moral precepts (Amish pacifism, Indonesian sacred and secular life) and tropes of genre narrative are imposed (justified violent action followed by the hero's departure, exotic romance and flight from a war zone). After the final interview, Brontë is seen adrift in the street. At first she stands motionless, as the sounds of traffic and voices of passersby threaten to overwhelm her. Successive shots show her walking along busy sidewalks, with the soundtrack filled at one point with Asian voices and music and later with a black man offering her "bijoux africains." This incident—an African immigrant speaking French—evokes too many of the couple's shared fictions for comfort, and by the time she reaches home and attempts to recover her equilibrium by working in the greenhouse, she (and we) can hear no Mozart. Street sounds dominate, and everywhere she looks in the greenhouse reminds her of Georges (the fish he bought for her pond and the tomato plants he gave her).

This recollection begins Brontë's acceptance of the preferred, romantic narrative in place of her own. The sight of Georges planting the tomatoes (framed by the greenhouse windows, since she stands outside on the roof at the time), with only his face not hidden among the leaves, accords with the posed photograph of the African safari, showing him similarly hidden among the more exotic plants. Seeing Georges for the first time through the window of the café and seeing him in another frame in her most private and special place link perceptions of him as urbanized immigrant, intruder, and French (film) hero in Brontë's mind once he has left the screen, recruiting her to the expected, satisfactory, genre conclusion. The film's narrative powers, in the form of his last letter read as a voice-over and the music she has inspired in him recurring with full orchestration, return him to the screen.

Where the film's and the characters' narratives combine, the happy ending is prefigured in the creation of a happy past. The short scenes and instant snaps that make up the pictorial record of their wedding day, honeymoon, beach vacation, and African safari add strength to the comedy and provide the impetus toward the romantic conclusion. These scenes, where the assumed roles and actual genre roles merge, illustrate the self-conscious narration of Weir's films. Another example is the photographing of the couple as they dance. The camera circles around them as they spin, recalling Keating's conjuring of Todd's rapture and foreshadowing the couple's quarrel on the morning of the interview. The reflexive nature of such scenes forms a visual counterpart to the thematic tensions of awkwardness in class and race inequality, which are similarly out of place in an ostensible romantic comedy. The characters take control of the camera and of their personas within distinct but connected levels of dramatic reality. We recognize well-known stars (McDowell and Depardieu) enacting the characters of Brontë and Georges at the moment in which those characters begin to believe in and assume in truth the "parts" they have been playing.[15]

Just as the comedic narrative relies on the separation of Brontë's and Georges' actual and pretended lives, so at least part of the appreciation of the performances, as well as a proportion of the film's reflexive impact (in toying with perceptions of the genre and the stars' personas), is dependent on recognition of the film's construction and its relationship with this conventional background. As in the mixed filmic tenses of *Picnic*, mixed screens of *Wave*, and mixed narrators of *Year*, Weir amalgamates the examination of a social and ideological problem with the laying bare of narrative technique, while at the same time making the scenes crucial to the outcome of the drama:

> Increasingly, the characters identify with the story they are telling themselves, and the fictional memories begins to interfere with their real feelings, just as the couple begin to become what they pretend to be. Alteration of the past entails a modification of the present, just as filming reality alters our perception of it. Thus Georges starts to believe in the rigged photos.[16]

The reliability and relevance of photos form another staple of Weir's films. Solutions to mysteries, judgments of value, and definitions of the future are sought from still images. In *Green Card*, the

Green Card   Andie MacDowell, Gérard Depardieu   (AUS-FR 1990)
Picture from the Ronald Grant Archive

photos show a "false" romantic narrative created by the characters. As in *Cars* and *Year*, the pictures are used to substantiate a preferred categorization of the world that the characters seek to control. However, the story line the pictures contain becomes the "true," conventional narrative that takes control of the characters. The albums Brontë shows Georges contain pictures from her past, building on his initial fascination with the picture of her as a dancer in the apartment and recalling Charlie's concentration on David's family pictures in *Wave*. The pictures illustrate Brontë's wish for her life "to continue as before"—her desire, in tune with Mrs. Appleyard's, for stasis. Georges' photos, by contrast, create a fictitious past while representing the only genuine past history, the preceding two days, that they shared. Above all, they symbolize his desired future, in accordance with genre anticipation, for a married life to come and his waiting for "life to begin."

Again, a Weir narrative stresses open-endedness rather than stasis in its ending, even when the basis for Georges' hopes is an imagined past. The film's last minutes, like those of *Dead Poets*, suggest the optimism of personal fulfillment against a background of authoritarianism. In the montage of close-ups that compose the final interview with the INS, Georges makes a third and fatal mistake, let down by his awkwardness with the spoken language. In comparison, Brontë seems at ease in the confined space and can act naturally, true to her previous reclusiveness. Yet the subsequent scenes extinguish the hopes for a conventional ending; just as the director refuses to allow the characters to outstrip the genre, so the genre must not dictate a conclusion to the film's problematic materials.

The obstacle of language, and the difficulty for the film and its characters in transmitting the correct message, have been identified by Weir and critics of *Green Card*. Both the director, in approaching an unfamiliar genre, and the star, in abandoning his native language, were stepping away from friendly territory:

> Peter Weir has not written sparkling dialogue in the manner of Hawks or Capra, since Georges has not mastered the language; instead he has concentrated his framing more on the body (tattoos, lips), on looks and behavior. The drama is born from the ill-mastered language rather than from comedy.[17]

Green Card's dissimilarity from its screwball comedy genre forebears in its lack of quick-fire dialogue is a direct result of the casting of Depardieu, which is central to the film's intention. The couples or romantic triangles of Cukor's or Hawks's films shared a common language, and their dexterity (or lack of it) in its use was an index of their compatibility as partners. This is illustrated by the pairing of Walter Burns with Hildy Johnson in *His Girl Friday* and Johnny Case with Linda Seaton in *Holiday*. Sexual, social, and moral differences are overridden by the characters' linguistic similarity. Social and moral dissimilarity are highlighted by conversational incompatibility of the characters' intended partners, such as Johnny Case and Julia Seaton. The very fact that Georges is not a fellow American makes the odd-couple comedy more odd, the attraction less understandable than the repulsion; the sexual and habitual differences are exacerbated by racial and language barriers. Conservative American society, personified by Brontë, is faced with a potential partner more different and unlikely than any seen in previous screwball comedies. Georges' otherness is indicated in his physical form (his bulk against her slightness), his dress (his black against her white), and his habits of eating, drinking, and smoking. The film's form constructs more obstacles (the door and window frames dividing the flat, the confining rooms of the INS), even as other aspects of Weir's characteristic style (Georges' mellifluous compositions and Enya's atavistic rhythms opposing Mozart on the soundtrack, the fabrication of a romance through the staged photos) seek to erode Brontë's antipathy. The language barrier becomes a coincidental factor in their incompatibility, and Weir's visual language announces these divisions while heralding their eventual convergence.

All of Weir's other films experiment with the expressive potential of the film medium and adopt a mixture of intertextual, genre and allusive references. The metalanguage that results appears ideally suited to address material such as the narrative of *Green Card* in postmodern and multicultural terms, illustrating the late-twentieth-century meeting point of cultural, historical, and artistic forces. Brontë's conservatism is shown through her seclusion in the apartment, her circle of friends, and her choice of music. Georges' difference is expressed through his expansive behavior and his lack of an apparent base: He has no home or address, and his aura of vagrancy is heightened by Brontë's insistence that he sleep on the sofa (or even outside the apartment) when she cannot just meet him in the park. His cultural association, while strictly French during the evening with the Adlers, is multiplied elsewhere (varied international dishes and Greek music at the restaurant, his facade of the safari inspired by the Afrika Cafe). This wedding of opposites is expressed through the eclecticism of Weir's idiom, which in the past had proved equally adept at elucidating the combination of British and Australian heritages in *Picnic*, the clash of Aboriginal and European cultures in *Wave*, the perspectival gap between 1915 and the present in *Gallipoli*, and the disparity of East and West in *Year*. Weir's inception and treatment of this multicultural comedy in America parallels the appearance of similarly variegated films (in ethnic as well as genre terms) portraying contemporary Australian multicultural society: *Death in Brunswick* (John Ruane, 1990), *Nirvana Street Murder* (Aleksi Vellis, 1990), and *Strictly Ballroom* (Baz Luhrmann, 1992).

Immigration control, social inequality, and isolationism were all features of American society of the 1930s, the era that saw the creation of screwball comedy in a Hollywood financed by a generation of immigrant businessmen. Ironically, it was these newcomers who established conventions of the American entertainment industry that have since pervaded all levels of morality and ideology in the social and political life of the country. That these outsiders became insiders appears to be the source of the compromise of the screwball comedy genre and the conservatism beneath its iconoclasm:

> [S]crewball comedy merely pokes survivable—status quo—fun at the eccentricities of the rich. While satire can and does exist, the screwball comedy viewer generally is allowed to grow fond of these wealthy wackos, in a superior sort of way. . . . Most screwball comedies minimize any socioeconomic differences of the leading duo and key on their initial conflicts concerning eccentric behavior.[18]

Green Card, a supposedly clear-cut commercial venture, offers little of this comforting comedy. The eccentricities are hardly endearing, racial and economic distinctions are emphasized constantly, and prejudice seems to be still in place, except in Brontë's case, at the film's end. The only solace comes from the suggestion of eventual happiness contained in the song accompanying the final credits. In the style of a Southern Methodist devotion sung by The Emmaus Group Singers, it assures us that from a "dream" we have hope that "everything's going to be all right." The song unites the dreams of Weir's other films, linking the allegorical solutions of the mysteries of *Picnic* and *Wave* with Martin Luther King's dream of harmony out of a Babel of racial discord, a fitting conclusion to a drama defined by its music. Ironically, the refusal of *Green Card* to manufacture a conventional ending can be interpreted as a latter-day realization of the screwball comedy's transgressive potential, in both formal and social terms:

> Without an artificial plot device to overcome narrative illogic and to resolve the sociosexual conflicts, the screwball comedy requires a precise handling of its opposed couple and their values if it is to finally unite them without appearing either cynical or naive. Because the more effective Depression comedies reconciled sexual and ideological differences involving fundamental contradictions in our culture, resolving the plot often demanded a rather severe narrative rupture.[19]

Gehring considers that screwball comedy is "conservative in the sense that to coexist in society is to know compromise."[20] Knowing compromise without embracing its consequences would be a limited compromise indeed, unsuited to the call for liberal concession and accommodation found in *Green Card*. The actions and intentions of Brontë, Georges, and Keating are not stereotyped as good or bad, laudable or execrable, and their complexity gives depth to the problems of contemporary life that beset them.

Brontë's idealistic concern for the ghettos contrasts with her conservatism toward Georges; Georges' artistic sensitivity clashes with criticism of Brontë's humanitarian efforts; Keating's ambiguous attitude to authority and education perplexes pupils and employers alike. The fact that their ideas are not "all from the same place" makes the portrayal of their moral choices, in individual or communal life, more complex and credible than commercial imperatives or genre convention may suggest. These factors of characterization, setting, and background indicate the presence of Weir's sensibilities and interests: Allied with his recognizable style, they provide a sure signature of authorship.

Shiach describes *Dead Poets Society* as a "well-crafted exercise in Hollywood emotionalism" that is "quite blatant in its attempted manipulation of the sympathies of the spectator."[21] He dismisses *Green Card* in similar terms, with the coda that Weir wrote and produced *Green Card* rather than work on it as a contracted director: "Perhaps Peter Weir is entitled to make *Green Card* as a sort of interlude in his career, a movie that has all the marks of a carefully crafted commercial product that hopes to do well at the box office."[22] Weir's own judgment of *Green Card* as an example of purposeful commercial pictures that "can become as interesting [as more personal work] at the time of doing them, not so much in looking at them later on,"[23] seems to bear out the argument that he was marking time during the making of what was, nonetheless, a privately conceived film. Commercial awareness need not entail the excision of all controversial material. Shiach notes that attitudes to gender in *Green Card* and other Weir films "have not always been politically correct."[24] It seems Weir's work can be criticized on the one hand for its achievement of commercial and melodramatic goals in *Dead Poets* and on the other for avoiding cliché and encouraging the controversial in the personal and commercial *Green Card*.

The personal signature of thematic controversy and formal inconclusiveness continues to mark Weir's individuality in the business of commercial filmmaking:

> Only in a society in which their position in a social hierarchy assigns individuals their human worth would a couple be deemed inappropriate simply because it violated such principles of social ordering. By criticizing restrictive romantic norms, the unlikely couple film questions the divisions of society into groups of differing social value.[25]

In an interview, Weir revealed his attraction to studio work and his conviction that he would have fit in well in Hollywood during the 1930s.[26] Conversely, Norman Lloyd (who played the headmaster in *Dead Poets* and who had worked with Hitchcock and Orson Welles) believed that Weir's selectivity in choosing work and co-workers would have made a prolonged contractual career intolerable for him.[27] While the art-cinema hallmarks of Weir's style in the 1970s have remained unaltered into the 1980s and 1990s, the integration of the contrary influences and aims discernible in his films is affirmed in *Green Card*'s proficient melding of form and content:

> *Green Card*, together with [Weir's] three earlier Hollywood productions, reaffirms the ability of this aesthetic system to assimilate distinctive talents and backgrounds. This does not mean that there are not recognizable Peter Weir "touches" in *Green Card*; it means that these "touches," involving the effective use of images, atmosphere, and milieu, are not isolated, as they tend to be in his Australian films, but are an integrated part of an overall formal system that privileges narrative, temporal, and spatial coherence, causality and motivation, climax and resolution.[28]

The characteristics noted in other works and periods of Weir's career attain a full integration in *Green Card*, unifying an individual idea and theme, a classical Hollywood genre format, linear narrative and melodramatic structuring, and components of the characteristic visual idiom that continues to distinguish Weir's work. Without recognition of the presence and significance of these stylistic structures permeating Weir's films, the appearance of these structures in *Dead Poets* and *Green Card* and their considerable addition to the reading of these films would be overlooked. Isolation of the structures associated with the directorial signature facilitates the interpretation of the films in which they appear. Such reading acknowledges the creative powers of the auteur, especially one as consistent and cerebral as Peter Weir, while giving credit to the reading audiences, the (re)creators of the text on innumerable individual interpretative bases.

Weir has succeeded in reaching a wider audience, but this has resulted in the refinement of his stylistic and thematic traits rather than their removal under commercial imperatives: "I see myself as—quote—*a Hollywood director of mass audience pictures*. At the same time, with the condition I do it my way."[29] Such individualism within the Hollywood establishment led Weir to his next studio project, being approached by Paula Weinstein to direct *Fearless* (1993), adapted from the novel by Rafael Yglesias. The summation of Weir's craft in *Green Card*, in its display of directorial style and genre inheritance, was followed by a purposeful return to the methods and mysteries of his Australian films.

Notes

1. Jean Douchet, "Le commerce de la poésie," *Cahiers du Cinema*, 430 (1990) pp. 40–41 (author's translation).

2. See L. Codelli, "*Le cercle des poetes disparus*," *Positif*, 345 (1989), pp. 54–55; Richard Combs, "*Dead Poets Society*," *Monthly Film Bulletin*, 56 (1989), pp. 272–273.

3. Mat Snow and Meredith Brody, "The French Connection," *Empire*, 22 (1991), pp. 50–56 (p. 52).

4. Carl Bode (ed.), *Henry David Thoreau: Collected Poems* (Baltimore: Johns Hopkins University Press, 1964), p. 21.

5. Henry David Thoreau, *Walden—or Life in the Woods* (London: Chapman & Hall, 1927), p. 78.

6. Emory Holloway (ed.), *Walt Whitman: Complete Verse and Selected Prose and Letters*, (London: Nonesuch, 1938), p. 26.

7. Don Shiach, *The Films of Peter Weir* (London: Letts, 1993), p. 169.

8. Michel Sineux, "*Le cercle des poetes disparus*," *Positif*, 347 (1990), pp. 66–67 (author's translation).

9. Francis Murphy (ed.), *Walt Whitman: The Complete Poems* (Harmondsworth: Penguin, 1975), p. 359.

10. Interview with the author, June 1993.

11. Wes D. Gehring, *Screwball Comedy: A Genre of Madcap Romance* (London: Greenwood Press, 1986), p. 155.

12. Snow and Brody, "The French Connection," p. 55.

13. Stuart M. Kaminsky, *American Film Genres*, 2nd ed. (Chicago: Nelson Hall, 1985), p. 3.

14. Gehring, *Screwball Comedy*, p. 165.

15. I. Katsahni comments on the "inspired moment" when the characters "take charge of their scenario": "*Green Card*," *Cahiers du Cinema*, 441 (1991), p. 73.

16. Thomas Bourguignon, "Le vert paradis," *Positif, 361* (1991), pp. 52–54; (author's translation).

17. *Ibid.*, p.53.

18. Gehring, *Screwball Comedy*, p. 154.

19. Thomas Schatz, *Hollywood Genres* (London: McGraw-Hill, 1981), p. 155.

20. Gehring, *Screwball Comedy*, p. 156.

21. Shiach, *Films of Peter Weir*, pp. 179–180.

22. *Ibid.*, p. 194.

23. Interview with the author, June 1993.

24. Shiach, *Films of Peter Weir*, p. 193.

25. Thomas E. Wartenberg, *Unlikely Couples: Movie Romance as Social Criticism* (Boulder, Colo.: Westview Press, 1999), p. 7.

26. Interview with the author, June 1993.

27. *Ibid.*

28. Geoff Mayer, "*Green Card*," *Cinema Papers, 82* (1991), pp. 53–54.

29. Snow and Brody, "The French Connection," p. 56. (Original emphasis.)

Chapter Seven

Fearless (1993) and *The Truman Show* (1998)

The apparent disparity between *Fearless* and *The Truman Show*, in terms of their commercial success and critical reception may appear to preclude their discussion in tandem. The tragic trajectory of the former and the comedic, satiric intensity of the latter may seem incompatible and opposed to an exaggerated degree within Peter Weir's canon. However, these films' preoccupations can be traced directly to the materials and perspectives of Weir's work during the 1970s. The association with dreams and subjective vision in *Fearless*, the conspicuous use of constricted framing in the compositions of *Truman*, and the emphasis in both films on renunciation of domesticity, dissatisfaction with the superficial world, and abdication of adult responsibility all work to reinvoke the existential crisis of *The Last Wave* (1977). Similarly, their foregrounding of the manipulation of the temporal, spatial, and emotional characteristics of the filmic world (in the representation of the subjective experience and recollection of the protagonist in *Fearless* and in the televisual fabrication of both personal and communal experience in *Truman*) connects with the awareness of the fragility of the normal (as in *Picnic at Hanging Rock* [1975], *Wave*, and *The Plumber* [1979]) and the enveloping and seductive power of the mythic (as in *Gallipoli* [1981]).

The additional similarity of these films to the pairing of *Witness* (1985) and *The Mosquito Coast* (1986) goes beyond their distinction in popular success and failure. The extension or subversion of star personas (in the cases of Harrison Ford's roles in the 1980s films and Jim Carrey's in *Truman*) represents a crucial factor in the

films' acquisition—or loss—of an audience. Such unusual handling
of leading actors fits the pattern of unexpected casting and characterization seen in Mel Gibson's and Robin Williams's roles in *The
Year of Living Dangerously* (1982) and *Dead Poets Society* (1989)
respectively. Reconception of the star is inseparable from the modification of genre convention and audience expectation, although
the malleability of structures and relationships within an essentially commercial cinema is finite, as evidenced by the disconnec-
tion of *Fearless* and *Mosquito Coast* from the mainstream audience.
While all the male protagonists of Weir's American (and Australian) pictures are non-conformists, the unsympathetic characterization of Allie Fox is not repeated in Carrey's portrayal of Truman
Burbank. Truman's unwitting stardom within his own living soap
opera vindicates both Carrey's casting and his performance, which
encompasses slapstick, sentimentality, and heroism and pleases
both diegetic and extra-diegetic audiences.[1]

Both *Fearless* and *Truman* maintain a trend of overt social criticism in Weir's American films. The examination of the western's
spectacle of violence in *Witness* and *Mosquito Coast*, and the consideration of historical and contemporary political and racial intolerance in *Dead Poets* and *Green Card* (1990), are succeeded by the
dissection of the American obsessions with litigation and therapy in
Fearless and the analysis of the dubious gratification offered by modern, globalizing media in *Truman*. However, the individuality of
Weir's films also needs to be seen in the context of contemporary
Hollywood films addressing similar concerns with comparable
rhetoric and metaphor. *Fearless*'s depiction of the white American
patriarch adrift and distanced from the certainties of professional
and familial existence is also found in a diverse range of contemporary films (*Hook* [Steven Spielberg, 1991] *Falling Down* [Joel Schu-
macher), 1992] *Mrs. Doubtfire* [Chris Columbus, 1993], *Forrest
Gump*, [Robert Zemeckis, 1994], *Jumanji* [Joe Johnston, 1995]),
and yet in such cases the status and significance of the father-figure
are almost invariably reaffirmed and reinstated. By comparison, the
alienation of the parent and partner in *Fearless* is both sought and re-
cuperated in highly ambiguous terms, and Truman's urge to escape is
fueled by a rejection of parenthood and yearning for romantic love.

Truman's critique of the mass media's coercive, conformist, and
nostalgic address is echoed in *Pleasantville* (Gary Ross, 1998) and

EDtv (Ron Howard, 1999). Similarly, a critique of the pursuit of bodily perfection, which leads in a future society to new, genetically motivated prejudices, is articulated through the science-fiction narrative of Gattaca (Andrew Niccol, 1997). As the New Zealand–born scriptwriter of Truman, Niccol was, like Weir, placed as an external and critical observer of American cultural mores.

Yet any critical reading of each of Weir's American productions also substantially outgrows any simplistic social or satiric commentary (if such were intended). Predominantly, they remain narratives of individual struggles against authority, constraint, mundanity, and conformity, of personal realization and the refusal to live "what was not life." Alongside the director's abiding thematic concern with individual experience and expression, Weir's stylistic pallet of visual and aural techniques (framing, allusiveness and intertextuality, and use of music) is present in and pertinent to the innovations and repetitions apparent in his films of the 1990s.

Fearless continues Weir's analysis of the role and responsibility of the American hero, and like Witness and Mosquito Coast, criticizes the modern filmic and social environment he inhabits. The impotence of Weir's heroes and their desire to evade societal regulation and genre convention reach their zenith in the figure of Max Klein (Jeff Bridges), who would rather die than face the social and emotional demands made on him by friends, family, and associates. Having saved himself and others from the physical danger of an air crash, he wishes to be "free of life,"[2] to be delivered from his own burdensome existence as a survivor/savior. He prefers to be a "ghost" among the living, evincing control over his existence through his refusal to be reintegrated with the lives of others and releasing himself from the myriad of life's requirements of a father, husband, and businessman. In this respect, despite their harrowing nature, the crash scenes that begin and conclude Fearless can be seen to be peripheral to its social and psychological analysis:

> The plane crash in Fearless performs the same role as natural elements in Weir's Australian films: [I]t reveals the fragility of human existence and prompts actions that would be impossible under normal circumstances. As in Picnic at Hanging Rock, however, Weir focuses on the changes that an uncontrollable occurrence brings to the protagonists' lives rather than on the event itself.[3]

Where *Picnic*'s title focuses attention on a superficially ephemeral occurrence that is transformed and immortalized by a freezing of time and narrative progression, and that of *Wave* suggests the significance of the event that motivates and is prefigured by the personal and domestic crises preceding it, the title *Fearless* foregrounds a desired emotional and existential condition that is attained accidentally, maintained imperfectly, and renounced resignedly. After the depiction of the oppositional unity of groups against controlling and restricting forces seen in *Dead Poets* and *Green Card*, *Fearless* and *Truman* return to the examination of the subversive, destabilizing, disenchanted individual seen previously in *Picnic* and *Wave*.

Initially compartmentalized within the genre of air-disaster movies, *Fearless* outstrips this framework to concentrate on the significance of near-death experience. As the hero seeks to evade everyday life following his escape from death, so the film diverges from narrative and genre expectation. Conspicuous stylization (such as the irruption of disconcerting sound, instances of slow motion, and the foregrounding of subjective, dream vision) reflects Weir's conviction that *Fearless* revealed him to be "drawing back to the earlier films."[4] *Fearless*'s clearest antecedent, thematically and stylistically, is undoubtedly *Wave*.

Fearless's stylistic distinction from the mainstream Hollywood product suggests its relationship with other earlier films also occupying the periphery of the entertainment cinema. Weir's film, like the novel by Rafael Yglesias on which it is based, reveals the air crash in a series of flashbacks that punctuate the narrative. The crash itself, treated chronologically and in detail by the novelist, appears primarily at the film's conclusion but is previewed intermittently through Max's recollections in dreams. The flashbacks to the crash are linked to Max's (and fellow survivor Carla's) subjective visions, with the result that the horrors of the event are revealed sporadically and unpredictably, making the film's structure particularly reminiscent of *Catch-22* (Mike Nichols, 1970). The possibility that the events between the aftermath of the crash at the film's opening and Max's return to life at its end are no more than the extension of his last moments of consciousness recalls the expressionistic horror of *Carnival of Souls* (Herk Harvey, 1962) and *Jacob's Ladder* (Adrian Lyne, 1990). Max's transcendence of and learning from traumatic experience also parallels a contemporary air-disaster movie, *Alive* (Frank Marshall, 1992), which focuses on the value of life to the extreme of sustaining existence by cannibalism in defiance of cultural taboos. *Fearless* embodies similar philosophical debates, but favors a more parabolic tone, after *Mosquito Coast* and *The Fisher King* (Terry Gilliam, 1991), which also starred Jeff Bridges in the role of outsider and pilgrim. Both Weir's and Gilliam's films exhibit a deep dissatisfaction with the condition of modern America. Their defamiliarizing gaze on contemporary hypocrisy and spiritual poverty is colored, like *Mosquito Coast*'s, by the idealism of the 1960s. The alteration in outlook between the counterculture of *Michael* (1971) and the retrenchment of *The Plumber* is also apparent in Max's disillusionment:

> Max understood something that had bothered him for a decade, that he had known only in a sleepy, evasive way. He was living in a reductive age, a time where any diminishment of person or goal was popular. The astronauts were considered to be frauds and no one believed racism could be conquered. The two longings of his youth, to live in peace with all the races and ethnics of his city, to see men walk on other worlds, were laughable, even stupid desires in the eyes of the smart and sophisticated and powerful people of his time. It wasn't the disappointment of designing discount electronics stores that had embittered Max; it was living in a nation without dreams that made reality so hard.[5]

The resemblance to David Burton's "loss of dreams" in *Wave* is apparent, precipitating a comparable desire for something beyond or apart from mundane existence. Where Burton the lawyer perceives the inadequacy of received rules in failing to accommodate the personal and the unpredictable, Max the architect comes to recognize the sand on which humanity's rational, consensual world is built. For both men, being separate from or "dead" to the world is a response to, but not a solution for, the denial or decline they detect in society and themselves following their encounters with the unknown.

The challenge in communicating the uniqueness of vision and experience through subjective narrative techniques was recognized and explored at length by Weir and director of photography Allen Daviau in their preparations for the film. Daviau, a frequent collaborator with Steven Spielberg during the 1980s, reviewed Weir's Australian films (in particular *Picnic* and *Wave*) as part of his own research.[6] Subsequently, Weir and Daviau experimented with ways in which to represent Max's personal vision. Some sequences were shot with 65mm film, and in other instances (again, as had been the case in *Wave*), zoom lenses and extreme close-ups were used.[7] Just as in *Wave* David Burton's subjective experience is relayed through combinations of visual and aural distortion, so Max's perceptions and recollections are signaled, rather than integrated, by dissociated sounds and by discernible and disconcerting shifts into slow motion or extreme close-up. These features are especially prominent during Max's first dream of the crash, as he lies on his bed and his wife Laura (Isabella Rossellini) removes his shoes. His unconscious recollection becomes an omniscient narration (in which Max himself is observed) ushered in by this conspicuous stylization:

> During a scene in which Max is dreaming, we see the rapid eye movements behind his clenched lids, and the shot ends with an incredibly tight composition isolated on just one ear. The move is choreographed with sounds of the plane struggling to survive, allowing the audience to enter Max's dream.[8]

However, the transition from the extreme close-up of Max's ear to an exterior view, in extreme long shot, of the plane at altitude does not separate Max's subjective flashback conclusively from the objective "present" of the film, which is maintained by intercut shots of Laura watching her husband sleep. This sequence, then, visualizes and foregrounds Max's alienation by keeping the images of his experience "secret" from his wife, but at the same time the intercutting of the sequence anticipates the film's climax, in which Max is ultimately recalled from his near-fatal, subjective exile by her intervention. The representation of the crash via Max's mind screen, recalled as dream images imbued with personal meaning and visions irrupting at the point of death, bears comparison with other films (such as *La Jetée* [Chris Marker, 1962] and *After Life* [Hirokazu Kore-eda, 1998]) stressing the indivisibility of the film image, human memory, and the questioning of existential meaning. Where *La Jetée* and *After Life* conclude with the recognition of the basis of life's meaning in emotional attachments, even when these are unconsummated or unreciprocated, *Fearless* focuses on a search for meaning derived from a deliberate, solipsistic isolation. The present (in Marker's film) and the past (in Hirokazu's) represent points of departure from which the activities of recollecting, summarizing, and concluding past existence are initiated. Notably, although in the novel Yglesias has Max revisit his past to establish the extent of his decline (in ambition and achievement[9]), in Weir's film Max's previous existence remains relatively unknown and invisible beyond the immediate past of the crash. The removal of any alternative existence for Max increases his isolation and presages his eventual return to conventional life.

Max's alienation is emphasized from the film's opening. *Fearless* begins without credits, beyond the title isolated against a black background and silhouetted by the smoke from the crash. The combination of the gradual rising of disconcerting string sounds (from "Polymorphia" by Krzysztof Penderecki, used previously in *The Exorcist* [William Friedkin, 1973]) and the incongruity of the crash survivors' dazed walk through a cornfield extend the sense of disorientation to the viewer. The cornfield might suggest a parallel to the idyllic opening of *Witness*. In that film, distancing was achieved by the unexpectedness of the date and place relayed by the title; in *Fearless*, a similar effect is produced by the nightmarish juxtaposition of images (passengers in blood-stained city clothes, stumbling along straight paths in a field wreathed in smoke) and sounds (the grating music).

Given the significance of soundtrack music within the Weir canon, and the weighting of diametrically opposed classical and popular pieces in several relevant instances, the selection of Penderecki's discordant, modernist composition for this sequence reinforces the film's depiction of materialism and rationalism undone by catastrophe. Similarly, the presence of this music in Friedkin's film connects as much with the disorientation attending on mundane crises (of bereavement and marital breakup) as with supernatural and spiritual ones. In a comparable way, the soundtrack music that accompanies Max's self-imposed tests (preceding his walk across the busy highway and on a skyscraper's roof) and Carla's memory of Bubble's death (in a flashback devoid of diegetic sound) is reminiscent of the unearthly choral compositions heralding the appearance and intervention of the black monoliths in *2001: A Space Odyssey* (Stanley Kubrick, 1968). The early scenes at the crash site, Max's later dream recollections, and the final revelation of the disaster as he again faces death function therefore in an identical fashion to the repeated premonitory and hallucinatory images in *Wave*. The subjective channel of the protagonist (Max and David) is used in each case for repetition and extension of the revelatory vision, in each film through the use of slow motion and the dissociation of sound and image, to "translate experiences of extratemporality in visual terms."[10]

The absence of naturalistic, diegetic sound is maintained while Max walks through the crash site. The foregrounding of slow motion in association with his perspective and the jarring sights of everyday objects among the detritus of the plane (a shoe and a severed limb, a charred body, and an unbroken champagne bottle) heighten the enormity of the crash. Surveying the crash amounts to viewing a cross-section of contemporary society and its artefacts. As in the case of the juxtaposition of horror and mundanity in the montage sequences of *The Cars That Ate Paris* (1974), Max's view appears distant and dispassionate, accepting the inconsequentiality of normality when seen against the ascendency of the unpredictable. Max exaggerates his distance and difference from normal society immediately, denying that he was on the flight and traveling away from the site while rescuers, reporters, and onlookers rush toward it. Later, he drives along a straight and empty desert road and walks along a deserted freeway as if, again like David Burton in *Wave*, he is the prophet or survivor of an apocalypse that has left him the only man "alive."

Max's revocation of his past roles (of father and husband) and of the new ones thrust upon him (as savior of the other passengers, the Good Samaritan of the disaster, and Carla's confessor) indicates his disgust for the society he attempts to leave and displays a prophetic stance similar to that of David Burton. The crash is a "senseless" happening, unless he can imbue it with meaning by using it as a springboard into a new life:

> Max felt something he hadn't since the explosion: irritation at the mosquito bite of the morally confused world. He had been free of it since the crash. Max hadn't measured the relief

of its absence until now as he felt the itch of its return. Why was this choice imposed on him? He was so near freedom.[11]

Max's effort to imbue the event with a personal and incommunicable significance does not prevent its rationalization within the wider community. His wife Laura is seen watching a television news bulletin discussing the crash and attempting to identify what it means for survivors, relatives, and viewers. In the novel, even in the midst of the event Max is able to imagine the complacent and self-serving investigation of the crash that will take place in the future.[12] Such retrospective evaluation recalls the insubstantial explanations offered for the bizarre weather in *Wave*. Similarly, Max's son Jonah is seen reviewing his scrapbook of newspaper cuttings on the disaster and his father's role within it, evoking Archie's study of reports of the calamitous events in the Dardanelles in *Gallipoli*. The rituals, patterns, and models that characters use to assert control over chance and irrational forces offer little or no protection. Max observes the preflight checks that will assure his safety on his plane ride home less than two days after his crash; the architectural computer model that Max's partner toys with on the flight is shaken by the plane's convulsions; and Laura's stage model, which she prepares for her dance class even as her marriage collapses, recalls the mayor's mock-up of the unrealizable "Paris of the future" in *Cars*.

Being summoned back to normal life is as traumatic as leaving it, as evidenced by Max's primal scream when the survivors' lawyer Brillstein (Tom Hulce) suggests he lies to gain greater compensation from the airline. When he is confronted with the same obligation to lie on behalf of his business partner's widow, Max emits a similar shriek of fear and release as he stands on the edge of the roof of Brillstein's office block. His behavior may appear suicidal (in Yglesias's novel, the incident on the high roof and his walk across the busy freeway are aggravated, in the first instance by Max's actually slipping off the parapet,[13] and in the second by his tempting of a mugger to kill him[14]), but Max's symptoms are misunderstood and misdiagnosed (by Laura and the therapist Dr. Perlman) as a loss of fear and a desire for death. Rather, Max is afraid only of the cowardice inspired by conscience, the guilt and shame of obligation and reciprocation:

What am I truly afraid of? Dying? Not loving my wife and
son? Loving them? Who cares what the real fear is? It was the
cowardice itself which appalled him.[15]

Max's impatience with society and his intransigence toward his
family is reinforced by the film's religious imagery and by his evan-
gelical stance, which is reminiscent of Allie Fox in *Mosquito Coast*.
Max's freedom from fear begins when a circle of light from a port-
hole on the plane plays on his face. He is the savior of other survivors, urging them to follow him toward the light beyond the
wreckage.[16] After the crash, he drives out into the desert for
Christ-like, solitary contemplation. Stopping by the roadside, he
spits into the dust and molds the sand into a paste, forming himself
into a new man in the manner of God's creation of Adam. Remaining incommunicado for more than a day, he is eventually tracked
down by the FBI and coaxed out of his motel room dressed only in
a sheet, like Lazarus called forth from the tomb. This miraculous
return from the dead has also been suggested earlier, when Max
checks into a hotel near the crash site. Examining his naked body
after he has been baptized and reborn by a shower, he discovers a
wound to his ribs on the right side, which matches the wound
Christ received on the cross. The addition of the detail of this
wound, not found in Yglesias's novel, represents an elaboration of
Max's messianic aura in Weir's film. On his arrival back home, Max
throws the ineffectual psychologist Dr. Perlman (John Turturro)
and the litigious lawyer Brillstein out of his apartment in an echo
of Jesus' expulsion of the merchants from the temple. When Max
walks down the aisle of the plane to join Byron in the moments before impact, he lays hands on and offers silent comfort to his fellow
passengers: a reassuring benediction for those he appears to know
will survive, and a regretful compassion for those about to die.

However, the circle of light also comes to symbolize Max's entrapment as he is forced to repeat his brush with death to reinstate
his alienation from those around him. When he opens the door to
the FBI agents, the harsh, intruding daylight on his face is a fitting
accompaniment to their demands for an explanation of his conduct. Again, a structural frame represents a conceptual or philosophical divide between the agents and Max, echoing the framing
through doors and windows, redolent of misapprehension or prejudice, in *Wave, The Plumber,* and *Green Card*. Forced to flee from re-

porters outside his home, Max is prompted to walk across a free-way by the reflection of sunlight on the base of a tramp's can of drink. The lights of a passing car illuminate one side of his face as he climbs into his car, before crashing it into a wall to prove to Carla (Rosie Perez) that she could not have saved her son's life by holding him in her lap. Ironically, this act frees Carla from her alienating grief and guilt. She returns to life and urges Max to do likewise.

Max's repeated encounters with mortal danger (both to his physical existence and his preferred but fragile solipsism) also are marked by intimidating associations of spirituality. His gaze fixes on the name badge of the waitress ("Faith") who brings him the first taste of potentially fatal strawberries. The symbol of an out-stretched, apostolic palm appears defamiliarized as a warning light on a pedestrian crossing, just before Max walks heedlessly through the freeway traffic. In these episodes, the religious allusions suggest the challenge to God as much as to secular conformity that Max's behavior articulates. The change between novel and film in Max's pronouncement after crossing the highway—from "They want to kill me . . . but they can't"[17] to "You want to kill me, but you can't," endows his actions with the same overreaching pride that precedes Allie Fox's fall. This tone also is echoed in Truman's successful con-frontation with his own creator. When the producer/director Christof (Ed Harris) summons a storm to thwart Truman's escape by boat, he responds defiantly, "Is that the best you can do? You're going to have to kill me!" The "mast cam" shot of Truman, prostrate on the deck after the storm, produces a graphic parallel to the overhead shot of Max lying prone beside a flagpole after crossing the lanes of traffic.

Both Allie and Max, while affirming their own preeminence and supposed invulnerability, acknowledge God's existence by de-fault through the zeal of their challenges to him. Max's attempts to distract Carla from her guilt focus on its religious source: Her de-vout Catholicism cannot explain the need for her son's death but does furnish the logic and rituals of her self-recrimination. The essence of Carla's belief and Max's loss of faith is articulated in the sequence showing their visit to the Church of Saints Peter and Paul. In trying to convince her that her son's death is not willed or perpetrated by God (in the same way that he strove to rationalize his own father's death in his youth), Max reveals his own, barely concealed vulnerability:

> Max: "If it makes no sense, if life and death just happen, then there's no reason to do anything."
> Carla: "There's no reason to love."
> Max: "What?"
> Carla: "There's no reason to love."

Unknowingly, Carla touches on the source of Max's regret and the obstacle to his hope, in his realizations that there can be no emotional connection without obligation, nor any salvation without the love of others. The evasion of their connections and emotional responsibilities does not return Carla and Max to a solitary existence supported by its own individual meaning, but isolates them in an asocial, disconnected state essentially devoid of all meaning.

By the time the intentional car crash takes place, Max's and Carla's isolation has become barren rather than liberating. The slow motion that portrayed Max's omniscient observation of the crash site has been used subsequently to emphasize his anxiety in the ruck of reporters outside his home pressing him for his story and for Carla's anguish at the sight and smell of another mother and her child. The safe haven of Max's car, from which he and Carla have observed the lifeless populace, becomes a site of helpless estrangement when Carla's guilt causes her to break down and Max to crash the car to save her. Crashing the car and breaching its private space coincides with Carla's release from guilt. Since she has recovered, Max's plea that they could still "disappear" from life's constraints when she visits him in the hospital appears naive to her. Max's solitude, in death, near-death or true life, is now complete. His experience has shown him "the meanness" of the world and convinced him that "to practice resignation" and "to live what was not life" are trivial and insincere, yet existing alone as a "ghost" is equally soulless and futile.

While Max's urges to remain anonymous and even disappear hark back to the longings for escape expressed by many of Weir's characters (especially by the vanishing schoolgirls and Sara's death in *Picnic* and the suicide of Neil in *Dead Poets*), the consistent urges to evade or abdicate from socially imposed roles are given a compositional as well as psychological motivation in *Fearless* through the examination of near-death experience. In reexamining the process and significance of his life to date, Max interrogates the meaning of his former existence and seeks a more fulfilling relevance in the present. Rather than being simply a series of anti-social acts, Max's disruptive behavior (his automatic telling of the truth, indulgence of a second childhood in a toy store, unexpected twirl with Carla in the mall in an echo of John Book's and Rachel's scandalous dance in the barn, his interruption of the Thanksgiving dinner) represents challenges to the meanings proposed and inculcated by others.[18] The sequence in the mall, which immediately precede Carla's release by the crash, appears as a structural parallel to the church scenes. The mall is a focus for secular meanings (based on the economics of consumption and banal family activities, which Max and Carla observe from a distance) that are juxtaposed with the religious rituals and iconography viewed in the church. In both locations, Max opposes or ironizes the dominant creed, suggesting the non-existence of God and buying Christmas presents for the dead.

Paradoxically, the awakening to Max's sense of his own mortality that is occasioned by the crash leads to the rejection of certain meanings to life and the reaffirmation of the need for others:

> The human being seems to require meaning . . . individuals facing death are able to live "better" lives, live with fullness and zest, if they are possessed of a purpose. We apparently need absolutes—firm ideals to which we can aspire and guidelines by which to steer our lives. Yet an existential concept of freedom . . . posits that the only true absolute is that there are no absolutes. An existential position holds that the world is contingent—that is, everything that is could as well have been otherwise; that human beings constitute themselves, their world, and their situation within that world; that there exists no "meaning," no grand design in the universe, no guidelines for living other than those the individual creates.[19]

The story of Max's and Carla's existence after the crash and their behavioral responses to the experience of the disaster follow the pattern of psychopathological symptoms of and defenses against a loss of life meaning detailed by Irvin Yalom. The individual's sudden grasp of his own mortality, his insuperable isolation, and the insignificance of the relationships and activities that occupy life in the face of an all-consuming death prompt a plethora of self-defensive measures. Max's characterization and development through *Fearless* manifest these obstacles and their cures in a way that, ironically but revealingly, perpipheralizes the role of the therapist Dr. Perlman, who is ostensibly responsible for the well-being and recovery of the survivors.

Max's decision to isolate himself in the aftermath of the crash is not so much a reaction as a realization of enduring, existential isolation:

> Individuals are often isolated from others and parts of themselves, but underlying these splits is an even more basic isolation that belongs to existence—an isolation that persists despite the most gratifying engagement with other individuals. . . . Existential isolation refers to an unbridgeable gulf between oneself and any other being. It refers, too, to an isolation even more fundamental—a separation between the individual and the world.[20]

The isolation Max creates after the crash forms a personal representation of the pervasive isolation that preexists that transformative event, vindicating its interpretation as a trigger rather than simply a trauma in its own right. In comparison, David Burton's dreams of the destructive wave expose a personal lack of fulfillment coterminous with the inadequacies and inequalities of non-Aboriginal society, which the heralded apocalypse will redress. The perception and invulnerability that seem to distinguish Max's messianic state after the crash can be interpreted as the first indications of his self-protective, psychopathological response, which disguises the anxiety provoked by the onslaught of meaninglessness. The belief in one's own "specialness,"[21] a sense of personal inviolability based on the denial of the threat of death, is accompanied in Max's case by compulsive heroism, expressed through repeated, deliberate confrontations with the fear of death to defeat and deny its power. However, what is proved by these rituals of disavowal is that he is "afraid of nothing because he, like all of us" is really "afraid of nothingness."[22]

The activities that Max undertakes in subsequent weeks to establish a new meaning in life follow the established patterns of self-defensive behavior enacted to disguise or distract from death anxiety.[23] In his care for Carla and the other survivors, Max displays altruism; the creativity of his profession (architecture) is redirected toward obsessive work on his own paintings; the trip to Oakland and the shopping excursion in the mall suggest a hedonistic indulgence. All these actions, along with Max's justification of his conduct to Laura, are related to the goal of self-actualization, the full achievement of his personal potential. However, the way back lies in self-transcendence, a (re)application to the obligation of relationships in place of a narcissistic insistence on the primacy of the needs of the self. This necessitates a recognition of the innate value of the relationship and the partner rather than simply their use value as bulwarks against isolation and anxiety:

> The problem of relationship is a problem of fusion-isolation. On the one hand, one must learn to relate to another without giving way to the desire to slip out of isolation by becoming part of that other. But one must also learn to relate to another without reducing the other to a tool, a defense against isolation. . . . Caring is reciprocal. To the extent one truly "turns toward the other," one is altered. To the extent one brings the other to life, one can also become more fully alive.[24]

Having previously cut himself off from his wife inside their apartment (by working on his images of vortices and eyes, epitomized by Goldsworthy's *Pebbles Around a Hole* and Bosch's *Ascent into the Empyream*), Max returns home from the hospital to ask her to "save" him. His earlier neglect of her need of him is replaced by renewed recognition of his dependence and of their interdependence in marriage and life. Laura's rapid action prevents Max's death when his allergy to strawberries, which had been nullified by his loss of fear, reappears with near-fatal results. The return to the crash (and the first appearance of these images of it) suggests how time has stopped for Max as it did for those on the Rock in *Picnic*. The visions of the mortal terror of the crash, released at last by his acceptance of the return of fear alongside meaning, are intercut with Laura's efforts to save him, accompanied by Henryk Gorecki's elegiac Symphony No.3 ("Symphony of Sorrowful Songs"). Like *Picnic*'s inclusion of the melancholia of the "Emperor" over the final scenes, the tone of mourning here is complex.

Fearless Jeff Bridges (US 1993)
Picture from the Ronald Grant Archive

Max's sympathy for the other passengers in the crash scenes is balanced by Laura's fear of bereavement in the present, but it conversely may be extended to Max's saddened resumption of normal life. The horrific images of the crash form Max's narrative; his absence from Dr. Perlman's therapy session, in which other survivors narrate their experiences to share and interpret them, means that the subjectivity of those images is preserved even while their significance (in precipitating Max's isolation and redefining his need for Laura) is focused in Laura's redemptive action. Max is seen in a center of light, in a nightmarish vortex formed by the dark tunnel of the wrecked fuselage, and he seems set to leave earthly cares forever until called back by Laura's love. The conclusion of the film omits the novel's insistence on the reimposition of fear alongside obligation ("I'm alive," he rejoiced. "I'm alive. And I'm afraid."[25]), but the film's juxtaposition of Max's salvation and the horror of the crash emphasizes the vulnerability and sanctity of the sources of meaning within life.

The untenability of moral and emotional freedom outside society dooms Max's attempt to abandon his relationships and responsibilities. Like Phil Connors, the cynical weatherman forced to reexamine his life in *Groundhog Day* (Harold Ramis, 1993), Max discovers that an irresponsible life is also a fruitless and meandering one. At once freed from responsibility and imprisoned by mundanity in the endless repetition of one joyless day, Phil embarks on a spree of carefree debauchery before being chastened by a Capraesque realization of true worth in the self-transcendence of a caring and considerate life. This lesson is inculcated through self-reflexive means, in the repetition of the day through the replaying of scenes and dialogue and in varied intertextual reference. Phil's heartless manipulation of his female co-worker earns him repeated slaps in the face which recall the rehearsals in *Day For Night* (Francois Truffaut, 1973), and his suicide attempts mimic the drive over the cliff in *Thelma and Louise* (Ridley Scott, 1991) and the fall from the clock tower in *Vertigo* (Alfred Hitchcock, 1958). Phil is transformed by living one day repeatedly until he has perfected his part in it and improved his character with numerous skills and qualities. Having entered the rural town as a "glass-is-half-empty kinda guy," Phil leaves it (and is only allowed to leave it) as an optimist and humanitarian, wiser than his years.

Max does not have an alternative "wonderful life" to discover, and his return to living is more ambiguous. His loss of freedom and selfhood may be spiritual and debilitating, like that of John Book, John Keating, Billy Kwan, and Irma, unable to disappear and returned unwillingly from the Rock. However, the transformation apparent in Max on being reunited with Laura brings the conclusion of *Fearless* closer to a conventional Hollywood ending than the preceding action has suggested, or any previous Weir film has ventured.

The Truman Show maintains and extends the existential questioning and self-reflexive characteristics of *Fearless* through its concentration on an isolated individual, who is subject to others' demands but who seeks individual meaning. The extrapolation from the stylistic and thematic consistency of Weir's 1970s films in *Fearless* is clearly discernible in *Truman*. Where *Fearless* evokes *Wave*, *Truman* exhibits echoes of *Michael* (in Truman's "teenager" rebellion against patriarchal control), *Cars* (in the depiction of the externally controlled community, based on and bound by a secret, evocative of 1950s science-fiction films), and *Homesdale* (1971) (in the portrayal of an experiment in exploitative control, perpetrated on an ignorant and defenseless individual). The extension of Weir's allusive and intertextual style to encompass this conglomeration of self-referential intimations suggests a reinforcement of the authorial signature within what is nonetheless a high-profile and high-budget studio project.

The setting of *Truman* in the near-future may legitimize its allusions to previous science-fiction films, but it also underlines the tone of nostalgia evident in "The Truman Show" itself. Like the "classic" series "Pleasantville," Christof's 24-hour docu-soap affirms traditional, conservative values even while it functions as a modern technical and commercial exercise. Just as the exploration of Cold War conservatism in *Dead Poets* connected with the political retrenchment of the 1980s, so the (re)creation of an idyllic 1950s community in Seahaven includes social observation within its reflexive quotation:

> The passersby circulate there with the awkward and falsely nonchalant gait of extras in an old B-movie. Their clothes, their haircuts, the women's makeup are a slightly exaggerated version of 1950s fashions . . . the film revives the paranoia of that period, but also reorients it. Truman recalls the hero of *The Invasion of the Body Snatchers* . . . the reference to Don Siegel's film is particularly obvious in the scene of the hunt organized by the actors and extras in order to find Truman to prevent him from leaving.[26]

While the film may function as a satire on contemporary television and its audience, its criticism of American parochialism is equally apparent. The newspaper headlines and advertisements (querying the need for travel, asking "Who Needs Europe?" and confirming Seahaven as the "Best Place on Earth" in which to live) that intrude into Truman's world as a subliminal, controlling element simultaneously recall the declamatory statements on view in *Michael* and *Cars* and reflect upon an abiding American isolationism. These statements are answered by the placards and slogans seen in Lauren/Sylvia's flat, related to her campaign to free Truman: "Abolish Media Manipulation," "Who's Next, Our Children?" Alongside such commentary upon general attitudes, Weir also draws an analogy between the attractiveness of Seahaven's apparently homespun but essentially manufactured insularity and the spread of walled estates in America during the 1990s.[27] In this respect, the interrogation of nostalgia and critique of conformity that dynamizes *Truman* operates in the same way as Weir's other treatments of disillusionment with and distance from the establishment:

> It latches onto the same baby-boomer nostalgia so many other of this summer's releases play to. Anti-utopia in *The Truman Show* is all about the same "little boxes" Pete Seeger sang of, and Carrey's discovery of self is really just another version of the sensitive-boy-escapes-oppressive-suburbia trope that filmmakers of the hippie generation return to time and again. . . . [With *Fearless*] *The Truman Show* can also be seen as an attempt to re-envision the perhaps simpler problems of the '60s in a future context.[28]

The critique of both the past and the present via the nostalgic evocation of the media is also at the center of *Pleasantville*. The opening of Gary Ross's film presents first a sound montage and then an image montage of contemporary television programming: news reports, talk shows, sports, advertising, and evangelism. This channel-hopping effect is succeeded by an extended trailer for the "TV Time" network, which only plays "old stuff in black-and-white" that is "fun for the whole family." The featured marathon screening of episodes of the "Pleasantville" show foregrounds its concentration of "family values" (the patriarch greeting his (house)wife on his return from work, the abundance of home cooking, and "safe sex" symbolized by a shot of twin beds). The show offers a nostalgic evocation of a non-existent idyllic past, which is almost inseparable from a reactionary distrust of the present. This is reemphasized by a sequence (reminiscent of the series of classes seen in *Dead Poets*) in which teachers present their students with depressing predictions for the future, in terms of their employability, the threat of HIV infection, and the consequences of global warming. When two 1990s teenagers, David and Jennifer, are transported into the world of "Pleasantville," their influence and experiences appear to be of dubious value. Jennifer's liberated attitudes play havoc with the existing characters' repressed sexuality, and David's accidental deviations from character also throw the town's unchanging routine into turmoil. As a result, the monochrome world of the preferred past is transformed into technicolor.

The show's image of a staid 1950s community is invaded by the 1960s culture of music, cars, and fashions, provoking an authoritarian backlash of repression and book burning. The color that invades the show's landscape seems initially to be precipitated by the release and acknowledgment of sex (in David's and Jennifer's mother Betty as well as in the younger generation), but subsequently has associations of passion and commitment, which replace both the conformity of the town's population and the former apathy of the insurgents from the future. Jennifer discovers that the pleasures of the mind outstrip those of the body. David, who has empathized with Betty as a cult fan (we see him anticipating her lines), gains a sense of purpose and commitment when he defends her from "colored" prejudice. The mayor of Pleasantville, who is depicted through low-angle shots and low-key lighting reminiscent of film noir, arrests David and Betty's lover Bill. They are subjected to Pleasantville's first trial, which, in an echo of HUAC, is deemed not to require lawyers. However, the mayor's impassioned hatred of the spread of color prompts his own spontaneous coloration, and the changes to the town become ubiquitous and irrevocable.

When the chance to return to their real lives becomes available, Jennifer prefers to stay and go to college within the world of the show. Back in his own home, David counsels his divorced, depressed mother in the same way he reassured Betty within the show. The ambiguity of the effect and meaning of "color" within "Pleasantville" (as a allegory of civil rights unrest and youth demonstrations against the establishment, but also as a representation of hidden feelings or opinions of every political shade) is carried over into a narrative uncertainty within the continuing show. In the final scenes, Betty sits on a park bench with her husband George and her lover Bill, and none of the characters can tell what will happen next. While the presence of the teenagers from the 1990s has forced the evolution of Pleasantville in parallel with that of American history (in acknowledging tension, conflict, and prejudice), the conservatism of the preferred past also has affected the modern youths (in taming Jennifer and in elevating David as a sensitive patriarchal figure supplanting the ineffectual or absent fathers in both the fictional, idyllic and factual, dysfunctional families). The repressive conservatism hidden within nostalgic and idyllic media representations is also imposed on Truman via the transmission of the "much-loved classic, *Show Me the Way to Go Home*, a hymn of praise to small town life," on the day he first becomes suspicious of his surroundings.

The inversion of values associated with female characters in *Pleasantville* (Jennifer's sexuality controlled by education, Betty's subservience overturned by sexuality) is comparable to the conflicting associations of female characters in the Weir canon. Women are seen to function not only as the symbols and guardians of establishment order (in the examples of Mrs. Appleyard in *Picnic*, Annie Burton in *Wave*, Jill in *The Plumber*, Brontë in *Green Card*, and Meryl Burbank in *Truman*) but also as the embodiment of escape and subversion of the establishment's power (Miranda in *Picnic*, and Lauren/Sylvia in *Truman*). Rachel Lapp in *Witness* may be seen to bridge or merge these functions. Meryl (Laura Linney) appears as a Stepford-like wife in her conservative costuming and robotic performance, but she acts as the embodiment rather than the victim of patriarchal authority. Lauren/Sylvia (Natasha McElhone) represents a visual echo of Miranda but also evinces a similar preternatural knowledge of the world's workings. Miranda's gnomic utterance, "Everything begins and ends at exactly the right time and place," suggests an understanding of and an ability to transcend a corporeal destiny in adolescence and a social destiny dictated to Victorian womanhood. Sylvia's knowledge of the show's imperatives of scripting and commercialism lies behind her seizing of the day with Truman ("if we don't go now it won't happen") and her efforts to derail the preferred narrative once she has been cut from the cast. Her activism is discernible even before her departure, as the slogan on her badge ("How's it going to end?") posits a moral, philosophical, and by extension political question to the show's manipulation of its star's and its viewers' lives.

The repressive control exerted by a script appears indistinguishable from a conservative and conformist conception of social order. Mrs. Appleyard's valorization of an unchanging England is echoed in the mayor of Pleasantville's insistence on a "non-changist" view of history in the school curriculum and in the repetitious schedules of dialogue, blocking, and even weather in Seahaven. Such controls are overthrown by unpredictable, individual action: unacknowledged or inarticulate desires in Miranda, David, and Truman:

> The only dramatic incidents worthy of the name . . . don't exist in the shooting script but are brought into it by Truman himself in his efforts to escape from the program's rarefied, sterile world. The show's utter tedium (one might say in its defense that it mimics the monotony of life itself?) allows us to feel superior to the huge herd of viewers who enjoy it.[29]

The restriction of the show's controlling vision is suggested by the consistency of composition that characterizes the show. The framing of the innumerable cameras within Truman's environment is assumed by the film at significant points to stress the observation and containment of Truman within Seahaven. However, this form of conspicuous framing is not maintained for every shot in the film. This inconsistency implies at once an observation beyond that of Christof's production (belonging to the film's and auteur's narrative, which displays the same tension between the protagonist's desires and the genre's demands seen in *Witness* and *Year*) and Truman's evasion of observation in the inauguration of his own narrative.

The iris of the camera's view appears as Truman greets his neighbors on the way to work on Day 10,909. The camera's zoom in on the star's face to frame his catchphrase continues this isolation of Truman within the frame. He is restricted to a small, shadowed sector of the frame by the camera's viewing him from the dashboard of his car and by the camera's observing his secret attempts to trace Sylvia through directory inquiries at his office desk. When Truman discusses the sighting of his father with his mother, the iris appears to frame him, but his point-of-view shots of her manipulative answers are unframed. The iris also appears in the shots showing Truman's and Sylvia's surreptitious departure from the school library and their escape across the parking lot to the beach, as well as in the "mast cam" shots of Truman battling the storm on his yacht. Just as the circle of light in *Fearless* initially suggests Max's liberation but comes to signify his entrapment, the graphic echoes of the iris, at first associated with Truman's objectification, also harbor suggestions of escape. The golf ball he uses to locate "Fiji" for Marlon (Noah Emmerich) suggests his desire for other worlds, and Sylvia's bracelet, decorated with jade globes, promises the existence of many beyond the studio.

In a similar way, the addition of other frames also marks the space for observation and a countering opportunity for spontaneous performance. A car wing mirror, recalling the one that trapped Guy in *Year*, moves anxiously to keep Truman in frame when he departs from his schedule during the morning rush hour. The camera behind Truman's bathroom mirror, which combines the iris with a square frame, records his impromptu sketches (detailing heroism in exploration on earth and in space). Under scrutiny, these improvisations reveal his desire for escape, foreshadow his departure from the show, and unwittingly suggest the implications for the viewers: "I'm not going to make it. . . . You're going to have to go on without me." Truman's subversion of the frames, placed around him in these examples, prompts a reevaluation of the key emotive sequences that ostensibly make use of the myriad observing cameras within his world but that may reveal the realization of his own narrative—of escape.

The flashback sequence showing the on-screen demise of Truman's father features the framing attributable to the cameras on the boat and in the water. However, this sequence is not identified as a retrospective sequence within the broadcast, as are the recollections of the meetings with Sylvia (prompted by Truman's discovery of her jacket in the chest in his basement). The first image of the flashback (of the boat setting out to sea) is unframed and initially unplaced as a single cutaway from Truman sitting alone on the beach. Only the subsequent addition of the show's images (with irises) and dialogue reveals the significance of the sequence. When linked to the orchestration of the later scenes of Truman's reunion with his father, this first flashback depicts an imposed emotion, a manipulated memory that has served to debilitate and control its star. The first image may be construed as a subjective recollection, but the irised images encapsulate the show's narrative, so it appears that there is no gap between the show's rerunning and its star's memory.

The flashback concerning Lauren/Sylvia again mixes framed and unframed images, to a differing effect. Truman's discovery of the jacket is followed by a cut to the waitresses in the "Truman Bar." They watch the wall-mounted screen, as the image of Truman in the basement dissolves to be replaced by the flashback to college. When Truman first sees Lauren, he is seen in an irised close-up while she is unframed, intimating that the shots of her are subjective. When Meryl is introduced clumsily, she occupies the irised image in an illustration of the show's preferred narrative, and, in a similar way, a soft-focus iris surrounds nearly all the shots composing the dance sequence, in which Lauren again catches Truman's attention but is spirited away. The iris is present for their escape from the library and for their descent to the beach but is absent during their conversation until the arrival of Lauren's "father," when a button cam records their forced separation. While they talk on the beach and in the library, however, and for the crucial close-ups of Lauren's badge and her eyes, the absence of the frame suggests the images belong subjectively to Truman, and they initiate his narrative.

Ironically, it is Truman's unforeseen interventions that create alternative and greater pleasures for the show's audience in place of its planned, bland certainties. His stolen moments on the beach with Lauren/Sylvia make it onto the show's "Greatest Hits" tape, and the expedient reintroduction of his father, Truman's disappearance from the basement, and his near-death in the storm at sea all act to raise the show's viewer ratings. Christof's orchestration of the reunion between father and son, as a tour-de-force of emotional manipulation through editing and musical accompaniment, requires the recollection of the producer's justification of the show's format in the behind-the-scenes documentary that forms the opening sequence:

> We've become bored with watching actors giving us phony emotions. We're tired of pyrotechnics and special effects. While the world he inhabits is in some respects counterfeit, there's nothing fake about Truman himself. . . . It isn't always Shakespeare, but it's genuine. It's a life.

Christof's comments are echoed and qualified by two leading members of the cast. Meryl remarks that the show is "a lifestyle" and "a noble and blessed life," while Truman's best friend Marlon insists that 'nothing is fake—merely controlled."

A question remains over what pleasures the show might offer and what emotions it manages to incite. Truman's genuine emotion in the reunion with his father may represent an authentic performance and unalloyed appeal, but it is facilitated (or exaggerated) by the show's representational mechanisms. Arguably, Christof's own ecstatic response (and that of his technical crew) belies that of the viewing public, as simply the recognition of artistry within the fulfillment of the expectations of narrative:

> In viewing films we play-act emotions, especially those we share with certain characters. . . . Acting as if one is experiencing an emotion, in a pretense play controlled by the film, also explains why viewers find sad or gruesome scenes so satisfying: these scenes make one act the emotion of fear. . . . [T]he institute of fiction is so firmly and massively established in our culture that total deception is all but impossible. Everyone is familiar with the signs and conventions of fiction, as well as the framework within which it is presented.[30]

This manipulation of emotion for maintenance (of the star's presence and the audience's loyalty) is based on a deliberately and recognizably clichéd soap-opera trope—the labored reintroduction of a lost character after a period of alleged amnesia. The emotion that the show's audience enjoys is therefore both play-acted and vicariously experienced and acknowledged as a formulaic, fictional convention that is nonetheless renewed with (and new to) Truman. It is indicative of Christof's conservatism that a disruptive event (the reappearance of an old cast member) and Truman's suspicions should be contained by a narrative cliché, a form of textual orthodoxy.

The extent to which Christof's control can be maintained through the furnishing of such familiar pleasures is tested by Truman's rejection of the "controlled" world and the audience's support for his efforts to escape. The acknowledgment that the show's first break in transmission and the resulting blank, titular card actually gain higher ratings underlines the commitment of viewers to the continuing and developing narrative. Even if the story is Truman's rather than Christof's, it remains recognizable and conventional (soap opera transformed into swashbuckler, familial conformity into individualistic rebellion) and, ultimately, resolvable in traditional terms (a journey into, through, and beyond the sunset). The scenes of viewers' reactions to Truman's disappearance from the screen, which range from communal rejoicing to apparent frustration, may be read in contradictory ways. The annoyance of the viewer in his bathtub might validate Truman's victory over narrative expectations in enforcing closure upon an otherwise endless, soap-operatic narrative. Conversely, the celebrations in the Truman Bar may reflect satisfaction with a decidedly conventional happy ending rather than support for the successful subversion of genre demands. Weir recognized the dubiety of the audience's relationship, and pleasure, in an interview: "Viewers have forgotten Truman's not aware, or else they've blurred the line in terms of all the other characters, believing *they're* [Weir's emphasis] real."[31] This ambiguity, in the nature of the conventional or oppositional pleasures to be derived from the show and its conclusion, persists to the film's last shot, which is not of Truman outside the studio nor of his reunion with Sylvia, but of two erstwhile viewers wondering "what else is on." Earlier, these fans, a pair of garage attendants, have discussed their dissatisfaction with the coy and hackneyed representation of sex scenes in the show: Their disappointment implies a reflection on the determined absence of graphic violence and sex scenes from Weir's films, as noted in relation to *Witness*. Their reaction to the end of the show (which even its star acknowledges as the swan song to a performance, through the repetition of his catchphrase), reemphasizes the conventionality of its characterization and conclusion, even when it is ad-libbed.

The satiric potential of *The Truman Show*, in offering a critique of media manipulation, commercialization, and consumerism, is more latent than that of Weir's films of the 1970s. Its comedic structure and its star casting undercut some of its darker, dystopian intensities. Weir discussed the exhaustive redrafting process of the screenplay, begun by Weir and Niccol in 1995, in an interview. The "Kafkaesque" nature of Niccol's original script was in part based on its setting in an ersatz New York, redolent of the paranoia of an episode of *The Twilight Zone*.[32] For Weir, the logic of Christof's vision demanded an alternative reading:

> I said no producer would build New York! Also, it wouldn't be an ideal community. Why would you create something that had all the problems of our world? Why not build an idealized world? That led eventually to [Seahaven], to a pristine community created in the style of the last century. . . . [T]his would be the way people would like to live, almost like a holiday brochure really, an ideal island somewhere. And every-

thing was for sale, everything from clothing to furniture to the houses themselves could be purchased in the mail order catalogue.[33]

The film's satire of the media and its critique of consumerism begin with the "documentary" footage shot with the producer and actors, which introduces the show as Day 10,909 dawns. The ironies of the documentary footage earn comparison with the mock-ad prologue to *Cars*. The background information provided in the documentary is extended later through flashbacks, trailers, and Christof's interview for "Tru-Talk," another television show that responds to and increases the popularity of "The Truman Show." Since it is transmitted without advertising breaks, "The Truman Show" relies exclusively on product placement for revenue. The inclusion of this detail may also reflect ironically upon the casting and quoting of brand names in contemporary feature films. Christof's vision embodies a tripartite merchandising of both the abstract and tangible aspects of Seahaven. The show's costumes and consumer items are available for sale but carry with them an ideological value combining aspiration and nostalgia: the consumption of the artefacts implies the assumption of the lifestyle. However, even as these items and their connotations are retailed outward from the show to its audience, simultaneously they are sold inward to Truman himself. He is addressed (by Meryl's and Marlon's product placements) as the intended consumer of the items his own presence endorses.

Weir's characterization of Christof, after the image of couturiers like Armani, Lagerfeld, and Versace, intent on creating goods and labels from which to fabricate an identity, encapsulates the control he seeks to exert both locally and globally:

> They have enormous influence on the world, and a very particular self-view, as if they were great artists and designers of more than just clothing. . . . Their "vision" is implied each time they come out with a new line.[34]

At the same time, Christof's and Truman's names invite allegorical and parabolical readings of the narrative. In a similar way to *Fearless*, *Truman* makes numerous, overt biblical allusions through its imagery. Truman awakens to his trials and tasks in his thirtieth year, and his equation with the Messiah is reinforced by his immaculate conception (as "the first child to have been legally adopted by a corporation"), his survival of the sea storm, and his walk on water prior to ascension through the studio's painted sky. Similarly, Christof's cueing of the sun and his raising and calming of the storm equates him with the God of the Old Testament, and Truman with Adam, Noah, and Jonah. In addition, the film can be interpreted via comparisons with other spiritual texts, such as Greek myths and Buddhist fables.[35]

The commercialism and nostalgia of Christof's project coalesce in the shadowless and saturated appearance of Seahaven, similar to the idealized images of television advertising but also reminiscent of the work of Norman Rockwell.[36] The purposeful mimicry of Rockwell's visual style provides another example of conscious imitation and quotation within mise-en-scène, and coincides with the quaint mannerisms of speech and dress exhibited by the island's residents. Rockwell's influence is also discernible in the mise-en-scène of *Pleasantville*, particularly in the film's satiric depiction of familial, social, spiritual, and political ideals portrayed unproblematically in Rockwell's *The Four Freedoms* (1944).

The critique offered by *Truman* of American culture and con-

The Truman Show   Jim Carrey   (US 1998)
Picture from the Ronald Grant Archive

servatism is perhaps attributable to the outsider's view and "Commonwealth sense of humor"[37] shared by the Australian Weir, New Zealander Niccol, Canadian Carrey, and Briton Peter Biziou, *Truman's* cinematographer. However, Weir also gave consideration to the symbolic equation of Seahaven Island with the Australian continent as another isolated refuge for a conservative (Anglophone) culture.[38] This analogy reconnects *Truman* with the lineage of Australian rite-of-passage films featuring naive and sheltered protagonists, from *Michael* to *Summerfield* (Ken Hannam, 1977) up to *Bad Boy Bubby* (Rolf de Heer, 1993).

The recognition of the Australian-ness, as well as the authorship, of *Truman* can be confirmed by the stylistic (and primarily visual) referencing of Weir's 1970s films. The symbol of the revolving door, which marks Michael's final refusal to conform, reappears as the entrance to Truman's office building. On Day 10,911, following his interception of stage-management instructions on his car radio, Truman also refuses to cross the threshold of his workplace, traveling around in the door twice before exiting to the street again. (Again this unpremeditated act causes a breakdown in the show's framing, as Truman is relocated outside the building by an unsteady zoom from a distant camera). Another echo of *Michael* is visible in the representation (and perpetuation) of Truman's family role through photographs. Just as Michael appears in and is contained by family pictures on display, so Truman's disruptions are answered by an evening spent reviewing photo albums with Meryl and Truman's mother. However, also as with Michael, these pictures ultimately reveal the invalidity of the memories they contain: Truman is puzzled by the picture of the prop department's scaled-down version of Mount Rushmore that he "visited" as a child and notices that Meryl has her fingers crossed in their wedding photos.

It is through the fashioning of his own image, as well as the crafting of his own narrative, that Truman's secret subversion of the show is expressed. Hidden behind his desk portrait of Meryl, Truman keeps a composite image of Sylvia, which he has assembled from fragments of magazine ads. This accumulation of remembered details (hair, eyes, and lips culled from different images) evokes the fetishistic imagination that attempted to recall the lost Miranda in *Picnic*. The montage represents Truman's attempt to overcome the disappearance and loss of the prescient girl who first instilled an awareness of his world's vagaries and duplicity. In re-crafting a face he can no longer see, which encapsulates his rejec-tion of the "reality with which he has been presented," Truman conducts his own Kuleshovian experiment, bent on creating a rela-tionship, identity, space, and time that otherwise, within the terms of his world, do not and cannot exist.[39] Ironically, this graphic counter to the show's principles, its preferred narrative, and its conservative, conformist ideology is fashioned from advertise-ments. Truman's riposte to having lived as an advertisement for everything (family life, marriage, consumerism), which he has ex-perienced simply as the containment, abuse, and debilitation of thought, choice, and action within the establishment, is to subvert everything through the disassembly and reassembly of convention-alized images in an order of personal significance. Redressing Sylvia's loss (in a way that Miranda's loss can never be compen-sated) anticipates Truman's successful rebellion and his own final disappearance from view.

Despite their differences in tone and success, *Fearless* and *The Truman Show* are united in theme, style, and authorship. While their upbeat endings still challenge expectation and cannot be classed as conventional (ambiguity still remains in Max's return to life and marriage, and the deliberate excision of scenes outside Tru-man's studio[40] deny us views of Truman and Sylvia reunited), these films continue the integration of Weir's style with genre material noted in relation to *Witness* and *Green Card*. The commercial and critical success of *Truman* reaffirmed Weir's place within contem-porary Hollywood, and yet its stylistic and thematic unity (with *Fearless* and the films of the 1970s) is equally evident, as is Tru-man's kinship with Weir's other, troubled protagonists: "Do you ever think . . . like your whole life has been building toward some-thing?" Where *Fearless*'s art-cinema style arises from its subjective, psychological concerns, the visual style of *Truman* evinces a com-positional motivation that both mimics television and foregrounds its reflexivity. If *Fearless* represents a full realization of the materi-als behind *The Last Wave*, then *Truman* asserts the assurance with which Peter Weir's signature can be imprinted upon the studio product: "A genre film, a popular film, *The Truman Show* is also, plainly, an auteur film."[41]

Notes

1. Weir discusses the strengths and dangers of Carrey's casting in Paul Kalina, "Designing Visions: Peter Weir and *The Truman Show*," *Cinema Papers*, *127* (1998), pp. 18–22, 56 (p. 19), and Douglas J. Rowe, "The Who, What, When, Weir, and Why of *The Truman Show*" at www.iowaalive.com/showing/movies/film008.htm.

2. Rafael Yglesias, *Fearless* (London: Penguin, 1993), p. 6.

3. Marek Haltof, *Peter Weir: When Cultures Collide* (London: Prentice-Hall, 1996), p. 123.

4. Interview with the author, June 1993.

5. Yglesias, *Fearless*, pp. 111–12.

6. Bob Fisher, "*Fearless* Explores Emotional Aftermath of Fateful Flight," *American Cinematographer*, *74* (1993), pp. 40–51 (p. 41). An alternative text of this interview with Allen Daviau can be found at www.cameraguild.com/interviews/chat_daviau/daviau_fearless.htm.

7. *Ibid.*, pp. 41–2.

8. *Ibid.*, p. 46.

9. Yglesias, *Fearless*, pp. 75–80.

10. Agnes Peck, "Etats seconds: Trois films de Peter Weir," *Positif*, *453* (1998), pp. 25–27 (p. 27) (author's translation).

11. Yglesias, *Fearless*, p. 137.

12. *Ibid.*, p. 39.

13. *Ibid.*, pp. 302–3.

14. *Ibid.*, pp. 211–13.

15. *Ibid.*, p. 300.

16. The religious significance of the light and its representation of the afterlife are discussed in Albert J. Bergesen and Andrew M. Greeley, *God in the Movies* (New Brunswick, N.J.: Transaction, 2000), pp. 19–20.

17. Yglesias, *Fearless*, p. 213.

18. The perception of the protagonists' behavior as irresponsible and the significance of Max's car as a subversive space was suggested in the film's working title, *Joyride*, reported in *Empire*, *42* (1992), p. 21.

19. Irvin D. Yalom, *Existential Psychotherapy* (New York: Basic Books, 1980), pp. 422–23.

20. *Ibid.*, p. 357.

21. *Ibid.*, pp. 117–121.

22. *Ibid.*, p. 122.

23. *Ibid.*, pp. 331–340.

24. *Ibid.*, p. 362, p. 373.

25. Yglesias, *Fearless*, p. 434.

26. Jean-Pierre Coursodon, "*The Truman Show*: Mirages de la vie," *Positif*, *453* (1998), pp. 16–19 (pp. 17–18) (author's translation).

27. Michel Ciment, "Peter Weir: L'image et le reel," *Positif*, *453* (1998), pp. 20–24 (p. 22).

28. Charles Whitehouse, "Bubble Boy," *Sight and Sound*, *8* (1998), pp. 8–10.

29. Coursodon, *Truman*: Mirages," p. 18 (author's translation).

30. Ed S. Tan, *Emotion and the Structure of Narrative Film: Film as an Emotion Machine* (New York: Lawrence Erlbaum, 1996), p. 228.

31. Kalina, "Designing Visions," p. 22.

32. Ciment, "Weir: L'image," p. 20.

33. Kalina, "Designing Visions," p. 20.

34. *Ibid.*, p. 19.

35. Ciment, "Weir: L'image," p. 24.

36. Kalina, "Designing Visions," p. 22.

37. Ciment, "Weir: L'image," p. 22.

38. *Ibid.*, p. 21.

39. Kristin Thompson and David Bordwell, *Film History: An Introduc-tion* (London: McGraw-Hill, 1994), p. 132.

40. Kalina, "Designing Visions," p. 21.

41. Coursodon, "*Truman*: Mirages," p. 16 (author's translation).

The Far Side of the World

Films are, above all, about something, and the question of re-makes and reworkings in the careers of major directors primarily revolves around reconsiderations and restatements of major thematic, ethical, and moral concerns. . . . The fact of authorship, then, the mere tracing of recurring motifs and formal repetitions, is less important than the question of authorship, the questions and issues with which an auteur struggles over the course of a career.[1]

A text does not derive exclusively from an author's individuality; it is replete with usages from elsewhere. It is a texture, a tissue for the articulation and distribution of various social discourses, cultural codes, and image systems. Any new text entails a recuperation of previous texts.[2]

Peter Weir's body of feature film work now spans nearly thirty years and amalgamates the experiences of production within the reemergent Australian film industry of the 1970s and the evolving post-classical cinema of 1980s and '90s Hollywood. Since the flamboyance of *Michael* (1971), Weir's filmmaking has drawn both positive and negative critical attention, but with the release of *Picnic at Hanging Rock* (1975) his place within Australian film history, and his eventual invitation to work in America, were assured. The Gothic and fantasy elements distinguishing his output in Australia, which may have appeared excised from his films of the 1980s, have been reasserted in his most searching, acclaimed, and successful films in America, *Fearless* (1993) and *The Truman Show* (1998). The persistence of thematic concentrations on the oppressive circumstances endured by isolated individuals, the exercise of iniquitous authority, and the intimations of and desires for experience beyond the rational and mundane world, unites Weir's protagonists across an otherwise disparate group of genre films (comedies, thrillers, horror films, period films). While his films remain grounded within genre narrative structures and expectations, their execution (in divergence from convention, the frustration of expectation, and characteristic stylistic expression) connects them strongly with the European art-film tradition and its emphasis upon auteurist structures of meaning interpretable on innumerable individual bases:

> While literary artists may work in non-narrative modes, the cineaste seems condemned to some form of narrative just to rein in the galloping connotations of images.[3]

Weir's filmmaking has charted the development of a highly individual form of narrative, which has often verged on non-narrative in its allusiveness, connotative meanings, and open-endedness. While his stated aspirations are toward a pure narrative craft and mass audience pictures (seemingly inseparable goals within the mainstream Hollywood industry), his work illustrates an evolving idiom of visual expression used to convey a consistent range of themes: liberty and repression, youth and innocence against age and disillusioned knowledge, clashes of culture, and the celebration of unique but unpredictable and inexpressible personal experience. These abiding themes are manifested in recurrent, recognizable stylistic features (the foregrounding and juxtaposition of soundtrack music, constriction of vision within the frame, and emphasis on the imagery and ideology of still photography and other visual art).

This characteristic style, persisting into *Truman*, accompanies patterns of genre imitation, revision, or subversion, based on the western (*The Cars That Ate Paris* [1974], *Witness* [1985], *The Mosquito Coast* [1986]), foreign romance (*The Year of Living Dangerously* [1982]), screwball comedy (*Green Card* [1990]), war film (*Gallipoli* [1981]), thriller (*The Plumber* [1979]), science fiction, disaster, and horror (*The Last Wave* [1977] and *Fearless*) and the European art film (*Picnic* and *Fearless*). *Truman* embodies many of these elements, in its moments of comedy, the paranoia of its conspiracy-thriller undertones, its evocation of invasion-narrative science-fiction film in the images of the dehumanized island population, and its art-film philosophy within a narrative structure indebted to classical Hollywood. Unity of style and consistency of treatment, set against a variety of genre sources, place viewers of Weir's films in several coterminous roles: informed readers of an auteur's art films; respondents to known genre materials in modified forms; and individual interpreters of the "genre" of Peter Weir films, which unites the poles of art film and genre, connotation and narrative. Whereas the formal and industrial operation of genre is founded upon the principle of "regularized variety,"[4] the auteur's manipulation of genre within the pursuit of a personal style produces a varied regularity in interpretation.

This eclectic visual language encourages connotative meanings, enlisting them in the interpretation of the narratives they interrupt. The pictorial compositions of *Picnic*, the Aboriginal mythology of *Wave*, and the religious imagery of *Fearless* and *Truman* point to the films' transcendence of narrative constraint even as the characters struggle to detach themselves from their disconcerting environments. The allure of escape from the restrictive practices of the world (schools, laws, historic events, business, families, life itself) does not hide its impracticality, and all but Weir's most recent protagonists have been singularly incapable of altering their destinies.

Perhaps the widest connotation of Weir's narratives, beyond allusiveness or reflexivity, is the recognition of life outside of their given temporal and spatial limitations. A significant proportion of the films' resonances derive from their unclosed narratives and their protagonists' uncertain futures. From *Michael* onward, they are specific episodes in the protagonists' lives that, through the narratives' open-endedness, can be presumed to continue (and be the focus of speculation) after they end:

> When the celluloid is projected those attending to it will not describe the contents of the projection as merely a jumble of flickering shadows and random sounds. Rather they will describe places, people, events, conversations, moods. If the film takes two hours to run, can we say that there were extra places, people, and events in the universe during those two hours, and that they have now, the projection having ceased, disappeared?[5]

If the allusiveness and unreined connotation of Weir's films may be classed as his most non-narrative characteristics, then his narratives' open-endedness (despite the distancing of a lack of closure being construed as an art-film trait) can be seen as one of his most commercial and illusionist hallmarks. Open-endedness urges the participation and submergence of viewers in the lives of characters, to the point of hypothesizing about their futures.

David Bordwell categorizes the viewing and interpretative acts as based on previous (film and life) experience, which facilitates the erection of expectations and formation of hypotheses as to future diegetic developments.[6] The two sides of Weir's filmmaking, the European auteurist vision and Hollywood genre revision, erode narrative conventions during the film's projection only to provoke hypothetical narrative debate after their inconclusive endings. The art-film trait of unclosed narrative has become a consistent feature of Weir's films, as much part of his audience's expectations as visual and musical stylization, and as such it underlines the unified structural reading expected of the viewers of an auteur's output or a studio's genre piece. The redrafting of *Truman* reflects the persistence of this authorial signature, as Weir explained in an interview:

> At the end of the film, there was a neat tying-up of every aspect of it: you saw the villain, as it were, punished, and you saw Truman with his girlfriend. It had all kinds of stuff going on for ten minutes afterward. I decided in that [last] draft that he shouldn't leave the studio, that it was interesting to [fade] into darkness, and for us to wonder what happened to him.[7]

Arguably, *Fearless* and *Truman* feature two of the most conventional, happy endings in the Weir canon (unions and reunions of heterosexual couples), but sufficient ambiguity remains (in the release of images of the crash in *Fearless*, and in Truman's walk into darkness and uncertainty in *The Truman Show*) for the continuation of the viewer's participation and doubt. While it both foregrounds and undermines the conventional function of closure in narrative, the open-endedness of Weir's films also restates the art cinema's demand for engaged and interrogative viewing:

> Text means Tissue; but where as hitherto we have always taken this tissue as a product, a ready-made veil, behind which lies, more or less hidden, meaning (truth), we are now

emphasizing, in the tissue, the generative idea that the text is made, is worked out in a perpetual interweaving.[8]

From varied artistic influences and national backgrounds (the Australian national cinema movement, the American entertainment film industry, a European cultural base, and contemporary films and filmmakers alongside past models of narrative craft), Weir has created a recognizable, multifaceted, but personal style. He has been responsible for some of the milestones of the Australian revival, producing some establishing texts in Australia and the more unusual (although still predominantly popular and commercially successful) films of contemporary Hollywood. He retains his independence and choice of suitable subjects but maintains a distance from the establishment that furnishes the forum for his "mass audience pictures": "Hollywood is just irrelevant. They just provide the room you play in."[9]

Hollywood represents the textual as well as industrial space in which Weir plays, as evinced by his transformation of well-known genres and the union of their tropes with the particularities of his own style and themes. This tendency, seen in the injection of pessimism into the western in *Cars*, *Witness*, and *Mosquito Coast* and in the disempowerment of the heroes of *Year* and *Dead Poets Society* (1989), reveals an awareness of genre conventions in the filmmaker and the assumption of similar knowledge in the viewer. Discussing the cult-film phenomenon with regard to *Casablanca* (Michael Curtiz, 1942), Umberto Eco analyses the different levels of intertextual and intermedia knowledge required for full readings of films by Woody Allen (which quote scenes and sequences from non-American art films) and Steven Spielberg (which rejuvenate past Hollywood genre cinema). For the former, ignorance of the sources eliminates enjoyment of the intertextual collage; for the latter, popular entertainment is not impaired by (or dependent on) acknowledgment of the antecedent genre. However, *Casablanca*'s "reunion of archetypes" represents an unpremeditated focus of genre and cultural motifs compared with the later films' deliberate intertextual quotation:

> What *Casablanca* does unconsciously, other movies will do with extreme intertextual awareness, assuming also that the addressee is equally aware of their purposes. These are

"postmodern" movies, where the quotation of the topos is recognized as the only way to cope with the burden of our filmic encyclopedic expertise.[10]

Although Spielberg's self-conscious reinvocation of adventure serials in the *Indiana Jones* films is not reliant on comparison with their source, *Year*, often compared to *Casablanca*, recalls specific genre motifs (such as the flight to freedom and enlightenment) while undercutting them simultaneously. Guy's flight from Jakarta is an admission of ignorance and incapability to act heroically within the context of an updated foreign romance. The genre, perhaps the specific film precedent, has been revised in a contemporary filmic and social context, a considerably more complex environment in which pat resolutions and simplification of pertinent issues prove inadequate. The suggestion of a classical source updated in *Year* underlines the way in which many of Weir's genre productions can be as allusions to, revisions of, and commentaries upon the work of the original studio auteurs: *Wave* and *The Plumber* mimic Alfred Hitchcock, *Witness* evokes John Ford, *Dead Poets* and *Truman* suggest George Cukor and Frank Capra, *Year* and *Green Card* recall Howard Hawks, and *Mosquito Coast* can be compared with Orson Welles and John Huston.

Year's recollection of the filmic model and its recourse to a similarly unproblematic conclusion of this narrative and historical drama underline a resignation to the impossibility of such a cure-all in the late twentieth century. *Year* was deemed unsatisfactory as an entertainment film, since it contained references to more than just the subverted genre. In Weir's opinion, such eclectic form is equally important and expressive as multicultural content:

> Some of the more didactic critics asked in their reviews, "What kind of film is this—is it a love story, is it a thriller, is it a political story?" You could say that it unsuccessfully fails to fuse these elements, but to ask why deal with all those elements together, why not choose one of them, reveals a view of life and films that is very different from my own.[11]

Weir's fusion of allusion and narrative and his openness to connotation and context supposedly alien to commercial cinema mark him as a contradictory figure, combining American and European concepts of auteurism in genre revision of mass audience cinema and personally realized, referential, and reflexive film. The mediation of other art forms through the cinema and of reality through all artistic processes is encapsulated in Weir's intertextual mode of filmmaking. This eclectic, allusive, and intertextual approach, pursuing authorial expression and individual interpretation through high art and popular cultural referencing and genre revision, epitomizes the work of modern and postmodern auteurs, including some of Weir's contemporaries and influences. Such an approach is particularly noticeable within films made by directors drawing inspiration from, but ironizing in their turn, the American cinema of genres: David Cronenberg, Akira Kurosawa, Wim Wenders, and Baz Luhrmann. The dual European-American lineage of Wenders's films, especially *Paris, Texas* (1984), a near-contemporary of Weir's first films in Hollywood, illustrates this fusion of art cinema and genre. As in the case of Weir's films, Wenders's style

> indicate[s] the problematic nature of the references that *Paris, Texas* makes to American cinema and American culture, while drawing on both as the material for structuring its narrative. The way it uses these sources generates much of the film's tension between the narrative and the images. This in turn displays varying levels of allegorical potential, but without committing itself to any overall scheme of metaphorical reference—which is in itself an ironic position.[12]

An ironic or ambiguous form of allusiveness marks Luhrmann's films, particularly his postmodern musical *Moulin Rouge* (2001). While evoking comparisons with the preceding texts of Jean Renoir and John Huston, this film also cites silent-film history (Méliès and *Metropolis-Rouge*), popular music in its soundtrack (Minogue and Madonna *Rouge*), and songs and images from previous musicals (a medley *Rouge*). The conspicuousness of this approach within the work of Canadian, Australasian, Japanese, and German filmmakers, whose film industries have been colonized (along with their subconscious[13]) by America, suggests this is as much a latter-day postcolonial as postmodern mode of filmmaking.

Weir's own experience forms a basis for his narratives of unique and personal events, which are inherently ongoing, inconclusive, and unclosed. Weir describes his films as "artefacts" or "phases" of his life,[14] which are the summation or by-product of the process of inspiration. The unclosed narratives provide a continuum, a series of causes and definitive acts without an envisaged final effect. This mode validates the characters' continued development in the diegetic environment, as well as the individual interpretative contribution of readers of his films:

> Most of my films have been left incomplete, with the viewer as the final participant: I don't like the didactic approach. One is constantly left wondering and I love it when that's done to me in a film.[15]

The difficulties experienced by Weir's protagonists in seeking to "narrate" their own lives and interpret unpredictable, unconventional circumstances do not disguise their desire, like that of the viewer, to "contribute a verse" to the polyphonous world they observe and in which they are immersed. They are provoked to participate rather than react, to consume and reflect rather than receive passively, reemphasizing the convergence of creative and interpretative acts of filmmakers, protagonists, and readers. Viewing in the cinema may be communal, but the significance of interpretation, particularly of texts that revel in unique experience and exclusive reference, remains private and untranslatable. Individual film reading in an audience can become as personal an act as film authorship within the film industry. Passive reception and individual activity are the choices confronting Weir's characters, as well as the filmmaker and readers. Communal understanding of unaltered genre motifs indicates an unquestioning stance by director and reader to the text and the society it reflects. An American auteurist input, reconfiguring genre, or a European auteur's vision, embracing personal meaning structures and cultural references, questions societal and cinematic constructs and allows wider, connotative, individual readings.

Weir's greatest art-film (*Picnic*) and genre (*Witness*) successes established his adaptive, allusive, and original style in the national and industrial cinema contexts. Their continuities, reflecting his enduring themes and style, validate his authorial signature in those films made without his usual collaborators (the commercial production of *The Plumber*, the personal project *Green Card*, and later studio films like *Fearless* and *Truman*). Sufficiently successful in commercial terms to continue in Hollywood and individual enough to be distinguishable from other studio directors and maintain an auteur's following, Weir unites the cultural and commercial aspirations of the Australian revival, and the exclusive and popular aims of European art film and American genre cinema. Art film and art quotation are merged with genre convention and narrative film in an evolving "Peter Weir" genre of consistent style, enduring theme, and constant questioning:

> While his films are overwhelmingly novelistic in their narratives, the fact that they refuse any final meanings or interpretations and maintain a firm reserve and questioning toward what they present gives the films both a popular place by virtue of their conventional novelistic structure and a modernist one by virtue of its thematics. . . . The films get doubly sold: within an art market (world bourgeois film festivals: Berlin, Cannes, New York), and as conventional mass entertainment.[16]

The films' success under both classifications reflects the uniqueness of the artistic consciousness creating them, the individuality of each viewer's reading of them, and the captivation of the personal and communal dilemmas portrayed within them.

At time of writing, Weir's next project, entitled *Master and Commander: The Far Side of the World*, is entering postproduction. This film is the first in a proposed series of adaptations from Patrick O'Brian's stories of seafaring and warfare during the Napoleonic era. As with *Truman*, at first sight this appears an unlikely vehicle for Weir's thematic interests or style, although the portrayal of the transformative journey in *Mosquito Coast*, and the complexity of the handling of the past in *Picnic*, *Gallipoli*, and *Year* may suggest otherwise. With a reported budget of $135 million (more than twice that of *Truman*) and a starring role for Russell Crowe, this production would seem to reemphasize the disparity between Weir's art-film reputation and his increasingly mainstream profile with the casting of contemporary stars. After another lengthy period of meticulous preparation, entailing another four- or five-year-gap between feature releases, *Master and Commander: The Far Side of the World* will again provide a test case for the presence and significance of Peter Weir's negotiation of artistry and popularity, Hollywood genres and non-(even un-)American perspectives.

Notes

1. David Desser, "Ikuru: Narration as a Moral Act," in *Reframing Japanese Cinema: Authorship, Genre, History*, eds. Arthur Nolletti Jr. and David Desser (Bloomington: Indiana University Press, 1992), p. 67.

2. James Goodwin, *Akira Kurosawa and Intertextual Cinema* (London: Johns Hopkins University Press, 1994), p. 21.

3. Dudley Andrew, *Concepts in Film Theory* (Oxford: Oxford University Press, 1984), p. 76.

4. Stephen Neale, *Genre* (London: B.F.I., 1980), p. 48.

5. Ian Jarvie, *Philosophy of the Film* (London: Routledge & Kegan Paul, 1987), p. 57.

6. David Bordwell, *Narration in the Fiction Film* (London: Methuen, 1985), pp. 32–33.

7. Paul Kalina, "Designing Visions: Peter Weir and *The Truman Show*," *Cinema Papers, 127* (1998), pp. 18–22, 56 (p. 21).

8. Roland Barthes, *The Pleasure of the Text* (Oxford: Blackwells, 1990), p. 69.

9. Pat McGilligan, "Under Weir . . . and Theroux," *Film Comment, 22* (1986), pp. 23–32 (p. 32).

10. Umberto Eco, "*Casablanca*: Cult Movies and Intertextual Collage," in *Modern Criticism and Theory: A Reader*, ed. David Lodge, (London: Longman, 1988), p. 453.

11. Sue Mathews, *35mm Dreams: Conversations with Five Directors About the Australian Film Revival* (Melbourne: Penguin, 1984), p. 107.

12. Stan Jones, "Wenders" *Paris, Texas* and the 'European Way of Seeing,'" in *European Identity in Cinema*, ed. Wendy Everett, (Exeter: Intellect Books, 1996), p. 46.

13. Wim Wenders, *The Logic of Images: Essays and Conversations* (London: Faber & Faber, 1991), p. 98.

14. Interview with the author, June 1993.

15. Mathews, *35mm Dreams*, p. 107.

16. Sam Rohdie, "*Gallipoli*, Peter Weir and an Australian Art Cinema," in *An Australian Film Reader*, eds. Albert Moran and Tom O"Regan, (Sydney: Currency, 1985), p. 197.

Peter Weir Filmography

Three to Go—Michael (1971, Commonwealth Film Unit)
Producer: Gil Brearley
Script: Peter Weir
Photography: Kerry Brown
Editor: Wayne Le Clos
Musical Score: The Cleves

Homesdale (1971, independent production)
Producers: Richard Brennan, Grahame Bond
Script: Peter Weir, Piers Davies
Photography: Anthony Wallis
Editor: Wayne Le Clos
Musical Score: Grahame Bond, Rory O"Donoghue

The Cars That Ate Paris (1974, Salt Pan Productions/Royce Smeal
Film Productions)
Producers: Hal McElroy, Jim McElroy
Script: Peter Weir, Keith Gow, Piers Davies
Photography: John McLean
Editor: Wayne Le Clos
Musical Score: Bruce Smeaton

Picnic at Hanging Rock (1975, South Australian Film
Corporation/Australian Film Commission)
Producers: Hal McElroy, Jim McElroy, Patricia Lovell
Screenplay: Cliff Green, from the novel by Joan Lindsay

Photography: Russell Boyd
Cameraman: John Seale
Editor: Max Lemon
Musical Score: Bruce Smeaton

The Last Wave (1977, Ayer Productions)
Producers: Hal McElroy, Jim McElroy
Screenplay: Tony Morphett, Petru Popescu, Peter Weir
Photography: Russell Boyd
Cameraman: John Seale
Editor: Max Lemon
Musical Score: Charles Wain

The Plumber (1979, South Australian Film Corporation)
Producer: Matt Carroll
Screenplay: Peter Weir
Photography: David Sanderson
Editor: Gerald Turney-Smith
Production Design: Wendy Weir

Gallipoli (1981, Paramount)
Producers: Robert Stigwood, Patricia Lovell
Screenplay: David Williamson, Peter Weir
Photography: Russell Boyd
Cameraman: John Seale
Editor: William Anderson
Musical Score: Jean-Michel Jarre
Production Design: Wendy Weir

The Year of Living Dangerously (1982, Wayang Productions/MGM)
Producers: Hal McElroy, Jim McElroy
Screenplay: David Williamson, Peter Weir, C. J. Koch, from the
novel by C. J. Koch
Photography: Russell Boyd
Cameraman: John Seale
Editor: William Anderson
Musical Score: Maurice Jarre

Witness (1985, Paramount)
Producer: Edward Feldman
Screenplay: Earl Wallace, William Kelley
Photography: John Seale
Cameraman: John Seale
Editor: Thom Noble
Musical Score: Maurice Jarre

The Mosquito Coast (1986, The Saul Zaentz Company)
Producer: Jerome Hellman
Screenplay: Paul Schrader
Photography: John Seale
Cameraman: John Seale
Editor: Thom Noble
Musical Score: Maurice Jarre

Dead Poets Society (1989, Touchstone Pictures)
Producers: Steven Haft, Paul Junger Witt, Tony Thomas
Screenplay: Tom Schulman
Photography: John Seale
Editor: William Anderson
Musical Score: Maurice Jarre
Production Design: Wendy Stites

Green Card (1991, Touchstone Pictures)
Producers: Peter Weir, Jean Gontier
Screenplay: Peter Weir
Photography: Geoffrey Simpson
Cameraman: Ken Ferris
Editor: William Anderson
Musical Score: Hans Zimmer
Production Design: Wendy Stites

Fearless (1994, Warner Brothers)
Producers: Paula Weinstein, Mark Rosenberg
Screenplay: Rafael Yglesias, from his own novel
Photography: Allen Daviau
Editor: William Anderson

Musical Score: Maurice Jarre
Design Consultant: Wendy Stites

The Truman Show (1998, Paramount)
Producers: Scott Rudin, Andrew Niccol, Edward S. Feldman, Adam Schroeder
Screenplay: Andrew Niccol
Photography: Peter Biziou
Editor: William Anderson
Musical Score: Burkhard Dallwitz
Production Design: Dennis Gassner
Design Consultant: Wendy Stites

The following films were unavailable for viewing, and therefore are not analyzed in the text:

ATN 7 Television Christmas Revue Films: *Count Vim"s Last Exercise* (1967)
  *The Life and Times of the Reverend
  Buck Shotte* (1968)

Commonwealth Film Unit Documentaries: *Stirring the Pool* (1969)
  Tempo: Australia in the '70s (1971)
  *Australia Colour Diary No. 43: Two Directions in Australian Pop
    Music* (1972)

Short Films: *Boat Building* (1972)
The Computer Centre (1972)
The Field Day (1972)
The Fifth Facade (1973)
Fugue (1974)
Three Workshop Films (1975)

Bibliography

Books

Andrew, Dudley, *Concepts in Film Theory* (Oxford: Oxford University Press, 1984).

Baldini, Umberto, *Primavera* (London: Sidgwick & Jackson, 1986).

Barthes, Roland, *The Pleasure of the Text* (Oxford: Blackwells, 1990).

Bean, C. E. W., *The Story of Anzac, from the Outbreak of War to the End of the First Phase of the Gallipoli Campaign, May 4, 1915*, 2 vols., 3rd ed. (Sydney: Angus and Robertson, 1934).

Belton, John, *American Cinema/American Culture* (London: McGraw-Hill, 1994).

Bennett, Tony, Susan Boyd-Bowman, Colin Mercer, and Woollacott, (eds.), *Popular Television and Film: A Reader* (London: BFI, 1981).

Bergesen, Albert J., and Andrew M., Greeley, *God in the Movies* (New Brunswick, N.J.: Transaction, 2000).

Bliss, Michael, *Dreams Within A Dream: The Films of Peter Weir* (Carbondale, Ill.: Southern Illinois University Press, 2000).

Bode, Carl (ed.), *Henry David Thoreau—Collected Poems* (Baltimore: Johns Hopkins, 1964).

Bordwell, David, *Narration in the Fiction Film* (London: Routledge 1988).

Bordwell, David, Janet Staiger, and Kristin Thompson, *The Classical Hollywood Cinema: Film Style and Mode of Production to 1960* (London: Routledge, 1985).

Braudy, Leo, *The World in a Frame: What We See in Films* (London: University of Chicago Press, 1984).

Brown, Dennis, and Jonathan Pedder, *Introduction to Psychotherapy; An Outline of Psychodynamic Principles and Practice*, 2nd ed. (London: Routledge, 1991).

Browne, Nick (ed.), *Refiguring American Film Genres* (London: University of California Press, 1998).

Bruzzi, Stella, *Undressing Cinema: Clothing and Identity in the Movies* (London: Routledge, 1997).

Cartmell, Deborah, Imelda Whelehan, *Adaptations: From Text to Screen, Screen to Text* (London: Routledge, 1999).

Caruana, Wally, *Aboriginal Art* (London: Thames and Hudson, 1993).

Caughie, John (ed.), *Theories of Authorship* (London: Routledge & Kegan Paul, 1981).

Clinch, Minty, *Harrison Ford: A Biography* (London: Hodder & Stoughton, 1988).

Coates, Paul, *Film at the Intersection of High and Mass Culture* (Cambridge: Cambridge University Press, 1994).

Collins, Felicity, *The Films of Gillian Armstrong* (St. Kilda, Victoria: AFC, 1999).

Coyle, Rebecca (ed.), *Screen Scores: Studies in Contemporary Australian Film Music* (Sydney: AFTRS, 1998).

Crouch, Harold, *The Army and Politics in Indonesia* (London: Cornell University Press, 1978).

Dalle Vacche, Angela, *Cinema and Painting: How Art Is Used in Film* (Austin: University of Texas Press, 1996).

Davies, Jude, and Carol R. Smith, *Gender, Ethnicity and Sexuality in Contemporary American Film* (Edinburgh: Keele University Press, 1997).

De Angelis, Rita, *Botticelli: The Complete Paintings* (London: Granada, 1980).

Dermody, Susan, and Elizabeth Jacka, *The Screening of Australia Vol. I: Anatomy of a Film Industry* (Sydney: Currency, 1987).

Dermody, Susan, and Elizabeth Jacka, *The Screening of Australia Vol. II: Anatomy of a National Cinema* (Sydney: Currency, 1988).

Dermody, Susan, and Elizabeth Jacka, *The Imaginary Industry: Australian Film in the Late '80s* (North Ryde, N.S.W.: AFTRS, 1988).

Dyer, Richard, and Ginette Vincendeau (eds.), *Popular European Cinema* (London: Routledge, 1992).

Eberwein, Robert T., *Film and the Dream Screen* (Princeton: Princeton University Press, 1984).

Ettinger, L. D., and H. S. Ettinger, *Botticelli* (London: Thomas & Hudson, 1976).

Evans, Peter William, and Celestino Deleyto (eds.), *Terms of Endearment: Hollywood Romantic Comedy of the 1980s and 1990s* (Edinburgh: Edinburgh University Press, 1998).

Everett, Wendy (ed.), *European Identity in Cinema* (Exeter: Intellect Books, 1996).

Fraser, Peter, *Images of the Passion: The Sacramental Mode in Film* (Trowbridge: Flicks, 1998).

Gehring, Wes D., *Screwball Comedy: A Genre of Madcap Romance* (London: Greenwood Press, 1986).

Gehring, Wes D. (ed.), *Handbook of American Film Genres* (London: Greenwood Press, 1988).

Gittings, Christopher E., *Canadian National Cinema* (London: Routledge, 2002).

Goldsworthy, Andy, *Andy Goldsworthy* (London: Viking, 1994)

Goldsworthy, Andy, *Stone* (London: Viking, 1996).

Goodwin, James, *Akira Kurosawa* and *Intertextual Cinema* (London: Johns Hopkins University Press, 1994).

Grant, Barry K. (ed.), *Film Genre Reader* (Austin: University of Texas Press, 1990).

Grant, Barry K. (ed.), *Film Genre Reader II* (Austin: University of Texas Press, 1995).

Guptil, Arthur L., *Norman Rockwell: Illustrator* (New York: Watson-Guptil, 1946).

Haltof, Marek, *Peter Weir: When Cultures Collide* (London: Prentice-Hall, 1996).

Heath, Stephen, *Questions of Cinema* (London: Macmillan, 1981).

Hedges, Inez, *Breaking the Frame: Film Language and the Experience of Limits* (Bloomington: Indiana University Press, 1991).

Hjort, Mette, and Scott Mackenzie (eds.), *Cinema and Nation* (London: Routledge, 2000).

Holloway, Emory (ed.), *Walt Whitman—Complete Verse and Selected Prose and Letters* (London: Nonesuch, 1938).

Jackson, Rosemary, *Fantasy—The Literature of Subversion* (London: Methuen, 1981).

Jarvie, Ian, *Philosophy of the Film* (London, Routledge & Kegan Paul, 1987).

Kaminsky, Stuart M., *American Film Genres*, 2nd ed. (Chicago: Nelson Hall, 1985).

Kaplan, E. Ann (ed.), *Psychoanalysis and Cinema*, 2nd ed. (London: Routledge, 1991).

Kawin, Bruce F., *Mindscreen—Bergman, Godard and First Person Film* (Princeton: Princeton University Press, 1978).

Koch, C. J., *The Year of Living Dangerously* (London: Grafton, 1986).

Kolker, Robert Phillip, *A Cinema of Loneliness*, 2nd ed. (Oxford: Oxford University Press, 1988).

Legge, J. D., *Sukarno: A Political Biography* (London: Allen Lane, 1972).

Lindsay, Joan, *Picnic at Hanging Rock* (London: Penguin, 1970).

Lodge, David, *Modern Criticism and Theory: A Reader* (London: Longman, 1988).

Margolis, Harriet (ed.), *Jane Campion's The Piano* (Cambridge: Cambridge University Press, 2000).

Mascaro, Juan (translator), *The Bhagavad Gita* (London: Penguin, 1962).

Mast, Gerald, and Marshall Cohen (eds.), *Film Theory and Criticism*, 3rd. ed. (Oxford: Oxford University Press, 1985).

Mathews, Sue, *35mm Dreams: Conversations With Five Directors About the Australian Film Revival* (Melbourne: Penguin, 1984).

McFarlane, Brian, *Words and Images: Australian Novels into Film* (Richmond, Victoria: Heinemann, 1983).

McFarlane, Brian, *Australian Cinema 1970–1985* (London: Secker & Warburg, 1987).

McFarlane, Brian, and Geoff Mayer, *New Australian Cinema: Sources and Parallels in American and British Film* (Cambridge: Cambridge University Press, 1992).

Moran, Albert, and Tom O'Regan (eds.), *An Australian Film Reader* (Sydney: Currency, 1985).

Moran, Albert, and Tom O'Regan (eds.), *The Australian Screen* (Harmondsworth: Penguin, 1989).

Mountford, Charles P., and Ainslie Roberts, *The Dreamtime: Australian Aboriginal Myths in Paintings* (Adelaide: Rigby, 1965).

Munsterberg, Hugo, *The Film: A Psychological Study* (New York: Dover, 1970).

Murphy, Francis (ed.), *Walt Whitman—The Complete Poems* (Harmondsworth: Penguin, 1975).

Murray, Scott (ed.), *The New Australian Cinema* (Melbourne: Thomas Nelson, 1980).

Narboni, Jean, and Tom Milne (eds.), *Godard on Godard* (London: Da Capo Press, 1986).

Nolletti, Arthur, Jr., and David Desser (eds.), *Reframing Japanese Cinema: Authorship, Genre, History* (Bloomington: Indiana University Press, 1992).

Neale, Stephen, *Genre* (London: B.F.I., 1980).

Nowell-Smith, Geoffrey, and Steven Ricci (eds.), *Hollywood and Europe: Economics, Culture, National Identity, 1945–95* (London: BFI, 1998).

Orr, John, and Colin Nicholson (eds.), *Cinema and Fiction: New Modes of Adapting, 1950–1990* (Edinburgh: Edinburgh University Press, 1992).

Palmer, William J., *The Films of the Seventies* (London: Scarecrow Press, 1987).

Pike, Andrew, and Ross Cooper *Australian Cinema 1900–1977*, 2nd ed. (Melbourne: Oxford University Press, 1980/1999).

Powrie, Phil, *French Cinema in the 1990s: Continuity and Difference* (Oxford: Oxford University Press, 1999).

Schatz, Thomas, *Hollywood Genres* (London: McGraw-Hill, 1981).

Sellers, Robert, *Sigourney Weaver* (London: Robert Hale, 1992).

Shiach, Don, *The Films of Peter Weir* (London: Letts, 1993).

Shirley, Graham, and Brian Adams *Australian Cinema: The First Eighty Years,* rev. ed. (Sydney: Currency, 1989).

Smith, Bernard, *Australian Painting, 1788–1970* (Melbourne: Oxford University Press, 1971).

Smith, J. C., and E. De Selincourt (eds.), *Edmund Spenser: Poetical Works* (Oxford: Oxford University Press, 1912).

Smith, Joseph H., and William Kerrigan (eds.), *Images in Our Souls: Cavell, Psychoanalysis and Cinema* (London: Johns Hopkins University Press, 1987).

Stone, Judy, *Eye on the World: Conversations with International Directors* (Los Angeles: Silman-James Press, 1997).

Stoltz, Donald, Marshall Stoltz, and William F. Earle, *The Advertising World of Norman Rockwell* (New York, Harrison House, 1986).

Stratton, David, *The Last New Wave: The Australian Film Revival* (London: Angus & Robertson, 1980).

Sutton, Peter, *Dreamings: The Art of Aboriginal Australia* (London: Viking, 1989).

Tan, Ed S., *Emotion and the Structure of Narrative Film: Film as an Emotion Machine* (New York: Lawrence Erlbaum, 1996).

Theroux, Paul, *The Mosquito Coast* (London: Penguin, 1981).

Thomas, Daniel, *Outlines of Australian Art: The Joseph Brown Collection,* expanded ed. (Melbourne: Macmillan, 1980).

Thompson, Kristin, and David Bordwell, *Film History: An Introduction* (London: McGraw-Hill, 1994).

Thoreau, Henry David, *Walden—Or Life in the Woods* (London: Chapman & Hall, 1927).

Traube, Elizabeth G., *Dreaming Identities: Class, Gender and Generation in 1980s Hollywood Movies* (London: University of California Press, 1998).

Tudor, Andrew, *Theories of Film* (London: Secker & Warburg, 1973).

Turner, Graeme, *National Fictions: Literature, Film and the Construction of Australian Narrative* (London: Allen & Unwin, 1986).

Verhoeven, Deb (ed.), *Twin Peeks: Australian and New Zealand Feature Films* (Melbourne: Damned Publishing, 1999).

Wartenberg, Thomas E., *Unlikely Couples: Movie Romance as Social Criticism* (Boulder, Colo.: Westview Press, 1999).

Wenders, Wim, *The Logic of Images: Essays and Conversations* (London: Faber & Faber, 1991).

Wollen, Peter, *Signs and Meaning in the Cinema,* 3rd ed. (Bloomington: Indiana University Press, 1972).

Wood, Robin, *Hitchcock's Films* (London: Tantivy Press, 1977).

Yalom, Irvin D., *Existential Psychotherapy* (New York: Basic Books, 1980).

Yglesias, Rafael, *Fearless* (London: Penguin, 1993).

Yoshimoto, Mitsuhiro, *Kurosawa: Film Studies and Japanese Cinema* (Durham, N. C., Duke University Press, 2000).

Articles

Alion, Yves, "Peter Weir," *Revue du Cinema, 474* (1991), p. 57.

Anonymous, "The Top Ten Films," *Cinema Papers, 44/45* (1984), pp. 62–65.

Berner, Robert L., "Old Gunfighters, New Cops," *Western American Literature, 21* (1986), pp. 131–134.

Bliss, Michael, "Keeping a Sense of Wonder," *Film Quarterly, 53* (1999), pp. 2–11.

Bourguignon, Thomas, "Le vert paradis," *Positif, 361* (1991), pp. 52–54.

Brennan, Richard, "Peter Weir—Profile," *Cinema Papers, 1* (1974), pp. 16–17.

Brown, Geoff, *"The Cars That Ate Paris," Sight and Sound, 44* (1975), p. 192.

Butler, Ivan, *"The Year of Living Dangerously," Films and Filmmaking, 345* (1983), pp. 34–35.

Carrére, Emmanuel, *"l'Annee des tous les dangers," Positif, 269/270* (1983), pp. 116–117.

Chion, Michel, *"Witness,* de Peter Weir," *Cahiers du Cinema, 373* (1985), p. 30.

Ciment, Michel, "Peter Weir: L'image et le reel," *Positif, 453* (1998), pp. 20–24.

Clancy, Jack, *"The Last Wave," Cinema Papers, 15* (1978), p. 259.

Clancy, Jack, *"The Plumber," Cinema Papers, 23* (1979), pp. 569–571.

Clancy, Jack, "The Triumph of Mateship—The Failure of the Australian War Film Since 1970," *Overland, 105* (1986), pp. 4–10.

Codelli, L., *"Le cercle des poetes disparus," Positif, 345* (1989), pp. 54–55.

Combs, Richard, *"The Last Wave," Sight and Sound, 47* (1978), pp. 121–122.

Combs, Richard, *"Witness," Monthly Film Bulletin, 52* (1985), pp. 166–167.

Combs, Richard, *"The Mosquito Coast," Monthly Film Bulletin, 54* (1987), pp. 52–53.

Combs, Richard, "Beating God to the Draw," *Sight and Sound, 56* (1987), pp. 136–138.

Combs, Richard, *"Dead Poets Society," Monthly Film Bulletin, 56* (1989), pp. 272–273.

Coursodon, Jean-Pierre, *"The Truman Show*—Mirages de la vie," *Positif, 453* (1998), pp. 17–19.

Dempsey, Michael, "Inexplicable Feelings: An Interview with Peter Weir," *Film Quarterly, 33* (1980), pp. 2–11.

Douchet, Jean, "Le commerce de la poesie," *Cahiers du Cinema, 430* (1990), pp. 40–41.

Fisher, Bob, "*Fearless* Explores Emotional Aftermath of Fateful Flight," *American Cinematographer, 74* (1993), pp. 40–51

Freebury, Jane, "Screening Australia: Gallipoli—a study of Nationalism on Film" *Media Information Australia, 43* (1987), pp. 5–8.

Fonda-Bonardi, Claudia and Peter, Fonda-Bonardi, "The Birth of a Nation—An Interview with Peter Weir," *Cineaste, 11* (1982), pp. 41–42.

Garsault, Alain, "Bienvenue . . . Andrew Niccol ou retour . . . *Gattaca*," *Positif, 453* (1998), pp. 28–29.

Gibson, Ross, "Camera Natura: Landscape in Australian Feature Films," *Framework, 22/23* (1983), pp. 47–51.

Glenn, Gordon, and Scott Murray "Production Report—*The Cars That Ate Paris*," *Cinema Papers, 1* (1974), pp. 18–26.

Hentzi, Gary, "Peter Weir and the Cinema of New Age Humanism," *Film Quarterly, 44* (1990), pp. 2–12.

Jaehne, Karen, "*Gallipoli*," *Cineaste, 11* (1982), pp. 40–43.

Kalina, Paul, "Designing Visions: Peter Weir and *The Truman Show*," *Cinema Papers, 127* (1998), pp. 18–22, 56.

Katsahni, I., "*Green Card*," *Cahiers du Cinema*," *441* (1991), p. 73.

Kemp, Philip, "*Fearless*," *Sight and Sound, 4* (1994), pp. 41–42.

Kimbal, George R., "*The Mosquito Coast*," *Films and Filming, 389* (1987), pp. 40–41.

Kinder, M., "*The Plumber*," *Film Quarterly, 33* (1980), pp. 17–21.

Kobal, John, "*Witness*," *Films and Filming, 368* (1985), pp. 45–47.

Koszarski, Richard, "Auteurism Revisited," *Film History, 7* (1995), pp. 355–6.

Leslie, Michael, "Edmund Spenser: Art and *The Faerie Queen*," *Proceedings of the British Academy, 76* (1990), pp. 73–107.

MacBean, J. R., "Watching the Third World Watchers," *Film Quarterly, 37* (1984), pp. 1–13.

Masson, Alain, "*La Derniere Vague*," *Positif, 259* (1982), p. 73.

Masson, Alain, "*Gallipoli*," *Positif, 257/258* (1982), p. 119.

Mayer, Geoff, "*Greencard*," *Cinema Papers 82* (1991), 53–54.

McFarlane, Brian, "The Films of Peter Weir," *Cinema Papers, 26* (1980), Special Supplement, pp. 1–24.

McFarlane, Brian, and Tom Ryan "Peter Weir—Towards the Centre," *Cinema Papers, 34* (1981), pp. 322–329.

McGilligan, Pat, "Under Weir . . . and Theroux," *Film Comment, 22* (1986), pp. 23–32.

Mulvey, Laura, "Visual Pleasure and Narrative Cinema," *Screen, 16* (1975), pp. 6–18.

Murray, Scott, "Hal and James McElroy—Producers," *Cinema Papers, 14* (1977), pp. 148–153.

Murray, Scott, and Antony I. Ginnane "Producing Picnic," *Cinema Papers, 8* (1976), pp. 298–301, 377.

Peck, Agnes "Etats seconds: Trois films de Peter Weir," *Positif, 453* (1998), pp. 25–27.

Roddick, Nick, "*The Year of Living Dangerously*," *Monthly Film Bulletin, 50* (1983), pp. 147–148.

Roddick, Nick, "*Witness*—Among the Amish," *Sight and Sound, 54* (1985), pp. 221–2.

Sarris, Andrew, "Notes of an Accidental Auteurist," *Film History, 7* (1995), pp. 358–361.

Sineux, Michel, "*Witness*," *Positif, 293/294* (1985), pp. 107–108.

Sineux, Michel, "*Le cercle des poetes disparus*," *Positif, 347* (1990), pp. 66–67.

Smith, M., "Mel Gibson," *Cinema Papers, 42* (1983), pp. 12–17.

Snow, Mat, and Meredith Brody "The French Connection," *Empire, 22* (1991), pp. 50–56.

Tessier, Max, "*l'Annee des tous les dangers*," *Revue du Cinema, 385* (1983), pp. 39–40.

Travers, T. H. E., "*Gallipoli*—Film and the Tradition of Australian History," *Film and History, 14* (1984), pp. 14–20.

Turner, Adrian, "*Gallipoli*," *Films and Filming, 327* (1981), pp. 33.

Ward, Kyla, "Weir'd Tales," *Tabula Rasa, 2* (1994).

Whitehouse, Charles, "Bubble Boy," *Sight and Sound, 8* (1998), pp. 8–10.

Internet Resources

Reviews, articles, and news:

www.peterweircave.com

Interviews:

www.splicedonline.com/features/weir.html

www.theavclub.com/avclub3321/bonusfeature13321.html

tipjar.com/dan/peterweir.htm

mrshowbiz.go.com/interviews/415_1.html

mrshowbiz.go.com/interviews/415_2.html

mrshowbiz.go.com/interviews/415_3.html

Index